Road to Kilimanjaro

Road to Kilimanjaro

Ruth T. Shaffer

the Four Corners Press
Grand Rapids, MI

Cover design by Daniel A. Shaffer

Cover photograph by R. David Shaffer, Jr.

Map by Grace S. Baker

Published in the U.S.A.
by the Four Corners Press
Grand Rapids, MI

ISBN 0-9615297-2-5

To Our Ilmaasai

FOREWORD

GOD, OUR FATHER, IN HIS WONDEROUS LOVE and mercy, enriches our lives through the touch of our friends. In my own pilgrimage, Ruth Shaffer, known much more affectionately as *Gokoo* (Grandmother in Maasai), has been an inspiration and encouragement beyond her knowing.

Clearly I recall as a small boy the warmth, the gaiety, the good cheer that tumbled from her during her holiday visit in my parents' home. Later, in my teens I in turn was to spend an adventuresome interlude in her home at Lasit, located at the foot of Mt. Kilimanjaro. There I made hunting forays into the Maasai Reserve and discovered a deep kinship of spirit with those free and magnificent people of the plains.

Some seventeen years later, when I was in my early thirties, she and her beloved husband sent me a heart-stirring letter. Would I possibly consider coming back to Kenya from Canada to work amongst their beloved Maasai? It was a call, a challenge, a charge, if you will, to turn from a life of self-gratification to serving others. It was God's way of speaking clearly to a very tough-willed young man at a crisis point in his career.

Not long after, when I went, along with my wife and children, she and Roy opened their arms, their hearts, their home to us in love and enthusiasm. She it was who taught us the rudiments of the Maasai language; who introduced us to their culture; who nurtured our affection for these lovely people.

Long, long after this, when others had taken up the work which they initiated, she came to reside in Three Hills,

Alberta. In characteristic fashion, she flung her energies into the work of the Prairie Bible Institute, leaving her own special mark and gaining the deep admiration of my whole family.

Thus, across the years we have in person and by mail kept in constant touch. She is a woman of wondrous goodwill, courage and enthusiasm. This vitality has as its source the gracious life of Christ's presence so apparent in her personality and character. So, to have known her is to have been uplifted and blessed in spirit.

Her book is in essence the narrative of a frontier missionary family. It recounts the resourcefulness, the initiative, the fierce faith in God which marked the lives of so many pioneer workers in Africa. Like a well-loved family album, it preserves in word pictures the heroic as well as the hilarious strands of life's tapestry in a tough territory.

Only those of us who have lived amongst the Maasai and learned to love them so profoundly as a people will fully grasp the pathos of these pages. It demands enormous tenacity, quiet resolution and enduring confidence in Christ to carry on His work when apparently the response to His Word is so greatly inhibited by tribal tradition and culture.

In His own gracious way, God has honoured the faith and faithfulness of those who, like *Gokoo*, laid down their lives for the Maasai, for today many of these splendid people are finding fresh life in Christ. This book tells something of the "plowing" and "planting" that often went unnoticed by any but by God Himself. May He honour its publication!

Blessings!
W. Phillip Keller

INTRODUCTION

As a little boy of eight, at Siyiapei, I recall very vividly my mother quickly getting ready to go and join the other mothers as they hurried to go and comfort Mrs. Shaffer on the loss of her baby daughter, Helen. And the talk when my mother returned, as she reported the whole episode to my father. It was no different from when she related any other sorrowful event in our home; it was the shared suffering of another mother, because, in actual fact, they were of the same age group. My own father was a soldier in the First World War, just like the Reverend Roy Shaffer.

The point is, when missionaries get into difficult situations, they become part of us, consciously or unconsciously. They affect us; but we also affect them. The Gospel of our Lord and Saviour Jesus Christ transcends all cultures and, as people get to know and love one another, they are knit together in love and sympathy and the loving kindness of our God.

What is related in this book in the life of one missionary couple has been reproduced many times in other missionary fields. What is unique here is that they, starting with John and Florence Stauffacher, covered an enormous area of two whole districts, Narok and Kajiado, each comprising more than eight thousand square miles, and they fully accepted the responsibilities of "... reaching all the people with the Good News of Jesus Christ."

The difficulties of travelling and communication are well narrated. But to my mind, by far the greater difficulty lay in communication; in making themselves understood. I recall as a little boy, how we made jokes and laughed at some of our elders who imitated the missionary way of speaking our own language. They did it out of sympathy for the missionary, to help him to understand. We mistook this as "being something else" on the part of our elders, and we were determined to speak our own language to the missionaries just as we spoke it to our parents.

I have also discovered, like many others, that the resistance to the Gospel among my people was not confined to a reaction to foreigners who spoke a foreign language; it was a resistance to the truth as a judgment against many of our unethical customs and traditions.

This made my sympathies with this group of pioneers deepen immensely. As the Maasai people are now accepting the Good News of Jesus Christ, their sympathy and gratitude to the pioneers who brought the News has deepened also. I am sure that many will treasure this book which will teach them what our salvation cost others who, out of love and loyalty to the Lord Jesus Christ, came and became Maasai that we might know, love, and obey the great Shepherd of the sheep. We thank God that Mrs. Shaffer is still with us to share our joy.

Rev. John T. Mpaayei

ACKNOWLEDGEMENTS

Like a live picture on my tv screen, there flashes before my mind a smiling mass of both African and white faces as I try to count up the many people who gave me inspiration, encouragement and help with these pages. I gratefully acknowledge and salute each one.

Little did Ted and Norline Rendall of Prairie Bible Institute know what they started when they asked me to write an expansion of a brief talk I gave at a staff meeting one Saturday, telling of the thirty-five years my husband, Roy, and I spent with the Maasai in Kenya. I typed ten pages. They asked for ten more, and ten more, and more, until I was swimming in a loose collection of memories. It became a family affair. Of our children, Esther S. Wilcox edited the manuscript and her husband, Ron, facilitated production arrangements; Grace S. Baker drew the map; Ruth M. Johansen, Harry D. Shaffer and his wife, Dorothy, provided strong and active support; and I owe much gratitude to Roy D. Shaffer and his wife, Betty, who made possible my two return visits to the Maasai. Roy also contributed valuable insights and happy recollections in addition to writing the Epilogue. His sons provided the cover: Daniel designed it and David shot the front cover photograph (while waiting for the 1985 Safari Rally cars to come by). Generous support and assistance were provided by my brothers, Frank H. Thiers and Wendell H. Thiers.

Special thanks go to the Africa Inland Mission International USA offices for their encouragement and assistance in arranging for publication. David Hornberger and Ed

Arensen provided photographs, and Hal Olsen initiated contacts with the publisher. There are many more friends who helped, typed, read and gave welcome criticisms; I am indebted to them all.

Finally, I pay tribute to the Moody Memorial Church in Chicago which has been our family of supporters since before we first went out to the field in 1923, and through whom God is still blessing the Maasai because of their faithfulness.

Ruth T. Shaffer

CONTENTS

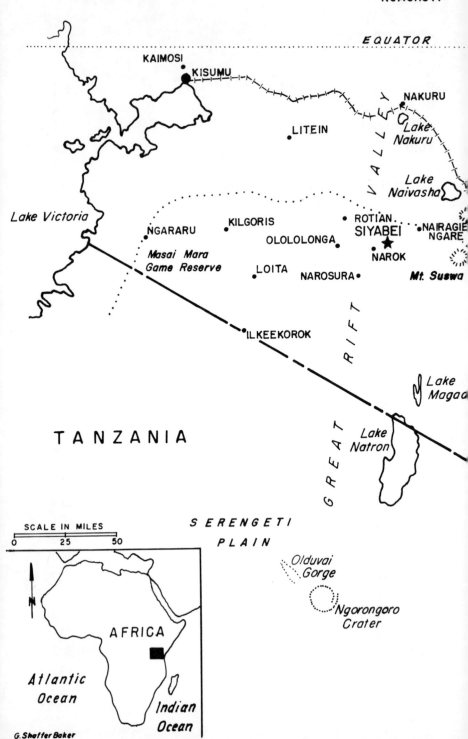

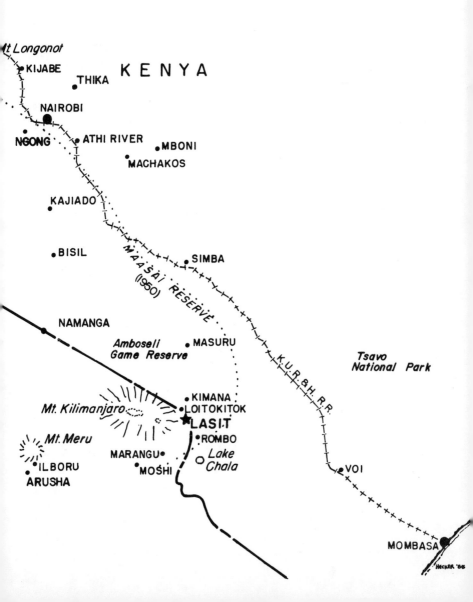

1 *Kuyoni and Wambui*

ON A DARK, RAINY NIGHT WHEN no one except the wild animals should have been out prowling, we heard a loud pounding at the back door.

"*Wou! Wou!* (Come! Come!)" someone called urgently. Roy picked up the lantern and went to answer the door. He opened it on two rain-soaked lads carrying a burning torch. One obviously had a broken arm.

Quickly, Roy brought them in by the fireplace and shut the door.

The torch-bearer was Wambogo, one of the school boys, and the other was his small brother, Kuyoni, who held a badly broken right forearm in his left hand.

Kuyoni never made a sound, though he was shaking with both cold and shock, while Roy searched his old Army first aid book for instructions. Soon Roy had the arm secured in a splint and sling and the fire had both boys warmed up.

I felt so sorry for Kuyoni I wanted to cry. But he was a Maasai and he did not cry. We were new missionaries in Maasai country. During our next thirty-five years there, we were seldom ever to see a Maasai cry.

During our four years of Bible school, Roy and I had also taken first aid and practical nursing at Moody Bible Institute in Chicago. Then we left for Kenya, East Africa, under the Africa Inland Mission with our two little tow-heads, Harry Daniel, who turned two on the ship going out, and Ruth Marie, six months old. Roy had also had a little training with the U.S. Army Fifth Medical Corps in France during the First World War. But Roy and I arrived at the AIM station, Siyabei, in 1923 as green, young missionaries never having actually set a broken arm. We could only wait and see whether Roy had done it right on Kuyoni. This was our first experience on our own after the departure of the station's senior missionaries, John and Florence Stauffacher, for a much needed furlough.

Ten-year-old Kuyoni certainly needed the use of his right arm, for he was already a dependable herder, as most little Maasai boys are by age five or six. He had the care of a flock of sheep and he alone was responsible for their safety as they grazed out on the plains in the midst of wild animals, some of which loved mutton. Like Jacob, he never let jackal, lion or leopard steal one of his flock. When they tried to, he would scream, curse, throw rocks and sticks, and bluff the predator into moving on.

One day, months before we had arrived, Kuyoni was herding on the mission station grounds, right up close to the little mud house called the *sukul* (school), and he heard some very unusual words being spoken by a Maasai man. He had heard the rumor about some news told in his own language by this tall man called Tagi, so he moved closer to the door to see if he could catch some of it.

Finding little or no grass around the *sukul*, his sheep wandered off while Kuyoni listened, enraptured by the strange words. When he suddenly realized his sheep had wandered off, he ran to collect them. Then he again brought them close to the door to listen. The sheep had no intention of standing there going hungry, so they moved out again and finally he had to go with them. But he began stopping by this way every day.

Sure enough, one day his old father, Kasura by name, caught him neglecting his sheep. Kasura was a short, scrawny man with a limp, but he was mighty. Not only was he a wealthy man with ten sons to tend his vast herds of cattle, sheep and goats, but he was also the local witch doctor. Kuyoni received a severe beating, both for his negligence and for his attachment to this *sukul*. When Wambogo also showed interest in the strange new words of Tagi, Kasura pulled up stakes. He burned down his whole village and moved away.

But it didn't work. Before long, both Kuyoni and Wambogo ran away from home. Kasura's older sons caught them at the *sukul*, punished them and took them back home. They became repeat runaways from their father's kraal, and repeatedly he punished them severely until finally he cursed them and disinherited them, a terrible thing in Maasai culture. He even took away Kuyoni's own one and only beloved sheep, raised by Kuyoni himself and loved as a brother.

This time the boys stayed away. They hurried straight back to our station *sukul* to drink in more of the *Irorei le Ngai* (Words of God) which Tagi told.

The local Maasai Christians gave the two lads cowhides to sleep on in their homes, just like all the other boys had. The people also gave them food, and in return, Wambogo and Kuyoni helped with herding their goats.

Other than soft, well tanned sheepskins to wrap around their loins, the lads had few necessities of life. If it rained, a piece of rawhide held over the head was adequate. Maasai consider rain a blessing from God. They accept it as a real gift, for they live primarily on milk. The rain means grass will grow, which means milk from the cows for the people.

Both boys asked if they might now go into the *sukul* and hold a flat black stone and a long slim stone in their hands and make marks, as other lads were doing. Tagi was, of course, very happy to let them come in and sit down on the dirt floor with slate and pencil along with the others. Both learned very quickly from this tall, engaging teacher. They, too, started to learn the songs he taught and they were astounded to hear—of all things—Tagi talking to God, something they thought only women did.

Tagi ole Loiposioki had been a top sergeant in a battalion of African soldiers called the King's African Rifles (KAR), around 1905. At the time, Kenya was a British colony under the rule of King Edward VII. Tagi was introduced to the mysteries of reading and writing through a little AIM class led by Miss Bertha Simpson near his army post. This was over one hundred miles north, at Rumuruti, where Stauffachers opened the first AIM work among the Maasai before the whole tribe was moved to its present Reserve. Bertha also introduced Tagi to the news of the story of Christ. The entire New Testament had already been translated into both Swahili and Kikuyu by early missionaries. Fortunately, both translations had been done with a phonetically pure spelling system, so that, although Bertha didn't know the meaning of the words, she could read them aloud phonetically. She was a smart girl and had studied phonetics while at college for two years.

When Tagi heard the Word in these two languages which he knew so well, he became a different man, for the love of God gripped him. He was never the same afterward. From then on he was determined to translate these wonderful words into his father's tongue so that the Maasai might also hear about the God who really lives — not just the god who sends rain, grass and cattle. The end result was that Tagi was perhaps the first missionary-minded African recorded by the AIM.

Tagi chose to resign from the KAR and work with the AIM. He and Bertha sat many hours daily, she learning Maasai and he learning English, meanwhile translating the New Testament into Maasai. Many years later, Bertha wrote to me telling how they triumphantly finished up translating the final pages in the school auditorium at the AIM's main station, Kijabe, just before Bertha left for furlough. They mailed the manuscript to the British and Foreign Bible Society in London for printing.

John and Florence Stauffacher had established their second station among the Maasai in 1918 at Siyabei, seventy-five miles southwest of Kijabe. Tagi and his wife now joined them there. As Florence's right hand, Tagi was very skillful at gathering into the school all the children who were not herding flocks and who were not afraid of white people. He was an able administrator. All the Maasai, both on and off the mission station, held him in highest esteem. Tagi lived and taught faith, hope and charity and fostered all that was just, good and upright to such an extent that he captivated the hearts and lives of men, women and children. They would have followed him through fire if need be.

One day he went out to shoot baboons which had been constantly devastating all the gardens. No one missed Tagi until evening, when he did not come home for food as usual. The whole village searched for him in vain. Early the next morning, somebody found his body. It appeared that his gun had discharged as he climbed over a garden fence and he was shot straight through his heart. The bullet had pierced the English New Testament in his left shirt pocket.

Tagi's sudden death was a stunning blow to the Maasai mission work and to the people all around, especially the school boys.

The Maasai never touched the dead nor buried them, by their own customs, but the Stauffachers told us Tagi was so loved that the Maasai broke their customs by sharing in the digging of his grave and gently laying his body to rest, in a Christian burial service.

While in London waiting for the ship which was to take us to Kenya, Roy and I heard of Tagi's remarkable translation work on the New Testament from Mr. Grimwood, manager of the AIM office there. Eagerly anticipating a meeting with Tagi on arrival, we were greeted, instead, with the news of his death. Yet truly, we were destined to meet him all through many later years because of the tremendous influence he had exerted on the lives of many young herders like Kuyoni who, in turn, grew into fine leaders of their own people. Tagi's stamp upon them was unmistakable.

The time came, after we settled in at Siyabei, when we needed help in our home with our own two little children. We needed help to cut wood; build fires; sweep the uncarpeted, crude wooden floors; to carry water up from the stream at the foot of the hill; or just to watch the children lest they wander off into the dense woods only twenty yards from our door.

One day I went out to greet a skinny, well-oiled young herder standing on a three-foot-high ant hill, watching his sheep and goats near the edge of the forest. I had previously seen him in Sunday School and had noted his attentiveness as well as his big, beautiful eyes. This was the lad Kuyoni. This time he flashed me a shy but very wide smile. After twelve weeks, his broken arm had healed and again become as useful as his left.

Somewhere, he had acquired what fragments were left of a man's coat. It looked like his goats had eaten the bottom off, clear up to two badly worn pockets. There were no sleeves and no buttons. He wore this coat constantly, during both the cold of the nights and in the heat of the African noonday.

With the bit of vocabulary I had acquired, I decided to ask this lad if he would consider helping me with my house-work. He was interested at once, for it would mean an income, something he had never experienced before in his young life.

"I don't know," he said, "I've never worked inside a white man's house. I'll go home and ask my brother."

The next morning he showed up without his goats, still in his beloved coat. We fixed the wage at eight shillings a month, top scale in the those days, especially for a tiny lad.

"Here is a bar of soap," I told him. "Go to the stream and wash yourself with it."

He had never seen soap in his life and did not have the slightest idea of how to take a bath as we know it. It was a very new experience for him but he obediently went to the stream. When he returned, he had wet himself all over in the stream and then smeared soap all over his body as a perfume. I am sure he must have itched all day. The soap was "Sunlight," a strong brand of laundry soap. Of course that night he slept on his borrowed cowhide bed as usual and when he came back early next morning, he again had all the aroma Maasai acquired from their beloved cattle, sheep and goats, since all the young lambs, kids and calves slept inside the hut with the people, for safety.

The following morning, Roy met him at the door and went down to the stream with him. He showed him how to get a good, soapy bath, then rinse, then put on fresh, clean shorts and a shirt. He was entranced and this became a ritual before each day's work.

Our children loved Kuyoni and he loved them. In no time he had Harry, our eldest, speaking Maasai.

We arranged the work so that Kuyoni could also go to school full time. In less than three months he and his classmates were reading out of the New Testament. After four years of school, there were six graduates: Kuyoni, Parmale, Kinyanjui, Wambogo, Shadrack and Sitoya — the first fruits of the little school begun at Siyabei by Florence Stauffacher and Tagi. Ten years later, Kuyoni, Parmale and Sitoya were to become my collaborators in translating the first revision of the Maasai New Testament for the British and Foreign Bible Society.

All during those first four years of schooling, Kuyoni was another Tagi: bright, cheerful, dependable, ready to care for the sick, to rescue a lost cow or sheep, and always ready with the right Words of God for any occasion. He repeatedly tried to introduce his father to God's love for him, even though it seemed in vain for he was only cursed and rejected. At Siyabei, in the homes shared with him, Kuyoni lived such a commendable life, even as Joseph in Potiphar's house, that he won many others to Christ. But his own father still resisted his words, so after awhile he seldom visited his father's kraal.

During this time I had engaged Wambui, a little girl about twelve years old, to help me with our babies. Her name means "the of the goats." Like Kuyoni, Wambui was quick to learn all the work in our home. She was half sister to John Tombo Mpaayei, another bright lad who later on not only figured prominently in our own work but who contributed significantly to the cause of Christianity throughout Kenya. We developed a high regard for their father, Mbae, as we called him, over the years for he lived an exemplary life.

However, it was an unbreakable rule that a Maasai father "make all the words" in arranging husbands for his daughters and, for obvious reasons, the father would try to select rich, older men.

Our little Wambui's husband had been chosen and Mbae had already started accepting payment for her, in cows. Three cows were standard, as a down payment. If a prospective husband were not already poor, he soon became so after paying the father of his wife-to-be. The prescribed bride price included many goats, wild honey, beer, a new blanket, a packet of tobacco and much else before he could finally lead her to his home after her ritual circumcision at about age 13. In addition to the dowry, a goodly white sheep was expected after the birth of each child.

But Wambui was a determined girl. First, she had heard enough of the words of God to give her courage to refuse the circumcision required of Maasai girls in those days. Two other girls attempted to stand with her in refusing this rite but their fathers beat them into submission and all three were circumcised.

Wambui then refused to marry the man her father had chosen for her. She said she hated him and would never marry him for he was not only a heathen but also well known to be of bad character. She held her ground this time. It was very daring for a Maasai girl to resist her father's authority. She even threw rocks at her prospective husband, a symbolic and unforgivable thing for a Maasai girl to do, but during all of this time she never missed a day of work for us.

Little did we know that, right in our home, Wambui had cast her eyes and hopes on Kuyoni, who was close to her own age, a most unusual thing for a Maasai girl to do. They adhered strictly to Maasai social regulations and never let anyone know of the feeling between them. One thing binding them closer together than anything else was their mutual love of the story of God's love for them.

Although we tried to discourage the Maasai from taking

foreign names at baptism, this custom had been started throughout Kenya many years before and had never changed. When Roy baptized them, Kuyoni chose the name "Peter" and Wambui chose "Eunice." We preferred the beautiful Maasai names, so we used both.

Eunice Wambui had made up her mind that she would marry Peter Kuyoni if he would ever ask her to do so. But no Maasai lad would ever dare directly ask a girl to marry him, so Kuyoni never did ask her until a long, long time later.

Meanwhile, just after the time Eunice was going to be taken by force and married off to the man who was buying her, she disappeared. We knew nothing of her real plans. She had a secret and she kept it well.

The day before she was to have been led to her groom in great ceremony, we left with our truck full of camping equipment, headed for the southern half of the Maasai Reserve where we were to hold meetings. But we went by way of Kijabe so we could visit other missionaries and, incidentally, Peter Kuyoni.

After his graduation from our mission school, Peter had enrolled in Bible School at Kijabe, where he would study, work and live with young men from many different tribes. We looked forward to visiting him there as well as his instructors, Charles and Mae Teasdale, who had been close friends from our own Bible School days back at Moody.

We made the long ascent to the top of the Mau Range, halfway to Kijabe, and set up an overnight camp at our out-school at Nairagie Ngare, just off the main road a few miles. Many wild buffalo roamed the tall grasses of this area. They were dangerous and very destructive to the village gardens. In those days the entire Maasai Reserve was a wild game preserve.

To our great surprise, the first person to greet us next morning at our campfire was Eunice Wambui. She had escaped from her home and walked all day and into the night to Nairagie Ngare by a shortcut. She knew how to cope with the tall grass and how to avoid the wild animals. Both were less threatening to her than her own father's wrath.

"Let me go with you," she pled. "I want to go as far as Kijabe where I can enter the work of the hospital."

Since we were only guests in Maasai country, we trod lightly. We had very much to learn of their culture, customs and habits and we did not want to antagonize or alienate them unwittingly.

"Should we take her?" we asked the Maasai Christians at the out-school.

Their advice was unanimous: "Yes, take her."

We did so and Dr. and Mrs. E. L. Davis and their staff at Kijabe's Theodora Hospital were very understanding and kind to Eunice. Fortunately she spoke fluent Kikuyu, having learned it from her own mother. Kijabe is in Kikuyu country. She was given work there and was safe from her father and anyone else. Furthermore, we discovered that she was not alone. There were many girls there who had run away from their parents.

Kuyoni, we found, was doing well in Bible School. He had quickly caught on to the Swahili language, the medium of instruction at the school being Kenya's trade language, and in his free time was taking organ lessons on the little pump organ we had given the Bible School the year before. He also worked part time learning to set type in the printing press.

The only time Kuyoni and Wambui ever communicated while at Kijabe was in shy looks covertly exchanged after church when everybody went outside to visit — women on one side and men on the other. African culture then did not allow a boy and his girl friend to stand around and talk together, nor of course ever to walk together anywhere. But the love these two held for each other needed no words to express. It was firm and true and they were willing to wait for each other.

After dropping Eunice off at Kijabe, we continued our journey through wide, sweeping Maasailand. The Maasai Reserve, as it was called then, which shaped the natures of these young people, straddles the Kenya-Tanzania border and alternates between low, hot, sometimes malarial plains, and high, cold bracing ranges.

2 *Sailing Away to Siyabei*

WE HAD BEEN APPOINTED AS MISSIONAIRES to the Maasai straight out of Bible School by Rev. Charles Hurlburt, director of Africa Inland Mission. Neither Roy nor I knew the Maasai from the Egyptians, but we were ready and eager to go.

We sailed away from New York for Africa on July 29, 1923, going first to England in what was then considered a palatial ship, the *SS Leviathan*. With our two little ones, we climbed in and out of the bowels of the ship by a spiral stairway. Our cabin was four decks below the dining room and there was no elevator in our tourist section.

"It is the largest ship in the world," Roy wrote home to his family. "It was built by Germany, then taken over by the U.S. during the war. Eight million dollars were spent on her . . . she's quite a contrast to what we had during the war days crossing in Army transports." We relished sitting out on deck chairs bundled up in steamer rugs.

In London we boarded the *SS Norman Castle*, which headed across the turbulent Bay of Biscay, through the Gibraltar Straits and into the Mediterranean Sea. We had hoped to see the Rock of Gibraltar but heavy fog prevented it. Every few minutes the ship's whistle blew, nearly scaring Harry Daniel out of his two years' growth each time. We did see high cliffs off the coast of Spain, as well as the hills and beautiful countryside along the Algerian coast.

I was quite seasick, in fact a lot more than Roy was. The ship's laundry room was down at the very bottom of the vessel. Roy was very good at helping me with the constant care of our babies and keeping diapers and laundry done during the next four weeks from London to Mombasa.

Port Said, at the entrance of the Suez Canal, was our first African port of call. The people were all Egyptian, not black. Everybody on board, settlers, government officials and missionaries alike, left the ship and went ashore to the stores to buy red-lined pith helmets for protection against the African sun. We couldn't find anything small enough that would stay on the baby's head, though. I tried in vain to make some sort of little sun cap for her but nothing worked.

We bought many yards of red material, for we were told that red counteracts the dangerous actinic rays of the sun. Back on the ship, I lined our umbrella and the baby carriage with red. I even made each of us a thick red flannel "spine pad" which we were told should be fastened on our underwear. It extended from the neck down to the coccyx, supposedly protecting our spines from those actinic rays. In addition to all this, some people even believed the red-lined helmets should be worn at night, just to be sure!

People ceased believing in the need for red flannel in later years, or perhaps just got too hot for that, and many whites went to the other extreme of wearing no hats at all. However, white skins do need protection and dermatologists to this day tell us that red or green are the best colors for screening out the sun's ultraviolet rays which are the chief culprits in causing skin cancers.

"More sand and barrenness than I ever saw," Roy reported in his letter home after we left Port Said one afternoon and entered the Suez Canal. "We glided along rapidly and silently through the canal. Our boat towered high over the surrounding . . . sea of sand.

"I was awakened . . . in the early morning . . . by the rattling and grinding of the hoisting machinery and went on deck to find out what was happening. The Egyptian canalman (pilot) was having his boat lowered into the water preparatory to leaving the ship. As the canalman and his two companions held onto the rope and towed themselves along by the side of the huge ship and then finally let loose and drifted off in the stillness of the clear moonlight, it seemed eerie and quite romantic and almost as if one were reading a book and not really travelling through this land of mystery. . . . Just after daybreak, we arrived at the city of Suez, where the Red Sea lay before our gaze and invitingly beckoned us.

"Bare, stark mountain ranges billowed up . . . on either side of the channel to the Red Sea. All eyes in the missionary party were eagerly looking for Mount Sinai. Early in the afternoon we came within sight of the Sinai Range, and later we could distinguish Mount Sinai, way in the distance, towering high in the dense grey atmosphere. . . ."

We have never again in our lives been as hot as we were in the Suez Canal and the Red Sea. We left our stifling cabin at night and tried to sleep up on deck.

Three roasting days later we docked at Port Sudan where we saw our first black Africans. They had decorative stripes down the sides of their faces, made by scarring. They were called "fuzzie wuzzies" because their heavy heads of bushy hair stuck straight out all over. They looked savage. Theirs was the authentic "Afro hairdo."

As they worked on the dock loading our ship with cargo, they started singing. What beautiful rhythm and, oh, how melodious to our ears! Then and there, God negotiated between me and the black people.

To tell the truth, I still had not resolved my apprehensions about going to Africa. But this singing of the "savages" melted my heart. It made me happy and willing to be on my way with Roy and our two babies to serve God, even in this hot, black Africa.

As soon as we rounded Cape Guardafui, a cool breeze came from the Indian Ocean. A furious monsoon storm followed, bringing refreshing relief from the stifling heat of the Red Sea — but rough sailing!

"We were glad to get out of the Red (hot) Sea," I wrote back to Roy's Aunt Zora, "but we were seasick as soon as we got into the Indian Ocean. Nearly everybody (with the exception of our children) was sick during those last four days on board."

Roy added a post script: "Our chief regret is that the monsoon caused us to lose a whole week's board and lodging, for which we had paid perfectly good money."

As we sailed down the east coast of Africa and approached Mombasa, the howling rainstorm quieted, and we even got out our steamer rugs again in the cool evenings. The skyline of that beautiful port was different from anything I had ever seen—a mass of tall, graceful palm trees. Today Mombasa is a modern port for oceangoing vessels, but in 1923 our ship had to dock far out in the ocean and small boats paddled by African oarsmen came to take us in to the shore. We climbed overboard on rope ladders, down into one of those tiny, rocking boats. Roy took Harry Daniel while I settled Ruth Marie on my lap. The oarsmen were ready to row us in to the shore, when a loud clamor broke loose from overhead:

"Cover that child's head up!" the people still on board the ship were screaming down at me. "That child will die of the sun! Cover that child up!"

Somehow, we had arrived still lacking a hat for Ruth Marie. Fortunately, I always wore middy blouses in those days because I was nursing her every three hours, so I simply pulled up my blouse and stuck her little head under there and tried to protect her that way. Harry, who had turned two years old on board ship, had his own little helmet and spine pad, so he was all right.

Thrilled and happy as we were to leave the ship and stand on land again, it still took us several hours for the Indian customs agents to clear us. The iron-roofed customs shed was like a furnace there at sea level on the equator. When we finally boarded the boat train, it too was hot. This ancient little narrow-gauged train came down to the coast from Nairobi, Kenya's capital city in the cool highlands, to meet ships every day. On the way, the train passed through desert where no man could live without protection in those days. Dusk brought the beginning of coolness.

The train took us up to Voi for our first stop, a 9:00 p.m. supper in a train station dining room, complete with white tableclothes and waiters. Then we got back on the train and tried to settle down for the night ride through the desert. The train rolled and rocked, going slowly upgrade.

All night long the creaking of the train was monotonous, and we just existed, six or eight souls in each compartment, sitting up straight, listening to the wind blow. The desert earth was a powdery red clay and the train was not at all airtight. The next morning we were all grotesquely covered with red dust. No one escaped this dust coating—passengers, stewards, and train men. Now we—Asians, whites and blacks—were all one color.

At dawn the Indian steward tapped on our compartment door.

"Open your window shutters and look out," he called. There on the west horizon we saw red dawn reflected on a snow-covered mountain reaching three miles into the sky! It was magnificent, two-peaked Mount Kilimanjaro. Its higher peak, Kibo, 19,340 feet, is a dome-like summit which contains a mile-wide volcanic crater that is perpetually ice-capped. The secondary peak, Mawenzi, 17,564 feet, is a jagged volcanic cone which seldom holds any snow.

It is written in history books that the German missionary-explorer of the Church Missionary Society, Johannes Rebmann, discovered this phenomenon of a permanent cap of blue ice on an extinct volcano that rises up suddenly from a low, hot plain only three degrees south of the equator. It is also written that when he wrote home telling his people of this discovery, they said the African sun must have driven him mad; there could be no such thing as a mountain with glaciers on top of it in the center of Africa.

Roy and I, with everybody else, hung out of the train windows gazing. Such a sight! We didn't even realize that we were already in Maasai country.

Soon, wild game began to appear in profusion as we

entered grasslands which stretched as far as the eye could see. Everybody got excited over huge ostrich running gracefully beside the train, fluttering their feathers furiously. We were passing through Tsavo, which today is a national park.

When lunch time came, the train stopped at Sultan Hamud, where the Chief Steward of the Dining Room, an Indian, got into a serious argument with the Train Officer, another Indian. They argued loudly in very circumspect English, obviously learned from books and distinctly pronounced.

"I have no food for them to eat," the Chief Steward protested. "I have received here a telegram with the number coming for dinner — so many adults, so many adultresses, and so many infants—but you have brought far more than that number!"

Our dusty little train still had to climb 2,000 more feet in altitude before we reached Nairobi, which was not an impressive sight in those days. Around the train station there were a few corrugated iron *dukas* (small Indian shops) some on stilts, some on the ground. There were also a few tents, mules and carts and many rickshaws, but almost no motor cars to be seen.

We all got off the train and took rickshaws into town. We found only one big store, a Whiteway & Laidlaw store, one of a chain of such stores all over the British Empire. There, at last, we found a tiny helmet that met our baby's need and I could stop tucking her head under my middy blouse every time we got out in the sun. We cleaned up and ate dinner in grand style at the old Stanley Hotel.

The boat train that had brought us from the coast had to return to meet the next day's ship. But our destination was still further up the railway line, so we transferred that same evening to another train that huffed and puffed up yet another thousand feet over a distance of some forty miles to Kijabe. This was where our Africa Inland Mission main station was located, high up on the west slope of a heavily forested mountain range.

The Maasai word *kijabe* means "cold wind." It surely

was cold! The altitude sign at the railroad station said 7,235 feet above sea level. We had cast off our steamer rugs in hot Mombasa, but here we got them out again to cover our babies and ourselves.

It was very dark and we were the only boat passengers to get off the train at Kijabe. A tall, thin man wearing a helmet on his head in the dark night stepped up:

"Hello, are you the Shaffers?" he asked. "I am Lawson Propst, from the AIM Station."

What a relief! Indeed, as our train had approached the stop we had seen a long line of kerosene lanterns coming single file in the darkness down to the railroad station. It was this white man, with five Kikuyu girls and five Kikuyu men leading five mules, coming to meet us and carry our loads up to the mission.

Mr. Propst soon got our luggage parceled out to the mules. One Kikuyu girl carried a box three feet long, eighteen inches wide, and about twelve inches deep with a little padding inside; this is where they put our sleeping baby, Ruth Marie. She never stirred. The girl carried the box on her back, suspended from a strap around her forehead. Her hands held the strap constantly steady and thus the baby was carried safely up the steep path in the darkness.

Roy and I were mounted on mules. We looked at each other dubiously.

"Could we please get off and walk?" Roy asked.

"No," Lawson said. "By one misstep you could easily land yourselves at the bottom of the deep ravine which is invisible to you in the darkness."

It was an odd experience, up on those mules, but this was just the beginning of many, many new experiences.

"The mules know the path," Lawson assured us. "They will never toss you off."

We stayed on. All the others walked, for they seemed to know the path blindfolded.

The Africans sang hymns in beautiful four-part harmony as we ascended three miles up the cold mountain path, to the mission station. They sang with more gusto the closer we got.

Four days later, when we would walk back down this mountain path, we were to see the treacherous hairpin bends in a dense enclosing forest and slippery, washed-out places where we strangers could so easily have slipped that night when we came in song.

Our entourage arrived at the home of a dear widow, Mr. Propst's mother-in-law, Mrs. Jane Myers, one of the earliest ladies to go to Kenya under the AIM. This grand old pioneer's family is still serving the Lord in Africa, well into the fourth generation, grandchildren of Lawson and his wife Clo. Mrs. Myers was so sweet, calm and friendly that the warmth of her welcome melted us right away.

"Take off your coats," she said in her deep, quiet voice, "and come over to get warm by the fireplace. Are you awfully hungry? I have food and a bath for you. We are so glad you have come."

What else could we ask for? We had no idea a big white bathtub would be found in Africa. To our amazement, Mrs. Myers took us to a little room where she had a lion-footed bathtub with hot water already in it! Everyone just off safari needs and wants a bath. We surely did, for we were covered thick with that powdery red dust.

Mrs. Myers then took us up to the attic room and showed us the beds she had made for all four of us. What a warm welcome in such a cold place!

Mr. Will Blaikie, the station superintendent, came at once to meet us. He was young, just three years out from New Zealand with his wife, Laura. They had charge of the boarding students in the school for missionaries' children just down the road.

When we looked out the window next morning, we discovered we were high on an escarpment overlooking a vast grassland: the fifty-mile-wide Kidong Valley three thousand feet below. And rising up sharply from the valley floor were two extinct volcanoes, Suswa and Longonot, silhouetted against clear sky with a hint of dawn tinting their peaks.

In the Kidong Valley was one tiny, meandering stream

called the Kidong, meaning "tail" in Maasai, and its course does look like a cow's switched tail. Usually it was dried up. This valley is one section of the Great Rift Valley which cuts up through northeast Africa and can be traced geologically to the Jordan Valley in Palestine. The panorama at dawn looked like a sea of glass with black mountains rising around it.

The school for missionaries' children at Kijabe is called Rift Valley Academy (RVA). Will Blaikie did a marvelous job at RVA feeding, bedding and schooling some twenty school-children from stations scattered all over East Africa. The school building was a two-story, cut-stone structure, 150 feet long and 50 feet wide, such as we had never expected to see here. It had wooden floors; no ceilings on the second floor (which was the dormitory) under the shingle roof; glass windows; and one bath tub for the girls' half of the building and one for the boys' half — complete with outside sanitation.

Missionary work certainly was not all preaching, we were discovering. At Kijabe we also found a large agricultural work directed by a Kikuyu named Maingi and Lawson Propst. They sent vegetables to missionaries all over East Africa into areas where it was too hot and dry for any to grow. I watched Lawson's wife, Clo, pack figs in fig leaf-lined wooden boxes that went to the farthest points and arrived in good condition.

There was also the Theodora Hospital where Dr. E. L. Davis, with his wife, Bernice, and Bessie Stevenson (both nurses) frequently worked far into the nights with no thought for themselves.

Dr. Virginia Blakeslee directed the Kikuyu Girls school. Miss Anna Zimmermann had the large African elementary school. There was a small industrial school as well. Kijabe's little printing press, small though it was, was serving all the other missions in Kenya. It printed songbooks, readers, reports, and letters of all kinds, and in all languages. Kenya has twenty-four main languages.

Africans streamed in from all directions on Sundays to the large stone church seating over four hundred, usually with an overflow congregation outside. Kijabe was the center of influence for a large surrounding area. Kijabe is now one of the three largest mission stations in the world — the other two being ELWA in Monrovia, Liberia, and the Christian and Missionary Alliance Station HCJB at Quito, Ecuador.

Kijabe presently has a large new medical center which was opened by Kenya's President Arap Moi and was built under the direction of Dr. Stanley Barnett. Stan is a son of Eric Barnett, for many years AIM field director, and a grandchild of early pioneers, Albert and Alma Barnett, who first worked with Stauffachers and Tagi at Rumuruti. There is also a large TV and radio work at Kijabe now. To accommodate over one hundred resident missionaries, the station has streets with names and numbers. In fact, Kijabe is today a young metropolis with many major departments.

But when we arrived in 1923, there were only about ten missionaries and six homes. George Rhoad was the field director.

Pleasant as our four days were among the folks at Kijabe in Kikuyuland, this was not the end of our line. We were headed for a tiny little station called Siyabei, out among the Maasai on the other side of the Kidong Valley, where we were to take over from the Stauffachers. Mr. Rhoad told us that John Stauffacher was on his way to Kijabe to get us with his Maasai co-worker, Molungit ole Sembele.

On the second day, John and Molungit arrived in a two-wheeled cart pulled by two mules, Nancy and Ned, covered with dust and full of excitement.

"We met a pride of five lions down on the plain!" John exclaimed. "Only divine intervention kept the lions from killing both mules, and us as well." After this first burst of excitement upon meeting, tall, wide-shouldered John, we soon discovered he was more often taciturn and quiet, a man who preferred to let his wife do the talking. Molungit was a tiny person with a broad, white smile. He also seemed to be a man of few words, but did, however, speak to us in English, having been to America with the Stauffachers on their first furlough. We all remained two more days at Kijabe to let Ned and Nancy rest and get filled up with good green grass.

John decided to have the mules spend only one night on the way back because of the danger of lions, so Molungit and the mules and the loaded cart stayed at Kijabe one day, while John, Roy and I with the babies in our little collapsible Montgomery Ward buggy started out afoot, threading our way back down the escarpment path and finally out to the edge of the dry, dusty plain where the road was rocky, rutted and rough.

Roy had very wisely put on his khaki overalls, a sensible outfit for this two-day tramp through volcanic dust and dry grass up to our waists. I should have used more sense and worn khaki too, but instead I wore my stylish, ankle-length black woolen skirt, and of course the middy blouse which had proven such a serviceable outfit for nursing Ruth Marie every three hours. I never once thought of giving my wee baby carrot pulp or so-called baby food. No such thing was available, and besides, "Mother's milk for babies and cows' milk for calves" was my slogan. The eyes, teeth and entire physique of all six of my children prove they lacked nothing.

With a tent borrowed from the Blaikies, we pitched camp the first night at the base of the escarpment. A cold wind kept our tent billowing most of the night. That, plus the howling and laughing of hyenas — you can guess how much we slept. But the volcanic dust of the earth made soft beds and we had good, warm blankets and a lantern.

The next morning, before dawn, Molungit and the mules arrived, fresh for the long day ahead over the hot, waterless Kidong Valley. A Kikuyu man took the tent back to Kijabe to return it to the Blaikies, who had to use it on safari. The next two nights we would sleep under the stars on the Kidong. Two adults rode in the cart with the babies and two walked, taking turns as we went. This was the longest walk Roy and I ever took—and oh, how we used to love to take walks in Chicago!

While we were attending Moody Bible Institute, the only place any of the young folk went out to was Moody Tabernacle. The Tab was seven blocks north of our home, across from

Lincoln Park, a nice long evening's walk. One of the popular songs of the day was "The Longest Way Round is the Sweetest Way Home," and of course many a time we circled a block or two on the way.

Of course it was not just the walks that drew us like a magnet to the Tab. It may have only had sawdust aisles, but the music and the messages and the dynamism of Paul Rader, the pastor, made the Tab a wonderful center of enthusiasm and influence. Just before graduation, Reverend Charles Hurlburt, director of the Africa Inland Mission, came for special meetings. He told of Peter Cameron Scott, the brilliant, inspired young man who founded the AIM in 1895 with eight dedicated companions. Scott's health gave out after only a little over a year of rugged pioneer work establishing several stations in Kenya with them. He died very young but the mission lives on to this day.

Charles Hurlburt, who took over from Scott, met with Roy and me while he was at MBI, as well as with several other couples who were hopeful candidates for the mission. He and A. F. Gaylord, who was on the MBI staff as well as chairman of the AIM Chicago Council, interviewed us. These two men gave us a long, rigorous oral examination, then ended with the request that *we* close in prayer!

The two men silently looked us up and down and all over, and finally Mr. Hurlburt broke the suspense: "I want this strong couple to come to the proud Maasai to take over from John and Florence Stauffacher while they come home on furlough."

So here we were, completing the long journey by car, ship and train, finally walking behind a cart across the Great Rift Valley into Maasai country with John and Molungit.

We had our chop box, food, lantern, a canvas water bag, a small trunk of clothes and a lot of presumption to cross that immense plain through the myriads of wild animals that parted to let us pass. Roy and I had been to circuses before, but this was the biggest one ever. There were herds of kongoni, tommy (Thompson's gazelles), zebra, and ostrich, with the young of each running right along with the older ones. Also eland, giraffe, greater bustards, granty (Grant's gazelles) and jackal. Scattered among all these wild animals were herds of Maasai cattle in the charge of young Maasai herders.

Near dusk, when the air started to cool a little, it was again Roy's and my turn to ride in the cart. John told us to stop at the first kraal we came to.

The tired mules trotted slowly after the long day. We went on and on, but saw no kraal.

When darkness came, Roy decided we should turn back. After he reckoned we had backtracked at least three miles, in the distance we could see the tiny light of a fire some one hundred yards off the track, to the right. It was John and Molungit at the kraal—a circular thornbush enclosure not more than three feet high. John had not told us what a kraal looked like and we were looking for huts with grass roofs!

This spot was known to everyone as "Quarantine," John explained. It was on a demarcation line between Kikuyu and Maasai country, past which neither side could take their cattle. It was designed to prevent the spread of rinderpest. Even ox transports outspanned here and hitched up to fresh oxen on the other side of the boundary. However, sheep could pass, apparently being immune. It was here that sheep traders kept their sheep at night when enroute from the interior to Kijabe where they could market their sheep for a good price.

We pulled up inside the thorn kraal and Roy tied the mules to the cart wheels for lack of any tree. Night swiftly descended and all the equatorial stars came out for a beautiful display, dominated by the Southern Cross, while we sat around the campfire where John was cooking some bacon he had bought at Ramji Kanji's *duka* in Kijabe, for a special treat.

Suddenly the stars left us. Lightning cracked close by, thunder rolled, and down came the rain. Simultaneously Nancy and Ned broke away from the wheels and ran out into the dark, frightened by the grunts and howls of lions and hyenas which had been lured close by the smell of the bacon.

While Molungit and Roy ran to retrieve the mules, John built up the fire and placed the high cart over the fire so we could have its shelter. With the mules safely back and tied more tightly, Roy threw his big army tarpaulin over the cart and this kept the rain off us. The hyenas kept laughing at us and hung around for a long time even though John and Molungit threw firebrands and stones at them.

People are funny. In the middle of all the commotion, our two-year-old Harry, who was housebroken, suddenly had to "go." I always carried a tiny little white potty just for him. At once I produced it and there he sat, under the cart, by the fire while it rained, very busy about his own affairs. I think this made John and Molungit laugh even louder than the hyenas.

This was our second night on the path. Who can possibly sleep, sitting with three other adults and two babies under a two-wheeled mule cart? We couldn't, so we were glad when dawn began to show faintly in the east. Roy blew up the fire and pushed the cart away. The rain stopped. John got some food and tea ready.

Molungit harnessed up the mules, and I nursed the baby and washed the faces of both children in the cup of water allotted to each of us. Even Theodore Roosevelt was rationed water when he went on his famous hunting trip across this very same road. Almost suddenly, countless wild game were all about us hungrily grazing on the rain-freshened grass.

We got an early start, for we would do well to reach Siyabei by nightfall even if we kept going steadily.

We went up out of the Kidong Valley, over the Mau Range, which is the west wall of the Great Rift Valley, through sagebrush, wild olive and cedar forests, then descended to the bridge across the rushing Siyabei River, our first water since Kijabe. We still had many miles to go to reach Siyabei station farther up the river. How gratefully we did bathe our dust-covered faces, hands and feet, and gulp cups of tea in a quick pause there on its grassy bank.

Then again we went up, up a steep grade where the road seemed to climb over itself on three levels. On and on we went, riders and walkers alternating.

Just before sunset the air began to chill. We were all together this time. Leaving a broad plain and descending a steep, rocky road into a sagebush area, we began to hear a continuous roaring sound.

"Do you see that over there?" John asked.

So camouflaged against the forest behind it that we saw nothing at first, there was a tin roof on a stone house, the same color as the rocky outcrop on which it was built.

"That is our house," said John, "and there is a stone building beyond, which is the chapel." Between us and the station was the Siyabei River once more, and a short walk downstream was a magnificent, roaring waterfall with about a sixty foot drop.

Just as darkness set in, the tired mules and tired people dragged their feet slowly up the last rocky stretch to the station. Florence Stauffacher came out on the road with her arms full of huge roses and a big "welcome weary travelers" smile on her face. She was a small person, with bright eyes and a keen mind. She had walked this safari many times before so she knew how tired, footsore, hungry, cold and covered with dust we were.

This was one of the happiest meetings in our lives, at the end of a two-day safari on foot across the Kidong. So restful to eyes and soul were the deep purple violets growing all around the veranda, and the thick red geraniums climbing the five posts to the roof.

Florence was a wonderful person; there was none like her. She had a hot bath ready for us in their tin tub in their bedroom, hot fires in the two fireplaces, and hot food on the stove, with Gashisha, their excellent cook, waiting to serve it.

In the bedroom, using the fire in the fireplace for light, I bathed the babies; then Roy fed Harry while I bathed; then

Roy bathed while I fed the baby. We all used the same hot water ferried from the kitchen stove in *debbies* (gasoline cans). The water was quite cool and dirty by the time Roy had bathed, but we felt good.

John waited for his own bath until after supper. Neither man had shaved for two days so we had fun about that. They looked terrible!

The hanging kerosene lamp in the center of the supper table lit up ten happy faces, for Stauffacher's teenage sons, Raymond and Claudon, and Dr. Davis' two sons, Phillip and Linnell, were all also there, on vacation from the Rift Valley Academy. (All four of these husky lads, as well as many of their offspring have become successful missionaries, some back to Kenya, some to Zaire and Tanzania and some to South America.)

What a feast Florence set before us: wild guinea fowl, well cooked and seasoned, several vegetables all out of their own garden, homemade bread and the inevitable pot of tea. For dessert she had a gallon of strawberries picked from their own garden—and cream! Few people in the USA have ever seen the thick, rich cream that skinny Maasai cows produce. Pure cream on strawberries was too good to be true.

After supper was over, we all sat around the roaring fireplace and listened to John recite to the others all about our safari. It had been only the first of many nights we were to sleep out under the stars, listening to the laughing hyenas, the roaring lions and the sawing leopards.

3 *Introduction to Maasai*

OUR FIRST DAY AT SIYABEI, a Sunday in late 1923, was a fitting start to our thirty-five years of living with the Maasai.

We sat with Florence in Sunday School and church in the little grass-roofed stone chapel. We felt relaxed to be in church again even though we didn't know a soul nor did we comprehend even a word of the language of the rest of the congregation, who were in every form of dress and undress imaginable, looking at us with big eyes, curiosity written all over their faces. We were an absorbing spectacle to them and they to us, especially those on the back rows, who wore the true Maasai garb: well-oiled, red ochre-impregnated skins and elaborate beaded decorations worn on all parts of their bodies—ankles, wrists, waists, biceps, necks, ears and shaved heads. These nomads who lived out on the plains in kraals, were constantly on the move with their livestock. In the front rows of the church were the local Maasai who had mostly adopted Western dress. Many of them had Kikuyu wives, lived in thatch-roofed huts and had made corn, bean, and potato gardens all around the station.

They all closely watched the new, young, foreign and ignorant missionary couple with two babies. They had brought babies to church with them too and each one was like a chubby doll, irresistible. Some carried their babies on shoulders, some babies were tied to mother's back in a sling, some were being led by the hand and some were not yet born. There were all sizes of little ones paddling their bare feet in the dusty path coming to Sunday School and church.

One striking impression we received was of the silent, reverent, worshipful attitude of every child and adult as soon as they entered the chapel door. If a baby started to cry, the mother got up quickly and went out with it, holding her hand over the baby's mouth as she went. If a man had to cough or spit, he got up, went out and expectorated, then returned. It doesn't take a Maasai long to learn the etiquette of a church service for he already has a built-in sense of honor and respect for others.

A few who could already read were singing the hymns out of a little red Maasai songbook the Stauffachers had had printed at Kijabe. Tagi, Molungit and another teacher, Milaun, had worked with them on the translation of this book, plus a catechism and some simple school books.

During that first church service at Siyabei, all was quiet, men sitting on the left of the aisle, women on the right. Everyone was listening to the message John Stauffacher was giving of the good news from God.

Suddenly we heard loud screaming and distressed shouting coming from the gardens nearby. We were startled. But everyone else knew what was happening, and sat still. We couldn't see what was happening through the windows because they were cloth-covered to keep out the cold on Siyabei's typically cool, misty mornings. During the final hymn, Florence discreetly whispered to us that a few watchers who had stayed home to guard the gardens, were routing a drove of baboons that came to raid. Given half a chance, baboons could and surely would, quickly clear out most of the corn in all the gardens. Furthermore, the baboons even knew when it was Sunday, their best raiding time! They feast in dead silence until detected, then scream like humans while being chased out. Baboons don't just grab an ear of corn and run. Each one puts an ear under each armpit, one in his mouth and one in each hand and foot—then runs for dear life back to the forest.

At the close of the service we all filed out into the sunshine and everyone greeted everyone else. This reception was our first introduction to the Maasai handshake, a very light brushing of the fingertips. Each tribe has its own type of handshake; not all of them grab and pump, as white folks do. If we had known, we could have said hello to the school-teachers, Soepi, Enok, and Olgoyai, for they were beginning to learn English. However, they were shy.

Following the church service, it came time for medical attention. As usual, all who thought they might be sick walked down the path to sit under a tree by Stauffacher's house, waiting in order until Florence would come to each one.

"Where are you dying?" she would inquire in proper Maasai terminology. *"Kaji nikieea?"*

Florence Stauffacher did a large medical work with very limited supplies; she felt fortunate if she had enough permanganate crystals, soap and water, and a salve she made up herself from sulphur and fat for the always-present itch.

Monday morning John started us right in on learning Maasai. Language study was of supreme importance because he wanted us to pass our first exam before they left on furlough. Every day he taught us new words, verb conjugations, grammar, short sentences and greetings, and made us talk, talk, talk.

He brought several Maasai to class to speak to us so we might hear them and reply. But all we did was stare blankly, for they spoke so fast we didn't comprehend anything they said. Book study, hearing and speaking are three different approaches to any strange language. Our ignorance and helplessness must have been really comical, though everyone was kind and tolerant and wanted so much to put the sounds into our lips and ears. We were as dumb and deaf animals.

Finally, I discovered one of my best avenues for hearing and learning Maasai was to attend the various prayer meetings and listen to the women and the men pray. One by one, I picked up my words, wrote them down, then tried to use them as my own. Later, I could hear sentences and understand them. It became a real blessing to hear especially the women, quietly yet fervently cry out to God to worship Him, praise and thank Him for all His mercies and to ask of Him their hearts' desires.

The process of the white man's trying to learn the African language affords great mirth and laughter to the Africans, in private of course, as they have too much honor and respect to show it in public. They are most patient and longsuffering when a white person mixes up the gender, tense and number of personal pronouns and verbs. It is uncanny how they can interpret what the white man means when he says, for example, "This women, he came tomorrow and bought his ten egg."

One day when Roy pinned a snake with a rake, he kept yelling for Kamau, the garden boy, to "go quickly" (as he thought) for the gun. Instead, all the time Roy was shouting "stand still, stand still," employing the word *"ntasho"* instead of *"ntasioi."* Of course Roy was upset when the lad didn't move. His consternation was equalled by the rooted boy's confusion at being shouted at for doing exactly as he was told.

After studying language for six or seven hours a day, we were a bit tense, so it was a genuine relief in the evenings to put the babies to bed early, then go sit in the livingroom at Stauffachers' and listen to wonderful classical records on their Victrola. Or John would play the organ and I the violin, also classics. John did not like jazz any more than I did. One thing he demanded of any and all houseguests, whoever came to their home: whenever he went to wind up the Victrola, everybody, old and young, had to sit down and keep absolute silence while the machine played. However, we looked forward daily to this real pleasure and enjoyment.

Florence would sit at the table and write her letters until the music ended. Nine o'clock was always bedtime and it was none too early, since six o'clock was always time to get up, and our days were full.

From the very first, in 1923, Roy and I were put to work at the little school held in the chapel on cedar benches, with a small blackboard leaned up against the whitewashed, mud-plastered wall. The students were all men and boys. Girls and women did not yet come. Each student had a slate pencil and a slate.

We were the ones who learned a lot. We had to pitch in and help teach *sukul* whether we knew how or not, and do all else by the same token. Missionaries surely do have a lot to learn on the field beside the new language. They don't learn it all back in Bible School.

First, we taught reading, writing and arithmetic. Fortunately, the early missionaries, government officials and others who reduced the African languages to writing, all used the International Phonetic Alphabet; consequently none of the African languages have been complicated with five or more sounds for each vowel.

John and Florence were eager to go on their furlough and we were striving to be able to stand on our own feet as soon as possible. They taught us what to do and not do, from their valuable experience. Roy found Florence's first aid work easy after his Army medical corps training.

John and Florence had established Siyabei five years before we came. During their first term on the field fifteen years before that, they had put in several years of pioneering work at Rumuruti, far north of Kijabe, with Albert and Alma Barnett, an adventurous Australian and his sweet Swedish bride, whose many descendents still serve on the mission field to this day. There were also two single ladies, Bertha Simpson, a classmate of Florence's from North Central College, and a tiny Englishwoman, Mary Slater. Rumuruti was where both Tagi and Molungit first joined the work; in those days the Laikipia Plains around it were Maasai country before they moved south to their present boundaries.

Then the Stauffachers' next term had been arduous years during which they covered hundreds of miles on foot with the party that walked from Kenya to Congo (now Zaire) over terrible terrain to establish the AIM in Congo. There, they lay flat with malaria for days at a time and endured other conditions modern missionaries would never dream of facing, to open a new field. Their many fruitful years are described in the book *Faster Beats the Drum* by their daughter-in-law, Gladys Stauffacher, first published by Kesho Press, Kijabe, in 1977 and distributed throughout the world from the AIM headquarters in Pearl River, N.Y.

When they first arrived at Siyabei in 1918 after their second furlough, John and Florence lived in a grass shelter while constructing a little two-room stick house. By the time we trekked across the Kidong to them, this was their guest house. To us, the stick house was a palace compared to camping under a cart on the trail. Animal skins on the dirt floor by a bed, table and chair, made it homelike and easy on tired feet.

The Stauffachers had long since moved into a large, rough-rubble stone house John had built of small boulders picked up right on the spot. The walls were almost two feet thick, laid up in mud and "African cement" (fresh cow manure). There was no real cement to be had. Absence of freezing and thawing allows the mud and manure mixture to hold as fast as cement, and when it dries, it is odorless.

In contrast, I was surprised to see glass panes in the windows and brass knobs on the doors! They had created a real mansion. The "little library"—as the latrine was called, for the Montgomery Ward catalogue was always there—was down the garden path a bit, also made of stone, roofed with flattened gasoline can *debbies*.

Roy, himself a good gardener, appreciated John's success in that line. Besides strawberries down the hill in the swamp, he had vegetables and fruit trees by the house. But baboons, bushbuck, monkeys, porcupines and other invaders raided his gardens continuously.

"Let's build a stone wall around the garden and put a high chicken wire fence on top of the stone," suggested Roy.

John and Roy quickly accomplished this, for Siyabei is on a very stony hill and, by collecting the stones for the wall, they cleared an area large enough to double the size of their garden.

The garden wall-fence kept out all species except the

monkeys and baboons, who climb over anything. But they were not eager to come that close to our houses. Before long we were eating plenty of custard apples, artichokes, avocado pears, oranges, peaches, and a variety of berries, head lettuce, fresh corn on the cob and many other vegetables. We enjoyed working in the garden and Roy brought many loads of sheep and cow manure from Maasai kraals to spread on it. This produced two-pound tomatoes, believe it or not. We later took bushels of huge tomatoes to help feed the children at RVA.

By now, our equipment from the USA had arrived safely, traveling the last seventy-five miles by ox transport, a huge cargo wagon drawn by twenty span of oxen. We had need now for a cookhouse to hold the Army field range we had brought out. Roy built a twenty-foot by twenty-foot rough rubble stone kitchen and sent to Nairobi for rolls of tar paper for roofing.

Although the garden was well fenced, our houses were out in the open. At night we could hear what sounded like deep-voiced men in the next room all talking at the same time. It was actually lions prowlng outside — whether hungry or well fed, we couldn't tell. In our stick house we could see the stars peeking at us from overheard; doubtless the animals peeked at us through the stick walls, too. If the rain fell, I put the umbrella over the babies and Roy put the tarpaulin over our bed. The roof was of porous shingles.

While we tried to keep our house dry, we had to keep the dirt floors wet! This was our introductin to Kenya's chiggers. They thrive in dry dirt floors. Each chigger is the size of a pinpoint and their favorite place to hide is under the corners of toenails where one can't get to them easily. They itch and burn like all Billyo! The only thing to do is remove the chigger with a needle, without breaking the sack full of little baby chiggers if it's a female. We became convinced that only the Africans know how to get them out without breaking the sack, and they do it best with a three-inch thorn rather than a needle. You can end up with hundreds of little chiggers from one if you are not exceedingly careful, and a bad case of chiggers can cause infection, fever and serious illness. So we learned to keep our dirt floors damp and, hopefully, chigger-free.

Soon we found that our routine was to be peppered with continual encounters with the area's wildlife.

One day at 3:00 p.m. a little herdboy gave a distress call over on the next hill.

"*U-wi! U-wi! U-wi!*" he called.

A lion was after his herd of cattle. Before fifteen minutes had passed, practically every man and boy of the community rushed with *pangas* (bush knives) and spears to where the lad was. A huge lion had taken a two-year-old bullock from the boy's flock and killed it, but he left it and ran to hide. He would reclaim it later.

Instead of waiting for sundown, within an hour all the people came home driving all their herds ahead of them. Roy and the Stauffacher boys went out and built a gun trap over the carcass. Just as we were going to bed at 9:00 p.m., we heard the gun in the trap go off. Before we could get dressed, there were seven Maasai at our back door with *pangas* and spears and fire brands, eager to get the lion.

It was dark, so we all advanced gingerly, for a wounded lion is desperately dangerous. All were disappointed, but relieved, to find no lion, but rather a silver jackal in the trap. The Maasai boys skinned it for us, then we left both carcasses, with the gun reloaded, but we never got that lion.

"*Bwana! Bwana!*" some schoolboys yelled, running to our house some days later. "Quickly, bring your gun to Enok's house!"

"To Enok's house?" Roy wondered why the school teacher wanted a gun.

"Yes, there's a snake in it!" they jabbered urgently. "We have speared it but it is still very much alive."

Roy and the boys disappeared with the gun. The punctured snake had taken refuge up in the rafters of Enok's

roof, where it glared down on the excited humans. Roy carefully shot it right in the head, then the lads paraded it back to
our house so we all could see. It was a seven-foot, poisonous,
black mamba.

Finally, a lioness got caught in the gun trap. We paid
eight shillings to the boys to skin it for us. They did it well
with no mutilation. Two women in the crowd watching,
pointed out her nipples and claimed they could foretell how
many cubs she had inside her tummy. A good guess. She had
four unborn cubs. This time, Roy had set the trap where some
sheep had been stolen and there was great rejoicing at there
being not just one, but five less predators abroad.

Leopards too, had been stealing many sheep. By now the
Maasai had utter confidence that Roy could shoot or trap all
the leopards in the woods. The truth is that too often the trap
caught jackals or hyenas instead. In this harsh, man-
against-beast environment where the people's herds and
flocks were their walking larders, it seemed only right to help
them out against the lions and leopards.

Here they came once more, one night, pleading for him
to come set a trap for a leopard that had been seen. He
decided he would not go and set a trap at night, as he had so
foolishly done before. It is too dangerous to go out at night
and take chances approaching a wounded or trapped leopard
or lion. This time he set a steel trap twenty-five yards from
our house, anchoring it to a tough wild olive tree, then baited
it with meat.

The next morning he went out early, and there sat a
beautiful big leopard with only his front paw caught in the
trap. Roy shot it and the Maasai were thrilled. They brought
us gifts of milk and once more held a big celebration,
which we found out they always did whenever there was
one less leopard or lion to kill their precious flocks and
herds.

4 *Home, Sweet Log Cabin*

A SHORT WALK FROM OUR HOUSE, at the edge of the forest which surrounded Siyabei, there was a pleasant pool formed by a spring of warm water. Gashisha, the cook, Ndilai and his wife, Naiyolang, Olduboi, Njoroge, Maringo, Murage, Milaun, and Olgoyai were the first nine who qualified for baptism, having attended *Kilasi* (catechism class) for two years. John asked Roy to baptize them.

The whole congregation walked down to the little pool for the baptismal service. The hymn singing was sweet, all in Maasai of course. It was a moving sight to watch their faces, even though we couldn't understand a word they were saying, as each one told of his or her faith and reason for being baptized as an outward expression of an inner experience. We could sense that their language has ample words to express it all. It was a lovely beginning to our many years with the Maasai.

Gashisha was black aristocracy itself, not only in his bearing and intellect but also in his upright, friendly spirit and rapid progress in learning. He had a good wife, Nyambura, and a doll of a baby girl, Besi, who remained a family favorite ever after.

Of the rest of the group, Ndilai and Naiyolang became our evangelists; Olduboi became a good elder of the church at Siyabei for many years; Njoroge and Maringo, who were more Kikuyu than Maasai, soon moved to Kijabe; Murage was our mule tender.

Milaun, our school teacher, was excellent at translation

of the Scriptures. He knew several languages. Olgoyai was also a schoolteacher, along with Enok and Soepi, whom we had been too reticent to greet in English that first Sunday after church. By now I had taken over their English lessons and had even taught them a little geography, which they loved.

Roy and I were still working hard on our Maasai lessons. One day John excused me from Maasai so I could finish some arithmetic drill cards before the arrival of an inspection team, the "Phelps-Stokes Commission on Native Education." We all worked hard and fast in preparation for their advent and arranged for folks to come in to help clean up the entire station inside and out. We expectantly waited for the Commission all day long. Finally, about 4:30 p.m. they arrived and stayed only two hours. An American Ph.D. from Washington, D.C., and an Englishman with his wife were the Commission. They were visiting all schools in Kenya to assess what was being done "for advancement of the African natives, physically, mentally, industrially and socially." They were very friendly, and made no critical comments on our station, but rather commended the Stauffachers on the results of their five years of work.

Now more than ever, the Stauffachers were ready to go home on furlough. But as is often the case with missionaries, they just didn't have the funds. The longer their stay at Siyabei was prolonged, the more we realized that we would have to have more space than the tiny two-room stick house with a detached kitchen.

Roy made up his mind he was going to draw up a plan and build a cedar log house; and he did.

First, he got permission from the government to go up into the forest three miles north of the mission station and cut red cedar logs. They were ten to fourteen feet long and twelve to fourteen inches in diameter. He took the mules, Nancy and Ned, up there, hitched those logs to the harness by a chain, then dragged them down to the home site where he had built a stone footing. It was on the opposite end of the garden from the Stauffachers' house.

Roy wouldn't stop when the sun set and he wouldn't wait for the sun to rise in the morning. He was a man who worked early and late. First, he positioned sleeper logs on the foundation, with cut notches ready to receive the next layer of logs.

I helped him lift the first twelve logs and then it began to look like a real house. Roy would hoist each log up on the top by rope, then I would hold the rope while he went up there and set it into its notch. As the walls rose, it grew into a beautiful log cabin.

The Moody Church, in Chicago, had sent us $250.00 to build a house, so we used that money to buy corrugated iron for the roof and glass for the windows. Roy made the window frames and the doors out of the local cedar. By hand he split the cedar slabs and planed them for our floor. There were no power tools. It was a little irregular and some of the slabs didn't quite meet, but it was beautiful. When we nailed down the iron roof, we felt that we at last had a "home." Our ceiling consisted of branches of sweet-smelling sagebrush.

John Stauffacher loved to work with stone and we were mighty glad he did, for he built us a stone veranda and fireplace to keep us warm in cold weather.

This log cabin is still standing and giving shelter sixty years later and many missionaries have reared their children in it during that time.

When we finally settled into it, we were very happy and we felt safer than we had for a long time. Soon after moving in, I recorded in my diary:

> It's 7:00 p.m. and I can hear the resounding call of Roy's cornet calling the Africans to their midweek prayer meeting. He blows Army bugle calls which they love. They do sound pretty as they echo and re-echo from the rising hills on both sides of our hill. Some of the youngsters are already singing the bugle calls. They love to sing — and always in a high pitch. On their way home after night services, they sing lustily for protection from night-prowling animals.

Two days this past week a bold lion was roaming about in broad daylight at the foot of our hill, just across the stream. He must have had a good feed. Olenaisho's wife told us a growling leopard tried hard to enter their kraal fence two nights ago. Silole, our nurse girl, said she saw a huge leopard over in front of the log cabin when she came to work at 6:00 a.m. today. It saw her then growled and ran down the hill out of sight. Lions have roared many nights recently. We feel so good to be in the house when we hear them!

We had to cancel the night meetings, for it simply was not safe to go out in the darkness when all the nocturnal animals prowled. In emergencies, if people had to go out they carried firebrands. Wild olive wood held the fire better than sage or cedar. Actually, wild animals are not interested in human flesh; they are after dogs, cats, sheep, goats, cows, calves and donkeys. A wild animal will seldom attack a person unless it is provoked or surprised. Then it will retaliate immediately and with vicious violence.

In the daytime it was safe to be out and about. Often on Sundays, Roy and I took a stroll through the woods leading to a nearby spring after both kiddies were off to their naps, or we joined John and Florence for a walk out on the new road which was being cleared through the brush toward the government post, Narok. Harry Daniel was enjoying life, but he especially loved it when the Stauffacher boys, Raymond and Claudon, were home for vacation and took him for a foray into the woods.

Many of our new Maasai friends came to look into the house we built of logs. One day I gave Gashisha's visiting mother-in-law a look at herself in the mirror hanging on our wall. She was shocked, half afraid to believe the mirror. She turned around as quickly as she could and rushed around the house to see what was on the other side of the wall the mirror hung on. When she came back, I offered her a closeup look in my hand mirror. She backed off, turned her head shyly, then leaned forward a little and finally dared to look in for one second, but no longer. In the end I persuaded her to enjoy a real look at herself in the harmless thing.

How we longed for the time we would be able to talk freely in Maasai. One Sunday I wrote:

> Went to S.S. and church and enjoyed both. Every now and then I am able to catch a phrase of their tongue as it clatters off so fast.
>
> Harry Daniel always insists upon studying his "mat sai" when his Ma does, and sit on her lap as well. Some chance Ma gets to really study!

And a couple of weeks later:

> I taught school from 11 to 12 a.m. today, also sewing class. The women have lots of fun out of me — they try to teach me to talk Maasai! They laugh to their hearts' content. I must say, I never know what they are laughing at.

We used to joke that we had hot and cold running water on our station. Tributary streams feeding the Siyabei River ran on each side of our hilltop homes. If we walked down the hill on the right side one hundred yards, we had a stream of hot water gushing out of a crevice in solid rock. If we preferred a cold swim, we walked one hundred yards down the left side of the hill where a cold stream ran. Both high trees and dense green undergrowth arched over the streams.

After we had been at Siyabei about six months, Roy succeeded in getting a water-powered mill wheel running down in our garden clearing near the cold stream. It ground wheat and corn very nicely and people on the station started bringing in their corn to be ground. The noise of the mill kept off the wild animals who had been robbing our unfenced garden, taking every bean and tomato. Only the big baboons never shied at the mill; they kept stealing the corn out of the neighboring gardens as usual.

Finally, there came the day I noted on a Monday:

> Language requirements came from Kijabe. We'll stuff on Maasai for three days to take the exam on Thursday.

And on Thursday:

> It wasn't quite as hard as I had expected. My grade was 92. Roy's was 86. Yet I still feel as though I knew nothing.

Only a few days later, a letter which had been eight months in transit, finally arrived informing the Stauffachers that funds had been provided for them and their boys to leave on furlough. Many Maasai came to say *Sere* (goodbye) to the Stauffachers. How we would miss them!

The day after they left, the women helpfully took an especially active part in their prayer meeting, making me feel good over the spirit they showed to me, a new, ignorant stranger.

The first Sunday after Florence left, we gave medicine to about thirty people for everything from croup to cuts, burns, sprains, sore eyes and chiggers. Roy named one boy "Chigger Toes" because he appeared too lazy to remove the chiggers himself and his toes were partially eaten off. A lot of sore eyes resulted from hugging close to the fires in their smoky huts. Blue spots on the eyeballs were common.

"Who has read the little black book since our last meeting?" I asked the Women's Bible Class that week.

"I can't read."

"I can't either."

"Will you teach us to read?" the women asked — almost in chorus.

I did. Until then our school had been for men and boys only. However, there were one or two women who could read, albeit haltingly, for they had been at the Girls School at Kijabe for a year or two.

How I enjoyed these women! I began to know quite a few of them by name. When you want to speak to a Maasai woman, you never address her by name. She is addressed as "Mother of (her firstborn's name)." I was called "*Ngoto Ai Danyo*" (Mother of Harry Daniel). Nevertheless, I still thought some of their own names were beautiful, such as: Nabiriganyua, Silole, Teteu, Nanjiru, Nyakeru, Nolminangai, Nolmusheni, Nyambura, and Waturie.

Soon I also started a class of eager little girls on the three R's as well as on some simple sewing. All the while, I was learning more Maasai words and phrases, and thrilled over each new one I mastered and made mine.

So far, our biggest problems had been learning the language and getting acquainted with the people. Now we started to encounter their customs.

First, we ran head on into polygamy and adultery.

One day Nakasema, a new wife of Enok the schoolteacher, brought me some khaki material. Then Waturie, his other wife, and I made her her first dress. It was a simple one and we finished it in an hour or two. She felt awkward as could be since at home she had never worn anything other than skins. But Enok had just acquired her and his house was now her new home and all the Siyabei women wore dresses, not skins.

Enok's taking a second wife caught Roy and me by surprise. We knew it was a Maasai custom to have as many wives as a man could afford to buy — but the Africans also knew that becoming a Christian meant one had to have only one wife. And in addition, it meant having a Christian wedding. There was no provision in the Church for marrying a non-Christian, let alone a second wife.

Not only had Enok bought a pagan wife, but he even refused to marry her Maasai style until she proved to be a "good wife." Proof, to the Maasai, is being able to conceive and bear a child, milk all the cows, dig the garden if she is a Kikuyu, build her own house, cut the wood, carry the water, cook the food and carry all loads.

Enok shifted back and forth between pagan and Christian living so often it became unsettling for the entire community. But we liked Enok very much. He was an elderly man who had some training under the Church Missionary Society at Mombasa. He was recognized as one of the wisest and most literate of the group at Siyabei, and he was a good teacher.

What to do? Roy decided to get counsel from fellow missionaries on how to handle Enok's *shauri* (a Swahili word meaning "situation," or "controversy," which had been fully adopted into other languages, including English, throughout Kenya).

However, before we could get counsel on handling

Enok, God had some tempering in store for us: a small family crisis.

One Tuesday I wrote in my diary:

> Harry Daniel went down to the stream with Gashisha to do the weekly laundry. He somehow stumbled over a stick that upset the *debby* of boiling water on the fire. It scalded both his little feet. We dressed his feet at once. This evening we started to dress the burns again but found it was much more serious than we thought, and have decided to take him to Kijabe.

Harry Daniel was three when this happened. He wore little sandals made of thin motor car tire rubber, just like the Maasai rawhide ones, with a strap around the ankle and a thong between the toes. When the accident happened, Gashisha had the presence of mind to plunge his feet into the cold stream. Both feet were a mass of puffed blisters. Then he brought Harry Daniel up to the house on his back.

Roy got the first aid book out quickly, then covered Harry's little feet with Vaseline and a light bandage. Gashisha wept with Harry Daniel. We did too.

When we decided we had better take him to Kijabe it was night, and no time to start out with mules over the Kidong. But we sent for Molungit, who agreed to go with Roy and Harry. We waited until 4:00 a.m. Molungit brought up the mules and cart. I filled the water jugs and Roy filled a bottle with kerosene for the lantern and put the chop box under the cart seat. Then, after a good, hot breakfast of oatmeal, Roy took Harry Daniel on his lap, well wrapped for it was cold. After asking God to keep them safe from the lions enroute, Roy told Molungit to tap the mules.

Nancy and Ned moved off by lantern light down the stony hill, up another hill, around the bend into the sage brush and out of my view, but not out of my heart.

They traveled 18 hours straight, across the Kidong. At 9:00 p.m. they had to stop and let the mules graze, for they were tired and hungry. For safety, they built a fire to keep the wild animals away. After an hour's rest, they completed the last ten miles and climbed the escarpment up to windy

Kijabe. At Theodora Hospital they found Dr. E. L. Davis and his wife still up, caring for the critically ill patients.

Doctor Davis assured Roy that his first aid had been exactly right for Harry Daniel's feet. Each time a new bandage was put on, the lad would whimper and say, "Wind it up! Wind it up!" for the cold air made it feel like it was burning more.

If anyone ever sacrificed, the Davises did. They lived in the hospital, so their own home was the emergency ward, the obstetrical ward, and the dental clinic. They were everything to everybody, night and day. Their hospital was meticulously clean insofar as possible. People of all tribes and tongues came from afar to get the healing touch of this *Dakitari*. Mrs. Davis did not lag behind him one step. She was right alongside wearing a trim, white uniform.

Their long veranda was always packed tight with the sick, wounded and dying. Added to all this, they delivered the missionaries' new babies as they came along, including three of ours.

"Looked for Roy all day," I wrote the Friday after Roy took Harry Daniel to Kijabe. "At 5:00 p.m. he arrived with Molungit, alone! I was scared when I didn't see Harry Daniel in the cart. But Harry is not well enough to come home. So I am taking baby Ruth Marie and going to Kijabe to help care for Harry Daniel."

Before leaving, however, I made a new pair of pants for my little boy and then we headed back to Kijabe.

It was to be a full month before he could walk again and we could go home. Possibly the compassionate care he received at Theodora Hospital during that time made a lasting impression on little Harry Daniel, for he grew up to be a dedicated pediatrician.

It was while we were still at Kijabe with Harry that Roy asked Harmon Nixon, who was an old friend, and Fred McKenrick, the current station superintendent, to help him settle the problem of our teacher, Enok, and his wives.

The three men rode speedily out to Siyabei by motorcycle, Roy in Harmon's sidecar. After listening to all sides of the affair, they reluctantly advised Roy to drop Enok as teacher, and find another one.

"You white folks ask too much of us," Enok sadly concluded.

Next, another cloud darkened our way after we all got back home again. Little did we know how often this sin would come up in the Church Council Meetings, but it got to be almost rote: Olgoyai, another teacher, confessed adultery with a woman whose husband had disappeared, and so Olgoyai was barred from communion for a time.

It was explained to us that, according to Maasai custom, if for any reason a husband were dead or gone far away, the Maasai women considered it their legal right to want to conceive and bear a child, no matter who the father was. To them, adultery meant little or nothing. Far worse was the stigma of barrenness.

Ample demonstration of this obsession came when one day a group of highly decorated Maasai women arrived from the north, dancing and singing to God, *Engai*, begging Him to give them children. All were women unable to bear children.

A Maasai custom is for them to make a pilgrimage in a group, taking a long safari on foot from kraal to kraal, singing and dancing and begging food, cents, a goat, meat, or anything to give to the medicine man or witch doctor who claimed to be able to cause them to conceive. Each woman wore hideous figures drawn in white chalk on her face besides the usual masses of wire coils and beads on all arms, legs, necks and shoulders and in stretched ear lobes. Of course each wore her well-oiled skin garb.

We were advised by Molungit to make no contribution to these women, who would just give it to the witch doctor. We tried to tell them that only God has the power to cause a woman to conceive. They left unimpressed. They knew so little about Him other than that He gives rain and grass and cattle — their chief concerns.

The next custom we ran smack up against arose right after I'd started the class for little girls. Some old men came one day saying they wanted to take our little mission school girls out among the kraal-dwelling Maasai to have them circumcised, "as proper heathen do," I recorded in my diary. They were afraid the Maasai would kill the girls if they refused this rite.

Only one man stood against this, again Molungit, who arrived on the scene just in time to sway the men against the plan and let the girls stay home and attend school. Two in our class, our children's nursemaid, Silole, and Nareyu, hid in the forest until the *shauri* was settled. The girls were not killed, but neither were they spared circumcision; it was simply postponed. At this time Molungit's daughters were not old enough to go through the rite. Sad to say, in later years when they grew up, he was foremost in having his daughters circumcised for he feared the threat of having his cattle hamstrung if he didn't follow Maasai custom. He, too, was a man who lived two lives.

It was about this time, very soon after Enok's affair, that we secured a new worker to live on our station, Miss Annie Grover, R.N. She was a former Moody Bible Institute student, too. She had been working in Stellenbosch, South Africa. We took her home from Kijabe and moved her into our new log cabin, while we lived in Stauffacher's stone house. We were so glad to have her with us! She took over all of the medical work and helped in the school.

Miss Grover was fifty years old; I was twenty-seven. While the missionized Maasai became reconciled to the truth, those from distant kraals couldn't understand a man's having only one wife and were sure that, according to their custom, the oldest one of us was Roy's first wife and I was his second.

5 *Safari Ways and Means*

ONE DAY SHORTLY AFTER ANNIE GROVER'S ARRIVAL,
when we had been at Siyabei one year, we decided it was
time to try to reach out to some of the outlying villages. The
church at Siyabei, which is a rooted community, could only
minister to a tiny fraction of the pastoral nomadic Maasai
who establish transient villages, or kraals, wherever their
search for grass for their livestock leads them. We packed up
gear in the cart for everybody: Roy; Ndilai, the Massai
evangelist; Harry Daniel; Ruth Marie; Miss Grover; Suguna,
the nurse girl; a *toto* (little helper boy); and me. Then we
walked ten miles to the largest Maasai kraal in the area,
wondering the whole way just what kind of reception
awaited us.

We reached the place just in time to pitch our tent, build
a fire, and eat supper before time for the meeting. But all
during this process of getting settled we were obliged to stop
and greet and shake hands with every person in the kraal.
They *all* came by.

We held the meeting right inside the kraal, in the midst
of the cattle and sheep by the light of our Coleman lamp. We
even took the portable Baby Estey Organ to stimulate the
singing. Their flocks were not disturbed in the least.

About half of the eighty people living in the kraal left
their huts and came out to look and to listen attentively to the
Words of God. They nodded their heads as if it were all true
according to their way of thinking.

We spent the night in our tent nearby. But we got little
sleep because of a roaring lion not nearly far enough away. In

the morning, we again read the Words of God and sang and prayed, and also gave out medicines to over fifty people.

As we left for home, they told us to come back again. They were all very interested in our children, the organ, our food, the way we ate, how we smelled and everything else about us.

We all left feeling a real call to village work. We laid plans to start village visitation throughout the whole Maasai Reserve. Hopefully, some day we would be able to establish some indigenous centers of influence if we could find places where people lived somewhat permanently. We could not take any extensive safaris right away, however, because I was expecting our third child.

Soon after Miss Annie's arrival, we had begun to have a daily prayer meeting together for our station work. Now we also began a daily hour of Bible study at our house from four to five in the afternoon.

"How we have all been strengthened," I noted in my diary, "blessed and spoken to by God since we began. Our station is so different. It pays!"

Mbae, Wambui's father, began to go out teaching in the nearby villages with Miss Annie, he leading the mule she rode.

The following February, Miss Annie was my great comfort and help when our third baby, Roy David, arrived in Dr. Davis' home at Kijabe.

Just before Roy David was born, his father had decided that mule transport was too slow, especially over the long, hot Kidong. Roy's fast ride in Harmon Nixon's sidecar from Siyabei to Kijabe had made the motorcycle look very attractive. Mr. McKenrick wanted to sell his old wreck of a motorcycle, with a weak wicker basket thrown in on the side. No one else wanted it. Roy bit. The initial cost was not much, but what Roy had to put into it to make it go cost plenty. After weeks and weeks of sweat and struggling, Roy triumphantly got it going.

This was the chariot we rode in, bringing two-week-old Roy David home to Siyabei! At no time did all three wheels of that motorcycle and sidecar ever simultaneously fit into the tracks or ruts on the road. Either Roy on the cycle was in the track or the baby and I in the sidecar were. Whichever way it was, the other of us was bumping along over camouflaged pig holes in the grass, anteater holes right on the track, or just plain rocks. The Kidong was always in one of two conditions: either covered with a foot of dust, or covered with a foot of mud during the rains. This time it was dust. While bouncing along, holding a new baby with one hand, and your helmet with the other you can't get a hold on anything! Regardless of chin straps, our helmets would blow off; then we had to stop, run back and chase them. The difficulty for the driver was that the holes in the rocky road were seldom seen until experienced. We would kerplunk down into one without any warning and stay there until Roy removed himself from astride the bike and lifted the front, back or side wheel out of the hole. I was so glad we had left our two oldest children farmed out with friends at Kijabe.

Mounted on their own mongrel motorcycle and sidecar were Clara and Harmon Nixon and their baby, Paul, coming home with us for their vacation. This was the first of several memorable vacations we would spend with these good friends from Moody Bible Institute days when Harmon was the president of my class and Clara was in the night school.

We arrived home just before dark, a messy sight covered with dust. It was no wonder that in those days the first gesture toward a guest on arrival was a bath, then tea, then talk and a chance to tell how they ever got across the Kidong. Good old Gashisha had fires, hot water in the long tin tub, hot food on the kitchen stove and a big grin on his face, happy to see our new baby, who actually looked like a little old man. Who wouldn't after coming through all he had?

We were famished. Food had never tasted so good. Home had never looked so good to me.

"E-Haw, He-Haw," brayed the mules when Roy went

out to see them. They seemed to ask him how he liked his three-wheeled chariot today!

Now that baby Roy David was safely launched, we embarked on our village visitation with Annie Grover.

Enter the Muleobus.

Our motorcycle and side car and the two wheeled cart were too small for our needs now; in Nairobi Roy found an old rusty World War I Ford chassis with no engine and nothing on it but wheels, some tires of questionable value and a brake that worked. He put boards on this chassis for a floor, built low sides and added cross boards to sit on. Above this he built a framework of waterpipes, roofed it with canvas, and nailed on roll-up canvas sides in case of rain. He bought two more mules to help Nancy and Ned pull this chariot, then named it "Mule-o-bus."

Now we were well off. We could live out among the Maasai for days or weeks at a time, taking with us Murage our mule driver, a cook, Ndilai the evangelist, and a nursemaid. The tires held air, most of the time, so we glided along in slow comfort.

Besides Tagi's New Testament, we always carried our little black medicine box. Few Maasai were without ailments. Especialy popular were the soothing eye drops for the chronic smoked eye problem. Dr. Davis at Kijabe kept us supplied with simple medicines. Until nearly 1930, there were no government medical services in Maasailand.

On our first few safaris, we whites slept in the Muleobus and our Maasai helpers slept in the kraals we visited. The people always gave us more milk than we could drink. Our mules were taken into their thorn enclosures at night to be safe.

First we took a long safari down to Kajiado, a small government post half way to the desert-like southern end of our Maasai parish. We had to plan well, days ahead, for we were three missionaries, five Maasai helpers and three babies, with all our supplies: food, bedding, lanterns, and even water and firewood. We had to pass through Nairobi.

How the populace did gaze at us in our Muleobus as we rolled down the main street, which was the only street across town at that time. There were few functioning cars in Nairobi and not very many four-wheeled wagons either. We felt aristocratic. At least, we had not walked across the Kidong this time!

As we passed through Nairobi, Roy saw along the road the wreck of another World War I Ford chassis with no top; but this one had an engine and body of sorts. Immediately he lost his desire for rapid transit via motorcycle and on our way back he bought this skeleton for a song and sent it out to Siyabei via ox transport.

Necessity being the mother of invention, our need of an adequate mode of travel caused Roy to invent many things. Out of this latest Model T, he finally created a car that would run at least part of the time, with tires that held air most of the time, and a "cranker" that would start the engine most of the time, if one got frustrated at it long enough. It went twenty-five miles per hour, which was better than mules any day. The first post-war new cars were just coming into the country and a new Ford could be bought for about $300.00 but we didn't have that kind of money.

We chose to be oblivious of the fact that we looked a bit odd in a car with no top. In this, we went all of 300 miles to visit the Nixons for Christmas. They lived high up on Mboni Hill in the Ukamba tribe. It took much puffing and huffing, but our Tin Lizzie made it. Enroute to the Nixons, we were spotted by a clever salesman in Nairobi who lost no time wooing Roy over to the idea that he should have a *new* Overland chassis he had there, instead of our pile of junk. Always looking out for something better, Roy listened. We talked it over with the Nixons, saying we would have to sell our mules, our motorcycle, our cart, our topless Tin Lizzie, and nearly everything else we owned if we bought the new Overland chassis for cash.

To us, this was a momentous decision. It meant we would still have to borrow about $140.00 privately to make up the cost. So far, we had always gone without until we possessed cash to pay. Since Miss Annie depended upon us for her tranport, we thought maybe she might loan us a little cash until we had funds to pay her back. This almost broke up our friendship.

"Mules are good enough for any missionary," was her reply. "If I did have any money to lend, it would not be for any extravagance like a motorcar," she added, smacking her lips.

We made no attempt to persuade her against her will; nevertheless we finally did get the car. When it was ready, she gladly rode in our new Overland. Roy had built a very serviceable body with two seats, a metal top that turned water if it rained, and lidded boxes on each side for tools, food, lanterns, or any kind of load.

Roy did all of his garage work in the backyard under the trees, using the tough, forked, olive trees as a vice when needed. He did his own blacksmithing on the spot, using charcoal made right there. As our boys grew up, they had auto mechanics training right in our back yard. They loved to help Dad with every contraption.

At the age of 13, Harry Daniel was able to take apart, mend, and put together again, an old truck which Roy had acquired by then for use in building. He also created a good battery out of several old ones, two hundred miles from any garage or town where he could get supplies. He was allowed to drive the truck everywhere in the bush, but not in Nairobi, as he had no license yet. Game trails were his highways. The same was true of Roy David, four years younger, when he became 13. We certainly learned to live with "What's next?" in the line of of transportation as our family eventually expanded from two little to five not-so-little children, plus our staff of helpers. There were great distances to travel to find our nomadic people. We took our food, bedding, lanterns, wood, water and every possible need for staying days, weeks, or longer. We had to be self-contained.

Day-by-day, we observed and learned how to greet in sobriety, not gaiety, to touch fingers instead of squeezing or shaking hands, how to gratefully accept and drink gifts of

sour milk from huge, highly polished gourds, without bene-
fit of cups; how to let people touch us all over and not be
embarrassed; and to admire their warmth which completely
routed the unfounded fears of white folks who sincerely
believed the Maasai were wild, arrogant savages. We found
them friendly, honest and hospitable; quick to give a visitor
the last drop of milk in their gourds, and a cowhide to sleep
on near the fire at night in their low, dung huts.

But right about this time there came an interruption to
our work in Maasailand.

6 *Kijabe Interlude*

ROY'S INVENTIVENESS AND PRACTICAL TURN OF MIND had not gone unnoticed. After our first two and a half years at Siyabei, the Field Council asked us to transfer to Kijabe so Roy could take over the Industrial Department which had virtually closed down for lack of workers. It consisted of a huge saw mill, a planing mill, a carpenter shop, a store for the Africans, a blacksmith shop and the printing press.

Mr. A.M. Anderson had run the Industrial Department for several years before going to work among the Kipsigis; then it was taken over by a Mr. Leasure, whom the Africans called *Bwana Nyundu* (Mr. Hammer). This was because once he threw a hammer when something too sorely tried his patience. Most whites were given an Africa name, whether they knew it or not. In later years, another head of this department, the effervescent Wels Devitt, who was known for always having a grin and a hearty handshake for everyone he encountered, was named *Bwana Jambo* (Mr. Hello).

Rev. Lee H. Downing, who first told us about the AIM back in our Bible School days in Chicago, had been trying to run the press, but as station superintendent he was swamped with so many other responsibilities that they took up all his time. Now it was time for his furlough.

"Roy, you have a way with tools," said Mr. George Woodley, the new station superintendent. "We need you to be maintenance man for the whole station."

So, besides breathing life back into the Industrial Department, Roy became "Our Boy Friday" on many unexpected types of jobs, as all good missionaries soon learn to do if they are to pull their share on the field.

Right away we started in again on language lessons. Kikuyu is completely different from Maasai, so knowing Maasai was no help here. In due time we passed our exams and dug into our new work. Our little Overland safari box body was the only car at Kijabe when we moved in, but not for long. Lawson Propst replaced his faithful four mules with a majestic International half-ton pickup, which his two boys, Charles and Herman (as Jim was still called then) were soon driving most expertly. Kijabe was motorized!

Roy used mules, however, to drag huge logs from the mixed hardwoods forest above the station down to the newly installed saw mill, 1,000 feet below. I loved going up to the forest with Roy for logs because the high trees were full of colobus monkeys whose long, straight, black hair is mantled with long, straight snow white hair on their backs, similar to the skunks we know in the U.S. Pieces of colobus skin are used all over Africa as dancing decorations on legs, arms, torso and heads at festivals and celebrations. Today these monkeys are protected by game laws, for they are now seldom to be seen swinging from treetop to treetop in the dense forest.

Roy introduced the first tiny 1-½ horsepower gasoline engine to power the Kijabe Press. Initially it frightened the pressmen, and Roy had to do the printing himself until they became accustomed to the noise and the speed. They dubbed it the *"tinga tinga."*. They were used to pumping the nice, quiet pedals of a stationary bicycle to power the press. But, once initiated, the *tinga tinga* delighted them.

Jeremiah, the head printer, who was a good typesetter, had had four years of schooling and spoke three languages. Whenever he worked, he worked well. But he also owned a *duka* (a shop) up in his village some distance away. This divided his time and attention. Soon his brother, Appolos, replaced him at the press.

Various missions in Kenya once more started sending

their work to our AIM Press to be printed: prayer letters, reports, song books, little readers, etc. It fell to my lot to proofread galleys after an African had proofed it once.

Most certainly I didn't know all the languages, so I could only proof letter by letter, or syllable by syllable. That was quite easy because, routinely in many African languages, a vowel follows each consonant. The translators who first broke these languages down into writing, put them down phonetically, just as they were spoken, using the International Phonetic Alphabet. This experience, my first brush with translation work, was to prove invaluable.

The variety of jobs Roy was responsible for included the station water supply. Every so often he had to walk two miles through the forest up above the station to a high, cold waterfall to clean out the cloth sieves on top of the two 1,000-gallon tanks which fed water through pipes by gravity to the station. Too often elephants tore up ditches that channeled the water to the tanks, using their feet and tusks, and then Roy would also have ditches to repair. From the tanks, the water was piped to each house and stored in a corrugated iron water tank with a faucet at the bottom of it. We still used good old fashioned pitchers and wash basins in every bedroom.

But times were changing. In those days at Rift Valley Academy each child had to carry his own lantern to his room at night after having been in study hall an hour under a huge kerosene lamp suspended from the ceiling. There were only fifty students. The School Board became divided over whether or not to buy a little electric engine to furnish a light in each room for one hour each evening. Many opposed the idea as too dangerous, but the affirmative won in the end and soon RVA could be seen at night from a great distance out on the Kidong because of the little electric lights powered by the new *tinga tinga*. In later years, Jim Propst and our son, Roy David, electrified the whole station from an ex-military searchlight power plant. Today, the station is connected to the national grid which is powered mainly by the Owens Dam generators at Jinja, Uganda, where Lake

Victoria pours out as the beginning of the mighty Nile River.

While we lived at Kijabe, it was my job to teach music in the African school. The children were naturally good singers. They inspired me. One small, shy lad with a bright face seemed to soak up the do-mi-sol scale faster than the others. He had a beautiful voice and sang out freely. When he grew up, he became the head of the Radio Department at Kijabe. His name is Timothy Kamau, son of the beloved, venerable Pastor Johanna Nyenjere, at Kijabe.

At Christmas, I was asked to teach four teachers to sing a quartet arrangement of "It Came Upon the Midnight Clear" in English. Andrew wa Mbare Gichuhu was one of the four. Andrew in later years became the Presiding Elder of the Africa Inland Church.

With some of the kids at RVA, I initiated the first little orchestra. We had no cello, so I strung up a guitar with cello strings and taught Jim Propst to pick the bass part. Ed Sywulka, Philip Davis, and Charles and Roxanna Propst played violin, or at least tried mighty hard. So, with Marjorie Bryson on the organ, we made happy noise, if not music, in the big old study hall-auditorium of Rift Valley Academy.

Beneath that large room was the cornerstone of the building, laid by none other than the famous "perpetual-motion-man" Teddy Roosevelt, president of the United States, in 1909 when he was on one of his hunting safaris in Kenya. The only evidence of civilization on the Kidong Valley where he did some of his hunting were ox cart ruts between Kijabe railway station and Narok, the tiny government post 75 miles to the west. When the telegraph line was put in paralleling the tracks it was strung very high, in deference to the many giraffe which populated the Kidong. For years it was the longest uninterrupted telegraph wire in the world.

Teddy bagged many fine game specimens on his hunts. You will find those animals "in person," both mounted and reproduced in beautiful bronze, in what used to be called the Field Museum (now the Museum of Natural History) in Chicago, Illinois.

His safari took him straight through our Maasai country, which was and is still, a game reserve. His book, *African Game Trails*, published in 1910, gives a hilarious account of his grand time out in Kenya.

When he walked to Kijabe to visit the AIM Station, he had such a good time among the young missionaries that he asked if there were something he could do for their work. Charles Hurlburt was quick to tell him that what the AIM wanted was permission to enter the Belgian Congo to open some Protestant missions there. He suggested that if Mr. Roosevelt might, enroute home, approach the proper offices in Belgium and secure an entry permit for the AIM, this would be most magnanimous of him. This is exactly what Teddy did. He visited the King of Belgium himself, and secured the permit!

John Stauffacher was the young man who carried that document with him when he walked to Congo, along with James Gribble, to scout out the area which eventually saw a string of AIM stations stretching into that land, now called Zaire.

Rift Valley Academy was constructed of limestone blocks cut in a quarry right on Kijabe station by apprentices in the Industrial Department. When Roy reactivated the department, he opened a new class of twenty-four boys from five different tribes, to teach them carpentry and stonemasonry. First, he built a new dorm for them.

"I am having the experience of a lifetime trying to take care of twenty-four African boys," he wrote home. "They are a clean, bright crowd of fellows. . . . I hope to send them out through the Colony in years to come as capable, well-trained Christian workmen. I believe it will tell for the cause of Christ in this land. Missions are criticized here because so many natives from missions are the dude, psalm-singing, good-for-nothing kind. . . . Carpenters and stone masons are greatly in demand now. . . . These boys are signed on for a three-year contract. . . . They are all very anxious to take up this work. I could have had a hundred, but had to limit the number."

The building stones these boys cut out of the limestone quarry were used in the construction of Moffat Memorial Bible Institute where we sent Peter Kuyoni ole Kasura for his training. We used to simply call it the Bible School.

Charles and Mae Teasdale, Moody graduates who had worked briefly in the Akamba tribe, were asked to open the Bible School in 1928. Mae was a smart girl with languages and a good organ teacher. Charles, who had more education than the other missionaries, was a gifted Bible scholar. They began the Bible School with only the one building. The attic was the dormitory, and the lower floor housed classrooms. They also took over the little old manual printing press and moved it into a classroom so some of the Bible School boys could start working at it part time.

The school's kitchen was just an outdoor fire ringed with three stones on which to balance a pot, and the dishwater drained down the hill. It was a bare-bones institution at first. Now it has several modern dormitories and classroom buildings. The press has its own new buildings housing up-to-date machinery operated by a large professional staff of both Africans and expatriots, as all non-Africans came to be called.

The steady growth of the Bible School has shown that tribal differences soon evaporate in an atmosphere where the love of Christ is allowed to permeate each heart. Through the years we watched the reflection of both Charles' and Mae's radiance and dedication shine forth in Bible School students.

Our two full years at Kijabe were highlighted by the birth of our number four baby, Helen Elizabeth, born on my 29th birthday, December 28, 1926.

When John and Florence Stauffacher returned from their furlough at the end of 1927, they asked the Field Council to return the Shaffers with them to the Maasai work at

Siyabei. We loved both stations and were willing to go wherever we were sent, so we moved back to the Maasai and settled into our log house. When we had left Siyabei, Miss Annie had moved to work at Litein with the A.M. Andersons in the neighboring Kipsigis tribe.

Andy Anderson was a great big Scandinavian man who spoke broken English. He was an inventive man who ran his truck on charcoal, and built posho mills at Litein so the Africans could grind their own corn. Andersons and their children seem as eternal as the mountains, considering the work they have accomplished along every practical line, whether it was Andy's industrial department, or their son Earl's extensive gardening, irrigation, and grain planting schemes, or their daughter Mary Honer's teaching school at RVA, or later, through their grandsons, Howard, Willard and Herbert, in construction and just about every imaginable activity involved in mission work. It was to be the Andersons who would gently take us in at a time when Roy would face the valley of death, a little further on down the road.

When we first returned to Siyabei, I began to get a look at another aspect of translation work from the sidelines. It had been several years since the British and Foreign Bible Society had published Tagi's Maasai New Testament. John began translating the Old Testament with the help of the three current Siyabei schoolteachers: Sitoya, who had a brilliant mind; Wambogo, Peter Kuyoni's big brother, who with Sitoya was in Florence's first class; and Milaun, who also had a very keen mind. They each knew three or more languages and could read the Bible in them in addition to English, so they did an excellent job of translation. Florence would give them huge pieces of brown wrapping paper to write on for the sheer lack of good paper. I only caught glimpses of the work, standing with Florence at her back door many mornings when they brought in another night's effort. She would take their work up to the attic room, where John edited it, then typed it into manuscript form.

7 *Helen and Grace*

WE WERE HAPPY TO GET BACK to Siyabei. Kijabe was too civilized for us.

"Surely we are living in the last days," Roy wrote to his family in far off United States, where the "Roaring 20s" were in full swing. "It is astonishing to see the clothes that some of the women and young ladies wear when they first come out here to the mission field. Needless to say, it does not take them long to add to the length of their skirts when they see what effect it has upon their work."

Far away from all that encroachment of the modern world, the comfortable little Siyabei log cabin was now partly covered with a lovely vine and surrounded by geraniums and nasturtiums.

One of the first things we did was to dam up the pure hot water spring back in the forest to make a tiny little swimming pool. We all jumped in. It was one way to get a good bath since we didn't own a tub yet. Besides, all our house water had to be carried up the hill.

The wheels in Roy's practical mind began turning again, and soon he sent to Salem, Ohio, for a water-propelled Meyers Hydraulic ram. It arrived many months later. He installed it and it pumped the pure, bluish water uphill in a one-inch pipe to our 1,000-gallon corrugated iron tank, which was mounted on a six-foot high stone base Roy had built. This furnished enough water to irrigate our gardens every day and all the water we needed in the two houses. No more running down the hill to the stream for water.

Back in Maasai work again, we eagerly resumed safari life, carrying the Good News further and further out into the Reserve. Yet, now God saw fit to bring sorrow our way. Life was not to be merely happy camping with the black book and black medical box.

On safari, toward evening, we always aimed for an area with wood for campfire and water, if possible, for even a mud hole meant water for our thirsty mules in our mule days. We found every combination from nothing to plenty for all in the way of water supply. One place might have white, sickly-looking water and the next place a cold, clear spring; the next, a dark and hot fast flow out of black rock; then the little brown Uaso Ngiro River. We always boiled our drinking water to avoid amoebic dysentery.

I honestly believe we were too interested and busy to become fearful of the myriads of diseases that probably were all around us. We had no screens on windows or doors at Siyabei, for it was too cold for flies to survive. Daily baths, no bare feet, warm clothing, regular sleeping habits, good food and plenty of love usually kept us and our children healthy.

But there in our log cabin, on February 28, 1928, our newest baby, 14-months-old Helen, took sick. She had eaten her supper as always with the other two pre-schoolers, Ruth Marie and Roy David. Then followed baths, pajamas, songs, scripture games and then prayers. This was our custom. They knew nothing else. I always put the children to bed soon after sunset as this gave me time to study language, write letters, mend clothes and a lot else that falls to a mother in love with her children. Helen loved her bed, never knowing it was just a packing box lined with cloth.

On this particular evening, I was alone with the children. Harry Daniel, age 7, was in school at RVA and Roy was back at Kijabe putting on the roof of the new Bible School. I was just sitting down to study when I heard a little cry, at 7:00 p.m. I went to Helen and found she had vomited blood. This was new to me but I did not let myself get alarmed. Again, at 8:00, 9:00 and 10:00 p.m. she vomited blood.

I awoke Ruth Marie, just turned 5, and gave her a lantern and sent her down the garden path to the Stauffachers, 25 yards away, with a note asking Florence what I should do for Helen.

"Give her some lemon," she wrote back. I had no lemons.

At 11:00 p.m., Helen vomited blood again and I sent Ruth Marie a second time in her little white nightgown, asking Florence for some medicine, not knowing what kind. I have so often wondered how I dared send my little girl out at night when animals were all about. I actually forgot this in my desperation. I do believe that children have their guardian angels who care for them. Certainly she was cared for that night.

Florence sent me some homeopathic pills to try, but I couldn't get Helen to open her mouth, let alone swallow any pills. In fact, she started acting so strangely I was afraid to leave her and go to Florence myself. I was told by doctors, later, that she was having convulsions; at that time I didn't know what a convulsion was.

I held Helen in my arms to keep her as warm as possible, for the night was cold. By 1:00 a.m. she was so unusual that I was frightened enough to run over to Florence myself. I banged on the door pleading for help. Florence was rather deaf, but John awoke her and sent her to the door. She told me to run home, make a fire quickly, get some hot water and she would come at once.

Our cedar wood burned hot and fast, so I got a good fire going and sat down on a low stool, holding Helen — now in a coma — in my arms before the fire.

Just as Florence came in, Helen drew her last breath, ever so gently, and then she was gone to join the angels who hovered over her. Even though I had three children besides her and I was expecting another, still I found it very hard to be reconciled to giving her up.

With Roy gone, I was heartbroken, alone, and could only weep heavily, but not bitterly. I had learned to trust God in the dark before this. So only He comforted me as I wept long and hard after Florence went home to John.

I still swallow hard when I think of this. Helen was a lovely child, just starting to walk and say a few words. The Maasai loved her so tenderly and sincerely.

From 1:30 until daybreak was an eternity. At dawn, faithful Gashisha came to build the kitchen fire and start the porridge. I gave him a telegram to Roy, to take to the little mud and wattle Government Post at Narok, eight miles west of us. He ran all the way. I sent just five words: HELEN DIED, WAITING FOR YOU, and signed my name. At Narok, the Goanese clerk spelled out each word over the wire to Kijabe.

By then, Florence had called me and my two little ones to come over and have breakfast with them.

The wire reached Kijabe that morning fifteen minutes after Roy had left for Narobi to get supplies.

"I feel led of God to open this wire," said Lawson Propst to several missionaries who gathered for lunch at noontime, so he opened it in their presence. At once he sent Charles and Herman to Nairobi with the wire to try to find Roy. They found him just as he was ready to depart for a distant section of town where it would have been impossible to locate him. When he read the wire, they all returned to Kijabe at once.

At 4:00 p.m. Roy, Herman Propst, age 14, and Harry Daniel left Kijabe to cover as many miles as possible before dark. As was customary, Roy and Herman took long enough in the Kidong to shoot a kongoni, a cow-like antelope, for our meat supply. After dark, they could make no speed over the awful road, it was so grown over and nearly impassable because of pig holes hidden in tall grass.

In the tropics we dare not keep a corpse overnight. Already, Helen's little cheeks had turned purple. A Maasai never touches the dead, yet our Maasai Christians came that day and helped John dig a grave under a big tree on stony ground. In the afternoon, as I sat by the door, I could see a long single file of women coming toward my house. This will always remain one of life's sweetest moments in my memory.

"We have come to eat sorrow with you," these dear women said (their exact words). I invited them in. All were dressed in their best, and barefoot. Most had a baby either on her back or in front. They entered silently, unable to get out the usual greetings. They could only look at me. All twelve women came in and looked at Helen in her buggy, as I invited them to do if they wished, knowing they were curious even though this broke all custom.

"Let us pray," said the leader, Molungit's wife Nya-keru, quietly.

They all knelt down on our bare cedar floor, and several talked to God, ever so briefly, asking Him to pour oil on my troubled heart; for didn't every one of them know the pangs of death as they, too, had had to give up their babies? They thanked God that death was only a step into real life, eternal life, free from all suffering and tears, into the presence of Jesus. I was unable to reject this comfort.

I thanked them all for coming. They had to go home to milk their cows and do the usual work of nighttime, so could not be at the grave service. Some Christian men did come and, by lantern light, they helped John bury Helen. They put a high pile of stone on top of the grave to keep hyenas out. Already, before dark, their howls were heard for they have the capacity to smell death from great distances. They are the only undertakers the Maasai know, since they never bury their dead.

I did not sleep that night.

Finally, at 4:00 a.m. I could see the car lights as they came around the bend two miles away. Soon they arrived, all dirty and dusty, but that was of no importance. I fell into Roy's arms and we wept together for a long time. This helped so much.

Births and deaths must be reported to the nearest Government Post. It was a thatch roofed mud hut where Roy and I went to report Helen's death. Narok was not yet out of its mud hut days. Even the hospital had no permanent buildings yet. The British doctor had just returned from a safari to distant Kilgoris and, from our description, he could only suspect Helen's trouble to have been lienteric diarrhea.

The next day, Roy chose a large stone off the ground and roughly straightened its sides. Then he chiseled the word: "KEPT," in large letters, on one side; and "HELEN SHAFFER," on the other. A poem sent to us by a dear friend said, "The little lass God keeps for me is just as safe as safe can be."

Six months after Helen died, I came down with a case of subtertian malaria. Although Siyabei is some 6,000 feet above sea level, where mosquitoes can't survive, yet we had to traverse low altitudes where they do, to reach other higher areas among our people. Often, nighttime caught us in the midst of these anopheles mosquitoes. It took only one bite to catch malaria. Our whole family had its share of this fever, which can recur in regular cycles once contracted. But my attack was different; it was the worst I had ever experienced.

Heavy with child and burning with a high fever, I had to be taken on a steamer chair in the rear of our box-body car across the Kidong to Kijabe.

Here, in their own home, Dr. E. L. Davis and his wife cared for me most graciously, though not effectively, for he was a homeopathic doctor and would not use quinine which was our surest medicine then. When I neared death's door, his wife, Bernice, and Bessie Stevenson broke the traces and insisted on giving me quinine. I was in a very low state, but the wooden coffin they had started for me, was never used.

At once I began to respond. However, quinine also precipitates labor, and I quickly gave birth to our fifth child. She was placed on a table and left for dead, for she weighed only four pounds, being a month early, and the umbilical cord was wound around her neck four times. The doctor, two nurses and Roy, gave me, the sinking mother, all their attention, to save me if possible.

Suddenly, they heard a squawk. They turned, realizing that the baby on the table had made the noise! She lived! Roy named her "Grace" right then and there because he knew it was only the grace of God that came to the rescue of us all.

We experienced a profound new sense of reliance upon God and trust in whatever He had in store for us as we returned to our work with our new, very wee, baby — Grace Evelyn.

8 *Warrior-Cattlemen*

"Bwana, we would all be very glad if all the laws of the white people were taken away," a Maasai warrior told Roy one day in the 1930s. The laws he spoke of had come with the start of British colonial rule, back at the turn of the century.

"Yes," Roy answered, "And you would soon be fighting and killing each other off again."

"Yes," he replied with a dazzling smile, "We like to fight and raid and secure many cattle."

It was a general joke among the white settlers when we first went out that even God had given up the Maasai as a lost cause for they were so slow to accept any of the ways of the white man, including his Christianity.

Just who were these people we were assigned to, sight unseen, back at Moody Bible Institute in Mr. Gaylord's office?

Well, hold your hats, as we used to say travelling in an open car when we were about to make a sudden turn, because I'm going to detour for a few chapters and tell you what we discovered about these warrior-cattlemen, these elders and prophets, these devoutly religious women, and above all the central role that the Maasai gave to cattle in their lives.

Once, while visiting the National Museum in Cairo, Egypt, on the way back from a furlough in 1948, we saw a mummy in a coffin which we were sure in the most minute detail was a Maasai warrior. But when we found the label it read: "King Tut Ankhamin." So many exhibits there made us think the Maasai could have migrated from that area.

Their origin is obscure. Their skin color is rich, brown-black and the pure Maasai have almost aquiline noses and thin lips. They are labeled "Nilo-Hamitic." Because they have stories similar to Biblical accounts, told from mouth to mouth, many think their origins were closely related to the Hebrews, or Semitic stock. With their countless herds they still look like Jacob did when he went to meet Esau.

Sir A. Claud Hollis wrote one of the earliest and best books on the Maasai, back in 1905: *The Masai, their Language and Folklore* (Clarendon Press, Oxford). In it, among many Maasai myths and traditions "all given in the words of the relaters themselves," is this account of how they became warrior-cattlemen:

> The elders tell us that long ago *Engai* (God) called a *Dorobo* (bushman) and said to him, 'I wish you to come tomorrow morning, for I have something to tell you.'
>
> A Masai heard this, and in the morning he went and said to God, 'I have come.'
>
> God told him to take an axe and build a big kraal in three days. When it was ready, he was to go and search for a thin calf which he would find in the forest. This he was to bring to the kraal, slaughter it . . . and the hide was to be fastened outside the door of the hut. He was then to hide himself in the hut and not to be startled when he heard a great noise outside resembling thunder.
>
> The Masai did as God instructed.
>
> God then caused a strip of hide to descend from heaven, which was suspended over the calfskin.
>
> Cattle at once commenced to descend, one by one, by the strip of hide, until the whole of the kraal was filled, and the animals began to press against one another and to break down the hut where the Masai was.
>
> The Masai was startled and cried, 'Ho! Ho!'
>
> He then went outside the hut and found that the strip of hide had been cut, after which no more cattle came down from heaven.
>
> God asked him whether the cattle that were there were sufficient, 'For,' He said, 'you will receive no more, owing to your being surprised.'
>
> Nowadays, if cattle are seen in the possession of the Bantu tribes, it is presumed that they have been stolen or found, and the Masai say, 'These are our animals, let us go and

take them for God in the olden days gave us all the cattle upon the earth.'

Acting on the axiom that God gave all cattle to the Maasai, they claimed the right to retrieve cattle from everyone else who had any. Their raiding parties up and down the country from the Indian Ocean coastline inland to the eastern shore of Lake Victoria had all other tribes living in fear and dread of these intrepid Maasai warriors and constantly alert for the next raid. All other tribes lived in mutually recognized boundaries, but the Maasai respected none.

To the south, the agricultural, nonviolent Chagga people around the base of Mt. Kilimanjaro were reduced to keeping their cattle imprisoned. Each family kept its one precious cow hidden in its own grass hut, day and night, where it gradually grew blind. Daily, someone in the family went down to the plain to cut grass and carried it back to the cow. The young boys of the more feisty Kikuyu and Akamba tribes, also agricultural, automatically became warriors and fought the Maasai when they grew old enough. Kipsigis and Nandi were also fierce in retaliatory battles. So it was hard to find Maasai kraals because they were always well hidden, even out on windswept plains, to escape discovery by the owners of the cattle they had stolen.

In the very old days, caravans of slave traders were repelled when they encountered the Maasai and had to go a safe distance around them to reach the interior of the continent.

With the start of British colonial rule, cattle-raiding and intertribal warfare were outlawed, and the Maasai were restricted to their own Reserve. This left the warriors with very, very little to do. They would still kill lions with their spears, braid their hair for days, and herd the flocks with their little brothers, but in vain did the government try to put them to work digging on water supply projects. This would have meant life and milk to their herds in the barren, dry seasons, but from boyhood they were trained for marauding and the white man's laws never were very popular. To this day, occasional raids are still reported and apprehended culprits pay heavy fines (usually in cattle, of course), and almost all young Maasai men still try to dress and look like the fierce warriors their predecessors were in their heydey.

Echoes of their reputation in that era survive two hundred years later and tourists travel thousands of miles to go to see one Maasai kraal and take pictures of a warrior. Some will practice up on a few words of greeting, hoping to be able to speak to a Maasai.

We knew of many instances where the warrior was quite capable of replying, "Good morning, Sir," and conversing with them in English but didn't.

Many of these strikingly-painted warriors at one time wore clothes, went through mission and government schools, and some even went abroad, only to return to their fancy red clay hairdos, their *shuka*, a yard of red ochre-impregnated cloth knotted at one shoulder, and their beloved six-foot spears. They chose their cattle, lion-killing sorties, and nomadic life in preference to the white man's wild way of life.

Whatever the white man had to offer, it didn't hold a candle to their own ways. In fact, when the Maasai first saw the white man, they spat and said, "We have never seen people like this before — these *Ilojuju* (hairy ones)."

Only cattle were important to the Maasai. Milk was considered precious because it came from cows; grass was precious because it fed the cattle. Cattle were wealth. They meant the price of a wife. To buy each additional wife, a man needed more cattle. So a family with several sons needed to have many cattle, of necessity.

But far above and beyond necessity, cattle gave meaning to life for the Maasai. Their customs were all built around cattle ownership. One of their sayings is, "A cow is as good as a man." They lovingly treated favorite cattle, sheep and goats as brothers or sisters. Which is what made it so terrible for the little boy Kuyoni when his father, in addition to disinheriting him, took away his one and only sheep.

Life revolved around the needs of their stock: herding them; milking them; tending to their ailments, births and deaths; bringing them all into the kraal nightly; and moving with them to new pastures according to the season. Their young men made great sport of killing lions, the worst predators.

To outsiders, the most arresting members of the tribe are the self-confident, laughing, irrepressible, handsome *Ilmuran*, or warriors, spelled "morans" in the English press. *Ilmuran* and *Olmurani* are the plural and singular of the noun for warrior, *muran* (the "r" is rolled), which might be built up from the verb root -*murat*, to circumcise.

A boy entered manhood and became a warrior only after circumcision in his teens, with all the other boys in the age group of his clan. Nobody knew his own birthday, or age; just his age group. The boys' circumcision ritual amounted to far more than simple removal of the foreskin and it took some time to recuperate from it. How well he withstood the pain was taken as an indication of his manliness. When a boy had healed well enough to walk around, he put on women's long skin garments and went around with a few of the other initiates, hunting birds. He only carried his *oringa*, a knob stick, and a couple of other slim sticks (no Maasai male is completely dressed until he has a stick or two in his hands). He would throw his *oringa* with deadly aim at small birds and the knob did the killing. He skinned the bird, stuffed the skin with grass, then wore it with the others he had killed, tied together and strung around the back of his head from ear to ear. A poor marksman was seen with only two or three birds on his neck.

After this ritual period, the young man became a warrior and he acquired his own long spear. He became well groomed, with no beard nor mustache. You never saw a dirty, slovenly, unkempt warrior. Wearing only his *shuka*, carrying his spear, sticks and *oringa*, he would stride along rhythmically with haughty pride in each step. He was either barefoot or wore thong sandals made of thin rawhide. There was never a chair nor a soft seat of any kind in his hut. He walked great distances, all day if need be, with the only meal being all the milk he wanted at night. He was princely, bold and brave. His crowning glory was his hair.

Only warriors let the hair of the head grow long. All others, men, women and children, shaved their heads to be well groomed. Warriors were vain, and proud of their appearance, more so than any modern girl just out of a beauty salon. They worked for days from dawn to sunset on each other's hair, winding it into hundreds of thin, tiny twists, each full of red ochre, mixed with oil of a wild castor bean. Then it was divided into front and back portions and two forelocks over the ears. The front portion was held together on the forehead by a beaded decoration or often a safety pin, sometimes three inches long; the back portion was gathered just below the shoulders and attached to a long beaded stick to make it look longer than it really was. This was called the *oltaiga*, of which they were very proud. It is the precise headdress we saw on the Egyptian King Tut Ankhamin.

Each warrior wore small beaded rings in his pierced and stretched ear lobes. The longer they were, the farther they could swing when he danced. The upper curve of his ear was also pierced and decorated with a beaded hoop or two. More beads decorated his throat, his upper arms, wrists, waist and ankles, and the red leather sheath carrying the *olalem* (long knife) at his side.

In our early days, each *muran* carried his own heavy buffalo hide shield, well painted in vivid designs proclaiming his clan, subdivision and age group.

But the warrior's most valued possession was his very slim six-foot spear. Each *muran* carried his with him everywhere he went. He couldn't take it into any hut, they were all so low, so he parked it outside at the entrance. He thrust its weighted, pointed end into the ground, where it stood alone, establishing his presence. The steel upper half of the spear, a double-edged, two- to three-foot long blade, was kept sharp and polished with sand until it looked like silver. Everyone had the greatest respect for the spear, and never touched it. Warriors were held in the highest regard by all the people.

Yet in one of our earliest newsletters home, Roy wrote: "Warriors present the greatest hindrance to the spread of the Gospel in Maasailand. Social customs make them degrading, demoralizing parasites on humanity."

Behind this harsh judgement lay the fact that, while the *ilmuran* absolutely would not do any work for their own society's good, still the tribe continued to support them as warriors, with a strict system of customs and privileges.

One of these was life in the warriors' *manyattas,* or free love kraals. The sole occupants of the *manyattas* were the *ilmuran,* the little girls of the tribe from age six to puberty, and a few old women, whose duty it was to school the girls to their role in the *manyatta,* and to milk the cows.

We believed the age-old custom of free sex within the manyatta to be one of the stumbling blocks to progress. Here we were once more in the direct confrontation with an entrenched Maasai custom.

One child named Dora, age 8, was brought to our girls school by her widowed mother who was a member of the catechism class and a devout believer in God's love for her. She was eager for Dora to escape the *manyatta.*

Four weeks after we got Dora, I looked out the window and saw her surrounded by three warriors with their spears.

I went out to greet them, not revealing the boiling sensation inside my stomach. Dora was trembling from head to foot, for she knew they had come to take her away to their *manyatta* and she didn't want to go. The warriors lied and said her mother had sent them to bring her home. I grasped her right arm and a warrior grasped her left arm; both of us pulled, locked.

Roy, over at the car shed, heard us and came over. In his disarming manner, he urged the warriors to let Dora stay until we could discuss the matter. They reluctantly picked up their spears and left. They were very angry because, according to custom, Dora did belong at their *manyatta.*

A few days later when we saw her mother, Ngoto Dora, she wept and held our hands in hers a long time. For many more years to come, it would be only the lucky few mission school girls who would escape spending their childhood in a warrior *manyatta*.

Once a young man has attained warrior status and moved into his *manyatta*, his biggest goal in life is to kill a lion. It counts as his kill if he is first to thrust a spear into a lion which warriors have surrounded, or the first to grab its tail, once it is wounded. They compete desperately for this honor. It is their equivalent to any graduate degree in a modern university. Not only has the warrior the thrill of making a huge headdress out of the mane of the lion, but he is given adulation and great honor and respect by all. The young girls make new beaded articles for him to wear on his arms, ears, neck and ankles, as well as a long, narrow leather bib, heavily decorated with designs in more beadwork.

One day when I walked into a kraal, all the women were buzzing over every detail of a lion recently speared "by a lad who was not even circumcised yet!" Because he was so big and responsible he had already been allowed to have a spear for protection.

This lad came into our yard and showed us his long spear, bent into a right angle with fang marks all over the wooden handle and he told us this story:

He was herding his cattle some three miles from our house. A lion grabbed one of his finest bulls. Why is it the lion always takes the biggest and the finest? A scrawny animal is never taken from the herd! The lion tossed the bull onto his back and started trotting off with it. The lad ran after him and thrust his spear into the lion. It entered the base of the lion's spinal column. The lion dropped the bull and just sat down, immobilized. The frantic lion pulled the spear out of his own body, yet the lower half of him was paralyzed and he was unable to get up. The lad retrieved his spear, took his bull home, then came and calmly told us his story.

Roy, with Harry and several Maasai *ilmuran*, went back with him to finish off the lion. The Maasai were so eager and quick to thrust their spears into the lion that he was soon like a pin cushion and drew his last breath. Roy didn't even need to shoot him to put him out of his misery. Harry cut off one of the paws with its sharp claws. He still has it.

Maasai kids are brought up on lion stories as Anglo-American children are on Mother Goose. Here is one our cook, Ngasotu, dictated to me one day:

EAR ILMURAN OLNGATUNY (OLOWARU KITOK)
The Warriors Kill a Lion (The Chief Beast)

The warriors go for a kill very early, before dawn, when the second rooster crows. They go to the plain and they hear a lion roar. One warrior says, " Listen! I heard a lion roar over there! Come, let's go that way."

They go that way and meet a lion eating a zebra. It stands up.

The warriors hurl their spears at the lion and they cry out, "U-wi!" The lion crouches down and enters a dense bush. The warriors go closer because the lion lies down.

"Let us pursue!" the warriors say. "We will not run away."

Then the warriors curse one warrior.

"Hold him back!" they say. But that warrior runs to the lion and he spears the lion with his spear.

The lion comes out right into the middle of all the warriors. He is speared! There are ten spears in his body!

The lion seizes the first warrior and throws him down and mauls him.

The warriors all pull out their swords and slash. They cut off the head of the lion and he dies. Two warriors seize the feet and rear end of the lion and they rip open the stomach of the lion, ripping with swords.

He is very fierce, the lion. He has twenty claws and four very sharp, long teeth. When he chews a person, he breaks the bone. He can rip open a shield. He is hairy.

The Maasai warriors are also fierce. Maasai warriors fear nothing. They can enter fire.

Each lion kill calls for a great celebration of dancing and singing. The dance of the warriors is like nothing else on earth and it can be terrifying to those who don't know the significance of it. It is simple, vehement, straight up-and-down jumping, keeping feet close together, hands to the sides, grunting like lions rhythmically with each jump.

The height of skill and accomplishment is when the dancer's *oltaiga* at the back and the safety pin in front of his hair both fly straight out, high in the air together. Each *olmurani* tries to jump higher than the others, with his *shuka* flying high in the air as well. The onlookers yell and cheer wildly when one surpasses the other. Each takes his turn, two or three *ilmuran* at a time. They do this for hours on end, just for the pleasure. It is spectacular, for they compete vigorously. The onlookers not only grunt like lions and bounce in rhythm, but also sing long, seemingly endless victory lyrics about lions they have killed and cattle they have saved, even if only the hide and meat and tail.

The wild exultance of this dance terrified the host of porters in the caravan of the adventurer Joseph Thomson, for whom the graceful herds of Thomson's gazelles roaming the Maasai plains are named. This brilliant young explorer was the first recorded white man to get into and out of Maasai country alive, and only by his quick wits and some trickery. Sponsored by the Royal Geographical Society of London, he launched an expedition from Zanzibar to hunt for a short route to Lake Victoria, straight through Maasailand.

If you want a good book, as authentic today as it was in 1885 when he wrote it, get *Through Masai Land*, by Joseph Thomson. When Thomson and his caravan, seeking water, approached the Engoitokitok Spring in the northeast foothills of Mount Kilimanjaro, they came upon a dance celebrating a successful lion hunt. The caravan turned and fled. They interpreted this to be a war dance, which was far from the truth, but they did not know it.

It was fifty years from the time Joseph Thomson's expedition visited the Engoitokitok Spring, to the time Roy was to dam it up for a new mission station water supply. *Tokitok* means bubble, and the spring did bubble forth.

Roy was careful to build watering troughs for the cattle to drink from a few yards below the dam. By that time we were well aware that a warrior's fierceness was reserved for lion fights and for any interference with his beloved cattle.

In fact, one *olmurani* killed a white man in a simple dispute over a cow, right out under the high, spreading *lasit* (acacia) trees between our house and the main road.

The victim was Major Grant, a government officer in charge of buying Maasai cattle as meat for the military forces during World War II. He was highly respected and even loved by the Maasai as their District Commissioner. Most of his *karanis* (clerks who recorded each sale of each cow and paid for it) had been lads trained in our little school at Siyabei, years before; among them was Stephen Sitoya ole Sankan. Roy and I were on the high seas, returning from furlough when this event happened, but on arrival I asked Sitoya about the details. By then he was one of the most trusted English-speaking Maasai in government service.

It happened at the close of day, he said. Major Grant had bought cattle all day and so was more tired than usual because of wind and dust. All were hot, sweaty and on edge; this included the cattle, for they know that when nighttime comes they want to be inside the safety of the kraal.

Grant had given all the elders and warriors good prices for the cattle and all were satisfied. He picked out the last cow to buy to complete his quota for the day, a white one.

"No, Bwana, this is my favorite cow," protested its owner, a 16-year-old lad. "I have sold you twelve already today. Choose any other, but not this one, for didn't I feed it with my own hands from the time it was born and its mother refused to give it suck? Isn't it white all over? Don't I need it to buy a wife with? No, not this one!!"

Grant well knew the love of a Maasai for a white cow, but he was very eager to get finished with the sale, for the sun was setting and all were anxious to get to their kraals before dark.

"What I have chosen, I have chosen," Grant said. He started to walk away.

The lad walked a few feet to where he had parked his spear in the ground, pulled it out, took precise aim and threw the spear at Grant. It entered Grant's back, went through his heart and on past his body ten feet to stab into the wood fence of the cattle corral, where it quivered several seconds. It all happened so fast that no one knew just what had happened.

Pandemonium set in among both the people and the cattle. There lay Major Grant, bleeding profusely on the ground. The several clerks' tables with the money on them were all upset. Everyone rushed in every direction, not knowing why, nor what to do.

Finally the Maasai got the cattle corralled, then they began to investigate.

The lad who had speared Grant had gone to a nearby tree and sat down. His brother ran to him and found him upset, but still calm.

"Was it you who speared the white man?" he asked, incredulously.

"Yes," quietly answered the lad. "I did it because I didn't want him to take my beloved white cow. I refuse to give it up, so I did it on purpose, and would do it again." The lad made no move to run away or hide.

The elders and warriors were ashamed by this affair. They wept with remorse and apologized in every way they knew. They gave many cattle to cover the cost of the air fares for Mrs. Grant and her three children to fly back to England. They gave much else besides in their desire to make restitution as far as possible.

Mrs. Grant took a marvelous attitude toward them, for she knew well how truly the Maasai did love her husband. She and her daughters remained in England but her son, upon finishing school, went right back to Kenya and worked among the Maasai in government service. Like his father, he too was loved by the Maasai.

Because the Grants were so special to the Maasai, the whole tribe had made not a murmur when the lad who speared Mr. Grant was tried in Nairobi in a court of law, found guilty and hanged.

By Maasai law, however, the payment of a heavy fine in cattle had absolved the crime. The Maasai have orally transmitted, well-defined civil laws of their own, almost Biblical in form. The affairs of the tribe governed by these laws were decided in council meetings. But the council meetings were definitely not in the hands of the hot-blooded young *ilmuran*. They were the affair of the elders. The *ilmuran* became elders only after periodic very elaborate ceremonial rituals were celebrated.

9 *Elders and Prophets*

ONE DAY ON SAFARI we happened upon one of their biggest celebrations. We were travelling self-contained in a new little house trailer Roy had built on the bed of a two-ton truck. The sun lowered westward as, hunting a good campsite, we were welcomed into a huge kraal of more than thirty huts.

The ground was littered with matted hair that had been shorn from the heads of warriors. One mother was still shaving her son's head when we arrived. But she was not using a razor and shaving lather. She just had crude pieces of metal, a little water and no soap. Everybody seemed proud of these cut and cast-off locks of hair even as they lay in the dry cow manure underfoot.

We had happened on a festival of *Eunoto*. This was the time of choosing a new *olaigwenani*, chief-spokesman, from among a clan's warriors as they went from junior to senior *ilmuran* status and began the transition to full elderhood. Each mother shaved the long hair off the head of her own warrior son. Now he was free to marry. At the end of this last half of his warrior days he would lay aside his six-foot spear and everything he had owned and treasured as a warrior, and become an elder. From then on he would carry the long stick and short-bladed spear of the elder, wear the blanket of an elder, and settle down.

Quite understandably, warriors are loathe to become elders.

Ever since circumcision, the young *muran* had belonged more closely to his age group than to his own family. Now, at *Eunoto* the age group would graduate together and choose a group name to stay with them for life. No matter where they lived, age group members were closer in spirit than fraternity brothers. Depending on their reputations as *ilmuran*, or how they wanted to be remembered, they would choose such group names as *Iltwati*, the rich ones; *Ilkishumu*, the raiders; *Ilkiponi*, those who add to, or increase; *Ilngarbut*, the gluttons; or *Ilseure*, the lucky ones.

The *Eunoto* is a ceremony of the greatest importance because, for months ahead of the actual choice, secretly and surreptitiously the right chief, or spokesman, is being sought and selected from among the warriors. We were told that the chosen warrior must meet certain requirements. The qualifications are very rigid and standards are very high. He also must be physically perfect, with no blemishes at all. He must have ten fingers and ten toes (some have extras, as did Chief Noolgimojek, who was chosen anyway), and good eyes with no blue spot on either (a common result of living in smoky huts). Besides, he must be one who is compatible and well liked by all his fellow warriors, brave, fearless and of good judgment. Very few can pass the tests. In fact, few even care to be chosen as chief; they glory in their bodily wounds received from some hand-to-paw fight with lions. They prefer the carefree life of no responsibility. The chief chosen must have living parents who are not blind. He must never have murdered a Maasai. The one chosen is not told until the last moment. Then a group of elders and warriors cluster about him and hold him for he will try to get up and run away and refuse to accept the awesome responsibility of the leadership bestowed upon him. Some of the well-chosen, outstanding *Ilaigwenak* we knew who came up through this system were Masagondi, Oimeru, Olegelisho, Kulale and Noolgimojek.

The *Eunoto* ceremony must always be held near a water hole, for they take countless cattle along to have plenty of milk for all, and cattle must have water to make milk.

The *Eunoto* we attended was at the place called "Olmoti," a temporary pool of water during the rains near Lukenia. These pools dry up after the rains. There must be plenty of wood with which to build hut frameworks and keep fires at night, as well as thorn bushes with which to build a high barrier around the kraal. Months ahead, the women go to the spot the men have chosen, and build the frames for the huts and construct the kraal enclosure. Next, the cattle are driven into the enclosure every night to ensure a continuous supply of fresh cow manure with which to plaster the huts. This takes several weeks, of course.

When all the huts are completed, the crowd of warriors, their mothers and some elders move in with their gourds and sleeping skins. The *Eunoto* lasts many days, with much meat eaten, much "doctored" milk drunk, and non-stop singing and dancing, all of which results in a high pitch of emotion. This brings on friendly fights, followed by unfriendly fights, between the younger and the older warriors, often resulting in a cracked head, the chief point of attack. Several times through the years, the wounded came to Roy to ask him to sew up their heads, which he did, using wildebeest tail hairs for thread. This seemed to foster healing faster than anything else.

Fierce fights also always took place between the younger and the older warriors after every circumcision year, for the younger wanted to prove to the older that they had become the dominant males. The older ones make the younger ones prove it in a fight.

The day we arrived at this particular *Eunoto*, we noticed the absence of spears. Not one was to be seen, which was most unusual. An elder told us that the day before there had been a fierce battle among the warriors and one was killed. The wise old Maasai elders advised the government police to come at once and take away all spears, shields and sharp knives to prevent the hotheads from spearing each other to death. They were in such a high spirit of agitation — being so drugged with their own concoctions — they didn't know what they were doing and friend was slashing at friend. They did love their pitched battles.

So it was rather ironic, after we had arrived and set up our camp at this *Eunoto*, that all the warriors were willing to sit down on their haunches and listen to the words Roy read from the little black book.

"Let's sing some hymns," they requested.

There were among them some who, as lads in our school,

had learned these songs in Sunday School and they never forgot them. We had Joseph Masaa as our evangelist with us and, like a magnet, he drew their attention to the simple story of God's love, and then prayed, talking to God in Maasai, which thrilled them.

"*Ashe* (Thank you)," they all said together at the close. This was a welcome calm after the chaotic day before.

Following the *Eunoto* ceremony, each warrior was expected to eventually move out of the *manyatta*, marry, if he hadn't already, and live in his own family kraal. His own opening would be established in the kraal enclosure, and his *oltimi*, or male seed symbol, which was usually a short, many-branched limb, was placed just outside his own entry every morning when it was reopened. It was never to be removed or disturbed. We did not know this until one time when Roy went to a kraal to collect manure for our garden. When he backed the truck up to an entrance he kicked aside a branch lying in the way, causing consternation to two old men standing there. Then one of them kindly revealed to Roy the importance of the branch.

All the young new elders started taking part in the *engigwana*, the tribal council meetings, usually called by the chief of the area. By the grapevine, word got around as to the time and location of an *engigwana*, often held under a large, spreading tree. Slowly, majestically, the elders began arriving in their skins or blankets, holding their flyswitches, spears and sticks, walking in groups or two or more, coughing, spitting and talking quietly.

After a while, all sat down on the ground, huddled under their wraps to keep warm as it was usually cold. When the chief arrived and sat down, they all courteously greeted him, but not all talking at the same time.

He slowly and deliberately opened the meeting.

WHACK! The chief struck the ground with his scepter of authority, a knobbed stick about two feet long and sometimes made of rhino horn.

"Our first word concerns —" (and he would name some affair on the agenda to be discussed.) "Say one!"

"One!" they would all say in concert. Then they would deal with the matter.

The only decisions taken were those which represented a consensus of opinion. The Maasai chief has no real executive power as we know it.

After settling point number one, he moved them on to the second.

WHACK!

"Say Two!"

"Two!"

And they discussed the second matter. There may be few or many "words" on the agenda. Being outdoors, if rain fell, they scattered and went home, to continue the next day. They were accurate and just about clearing any innocent person brought up for trial. It was uncanny what kinds of evidence might be produced to persuade the elders. For example, in the case of a cow theft, such items as a burnt hoof, or hairs from a cow's tail seem to be convincing. When a person was found guilty, punishment usually was payment of a fine in cattle. Cattle were more precious to them than our silver or gold, so they hated to give up even one for anything.

What held the Maasai in even more awe, respect and fear than their own laws and chiefs, were the *iloibonok*, the prophet-advisors. The position was handed down from father to son. We soon realized that if we were ever to be effective, we would have to learn about the power of the *iloibonok* (whom we called medicine men) and study it closely.

In July 1931, we wrote home in our newsletter "Echoes from Masailand" (the spelling of Masai was later changed to Maasai, reflecting the root word *maa*, meaning the people):

> We have just completed another trip of nine days out in the Masai Reserve. We traveled most of the way with no roads, so at times it was difficult going. We managed to get to our destination, which was the kraal of Sendeyo, the Chief Medicine Man, about 75 miles from home. Sendeyo and his brother, Lenana, are the last survivors of a long line of

medicine men who have been very powerful in the Masai tribe.

When we approached Sendeyo's kraal, he and his fifteen wives and all the people from his forty huts came out to greet us. Sendeyo was a huge, full-faced man, with his slow-moving hulk of a well-greased bronze body all draped in a blanket. He carried the ever-present wildebeest tail fly switch and small stick carried by a man of importance. He wore two big rings on his fingers, one in each ear, and some large beads strung around his neck (not small beads such as the younger people wore). He was quite old and feeble, but his slightest wish was obviously obeyed promptly.

No white man could ever have been more friendly and hospitable than he was to us, a party of total strangers arriving completely unannounced at his kraal. On the evening we arrived and also the next dawn, he sent us many gourds of milk — all we and our helpers could drink.

We held several meetings in his village and the people all heard the words with keen interest. Then Sendeyo gave us an elaborate blessing and said he was pleased that we had come to see him.

"Your words are very good," he said, "but they show that we Maasai are very great sinners." As we left, he begged us to return sometime.

Sendeyo was following the pattern set by his father, Mbatian, whom the Maasai considered the greatest of all *iloibonok*, or prophets. Legend has it that a century ago he foretold the coming of the man with no coloring in his body.

"Be good to him," Mbatian is alleged to have said, "for he will not harm us. He will come only for good."

Over the years, very few white people have ever been killed by the "murderous Maasai," as they were previously known, and they have always since had harmonious relations with the government.

The highest peak on Mount Kenya was named Mbatian, and one of the streets in Nairobi was named for his elder son, Lenana. One of the fine secondary schools, grades 6 to 9, in

Karen, a suburb of Nairobi, is named Lenana School. Over 1,000 students attend, all looking so trim in their uniforms. Their sports program is excellent. They and Rift Valley Academy often compete in rugby. Lenana took over the north part of the tribe when Mbatian died, while Sendeyo, the second son, lived in the south part of Maasailand.

But we found that, while the chief *iloibonok,* or prophet-medicine men, may have been kind to us missionaries, the lesser ones cursed us and worked against us as did Kasura, Kuyoni's father, for so long. The people consulted them on all issues, paid fat fees for their edicts, and obediently went through painful ordeals on their orders. Our cook's baby, along with every other infant in the district, once had circles burned on both cheeks "to keep away an impending drought and locust plague."

The name *iloibonok* (for which the singular is *oloiboni*), comes from the verb stem *-ibon,* meaning to prophesy or foretell events. We called them "witch doctors" or "medicine men" because they claimed healing powers. Generally, we found that our best course of action against them was to ignore them and before long we had a nucleus of Maasai whose hearts the Spirit of God had opened to the Light, who no longer consulted the witch doctor on any issue and who no longer feared him. But this was at great cost.

There was one fine elder who had been teaching himself to read by studying the printing on petrol boxes. He waited a long time before he publicly declared his desire to look into the *kilasi* (catechism class), and learn more about *Yesu* (Jesus). Very soon after he joined the *kilasi,* the *oloibani* secretly arranged for the maiming of three of the elder's best cows by houghing, or severing the hamstrings in their back legs, which meant he then had to slaughter them, of course. This almost broke his heart, for he loved his cattle individually. But he did not leave the *kilasi.* Later, he did move away, but we were told he never gave up his love for Christ, to his dying day.

Olenaisho was one *oloiboni* whose wife dared to join the

kilasi. She listened for some time, then broke through into the Light. She decided to cut away from her old life, for the love of God had really flooded her mind and heart. She asked me to teach her to read God's Word, which I did. One day she brought all of her beads, wires and skins and asked me to destroy them and give her instead, a cloth garment to wear, saying she would bring milk in her gourd to pay for it. On my little hand sewing machine I made her a blue dress of new, strong material which she loved. She loved to turn the handle of my machine for me, as well. All the paraphernalia she had been wearing weighed 20 pounds when I put it on the scales.

"Nolminangae" was her name, meaning "one who has not been cast aside." She was Olenaisho's favorite wife, even though she was barren, the greatest curse a Maasai woman can bear. Very quickly, Nolminangae learned to read and was soon accepted as the leader of the women.

Olenaisho, meaning "the of the fermented honey," loved her as Jacob had loved Rachel. He did not cast her out of his kraal even though he should have according to custom, since he was the local witch doctor. In God's wisdom, He drew this man Olenaisho not only to attend church where his wife went, but to enter the *kilasi* to find out something about all these new Words of God for himself. He found Christ, not by any high-powered persuasion on our part, but by the Holy Spirit of the Living God.

So then he took the bravest step for any Maasai: he brought all of his witch-works of chicken bones, leopard teeth, gourds, stones, bits of fingernails, claws of lion, wood ashes and much else for Roy to burn in a public ceremony outside the church. He had bought a pair of khaki shorts and a shirt which he wore to this burning ceremony.

All of the people laughed with him as he chided himself about feeling so funny in the white man's clothes. He looked and felt very awkward, but the broad grin he wore from ear to ear bore witness that he was pleased from his heart down inside, clear to the outside, and was not shy about saying so. Today, this couple's granddaughter Joyce is a highly placed graduate nurse with the East African Flying Doctor Service.

During our time out there, the days of the power of the *iloibonok* were passing. But there was one accurate, final prophecy attributed to the great Mbatian: that when the white man came, he would bring with him two long, glistening snakes lying side by side on the ground, which would never come together, neither would they separate, nor would any man be able to find their tails or heads, and they would glisten and shine like Maasai spears. No one would be able to harm them, nor would they harm anyone for they would be strong and never move.

Mbatian did not live to see the coming of the shining railway tracks of the Kenya-Uganda Railway from Mombasa on the coast, inland to Lake Victoria.

Very soon Kenya was flooded with settlers from England and most of the European countries as well as South Africa, India and Australia. All of the good and the bad effects of civilization poured in with them to add to the already complex diversity of the people of East Africa. But the adaptability of Africans is one of their greatest strengths. Their knack for quickly learning a new language is notable. Perhaps it is because most of them already know three or more languages of their own.

There are many vernaculars in all countries of Africa. Kenya alone has twenty-four main languages and many other dialects. With eight hundred languages and eight hundred cultures, it may be a long time before there is any political unity in Africa. There is only one area in which there can possibly be unity and that is centered around Christ and His love for mankind and mankind's love for Him in return.

This, then, was our mandate for taking the Good News to the Maasai. With little published for us to read about them and much wild rumor about their ferocity, we set about getting to know what were, by now, "our" Maasai.

"Is it worth the time and effort to try to change these Maasai?" folks used to ask us.

"No," we liked to answer. "We never expect to change them." But the power of God's Word has already done just that and continues to do so.

10 *Women of the Maasai*

WE QUICKLY DISCOVERED THAT among the Maasai a woman was rated below a cow in real value to her husband. She seemed never to live in any state other than utter subjection to men, always seen but never heard. It was as though she must never have any desires or plans of her own.

Each grown Maasai woman wore a set of closely wound, heavy-guage, shiny wire coils encasing her upper and lower arms and her lower legs. She received them after she left the *manyatta* as a girl, was circumcised, and was led to the kraal of her husband. There, she put on these spirals of heavy iron, brass, or, in later years, aluminum, which denoted she was now a married woman. They weighted her down for the rest of her life.

I have seen young matrons in agony as they tried to scratch an itch up under the wires. They had to take long, thin sticks to try desperately to scratch where fingers couldn't reach. Some women had even been killed by rhino just because the heavy loads of wire prevented them from running to get away from the wild, nearsighted animals. So the Maasai elders began to change and not require their women to wear these heavy coils which restrict walking, let alone running.

The most attractive part of the usual Maasai woman's appearance, to us, was her multiple necklace of colored seed beads strung on fine wire hoops that formed a large, flat circle reaching to her shoulders in diameter, with a hole in the center just large enough for her shaven head to go through.

The women delight in dancing up and down, making

these beaded necklaces bob up and down as they hum and sing monotone lyrics in rhythm with the bobbing. Ear lobes and tops of ears are pierced to hold even more beaded wire hoops in fancy patterns. But only the older women are allowed to wear heavy, flat brass spirals that are suspended by rawhide straps from their long, stretched earlobes and rest on their breasts.

Besides all the jewelry, the girl or woman wears the *engela*, a skin or cloth garment in two pieces. One is draped closely from her waist to her feet, overlapping in front and held on by a rawhide belt. The top part is draped around her shoulders and knotted in front, covering what part of her breasts the beads miss. The skin garments are usually decorated around the edges with double rows of beads.

One time when I was travelling all alone after retirement in the U.S., my train reached Grand Central Station in New York City at 2 a.m. I will never forget the grandeur of this huge station. The first thing I saw, besides the milling around of countless people rushing about everywhere, was a 50' by 50' colored slide show high up on one wall. Of all things, what did I see flashed up there momentarily but a closeup of one of our beautiful, bead-bedecked Maasai women in her shaven head, smiling down at me! Brass coils covered her arms. I let out a loud, affectionate greeting: "OI!! TAGWENYA PASENAI!!" Then she was gone. Thrills ran down my spine. No one even heard me yell, the place was so noisy.

A Maasai woman is envied if she is lucky enough to have her own baby slung in the skin on her back, next to her body, where it stays until it is swung around in front to be nursed at mother's breast. No schedule here—just anytime.

Of course, civilization and education are fast changing dress codes of the Maasai, both men and women. This is true of all tribes everywhere. Today there are many Maasai girls going through the Girls School at Kajiado who dress just like any American girl, for they never did dress as the original Maasai girls did during our days there. Some still do, however, in areas far from towns.

In the kraals, women do all of the work of putting up huts. First, they cut wood for the uprights and collect sticks and saplings for cross strips. I saw a woman laboriously put a wet handful of fresh cow dung on the dry, hard ground, then use a sharp stick to dig a hole a few inches deep under it. Water was scarce, so she used wet dung. Into this hole she put an upright, which was about four feet high and curved at the top to start the rounded roof. Several women worked together setting uprights in an oval outline on the ground before weaving the cross strips like a basket up the sides and across the top. If leaves were available, they were woven in too.

The entrance is built so low one has to bend down to go in and out. However, Mary Slater, who worked among the Maasai in the early days with the Stauffachers and the Barnetts at Rumuruti, was so short she didn't need to bend. The Maasai named her "Nakwetiaji" (the who can run into the house).

Over the whole framework of the hut they now spread, by hand, a layer of moist dung, then wait for this to dry. After the dung is dry, they put on another layer, then another. During rains, the huts are kept freshly daubed with fresh dung, which keeps the rain out.

Inside the hut, they weave a basket-like partition to divide the area for the lambs and calves from the raw hides which are laid over grass and sticks as a sleeping place for the people. A three-stone fire is always kept burning in the center of the hut.

Often women came to our back yard and just sat there waiting patiently until I could come out to greet them. Many came for medicine, but many others came just to "eat the words of the day."

"When is it going to rain?" was one of the invariable

questions, as though they were sure that white men and women knew this secret. Their greatest concern in life was not money in the bank, nor new clothes. Rather, they had two desires: first, to be able to conceive and bear children; and second, to have rain, which meant grass, which meant food for cattle, which meant milk for her children and family.

If a Maasai wife is fortunate enough to conceive and bear a live child, everyone is delighted and her new baby is immediately plastered with sheep fat instead of soap and water. A rawhide string is placed around the baby's neck, with a tiny pouch containing various charms made by the medicine man. This is not to be removed.

I often would like to have given a dress for the new baby, but I soon learned that a baby never gets a dress. Baby gets just a string of colored beads to wear below its fat little tummy. Its sole protection is its immediate proximity to mother's body. When not nursing in front it is carried on mother's back, inside her skin garment, where baby keeps warm as toast. Later, as baby grows, its head dangles outside looking like it would drop off backwards!

Baby's head is not shaved like everybody else's until five or six months of age. During that time the mother does not shave hers either. And aside from the string of beads and the pouch of charms to keep away evil spirits, the baby has nothing to cover up its beauty.

Babies are really never "bathed" as we know it. I have often watched a mother use the unique Maasai method of bathing a baby. In her left hand she held her baby up in the air. She swigged a mouthful of water from a gourd, warmed it in her mouth for a moment, then spewed it over the shrieking baby's head, rubbing it with her right hand. The next mouthful went to baby's eyes, then face, then neck and arms, then the tummy, then legs, clear down to the ten toes, with equally as many mouthfuls. This was up on the Mau at seven thousand feet altitude, where it is cold and windy. No wonder the lungs of Maasai babies rattle most of the time! But after baby shivered and cried lustily, mother tucked it back into the warm, greasy pouch on her back. There was no question of something clean on baby — not among the nomadic Maasai.

Besides achieving good grooming, shaving heads helps to control head lice. I often watched a mother give her baby his first shave. She spat on a spot, then scraped it with a piece of sharp metal. This spitting and scraping continued until she had shaved the whole head. Maasai never saw razor blades until the Indian *dukas* brought them in, and some sold packages of used blades for the high price of new blades. Because the razors are dangerous, Maasai mothers prefer to use their own pieces of metal. All women shave off their eyebrows and they don't paint others on, as white women do. In fact, they shave off all body hair.

If the baby is a girl, at five or six years of age she is well greased and painted from head to foot, then led by her mother with great ceremony to the *manyatta* where she will stay until she reaches puberty. Then she must go home. As the child develops she will try to hide any sign or evidence of puberty, for by this time she will have developed an adoration for the warriors and will not want to leave them.

When the girl reaches puberty, she is taken back home to her parents, who arrange for her to join a group of four or more girls who are to be circumcised, in many cases against their will.

The clinical term for female circumcision is "clitoridectomy." The excision of the clitoris was done by an old *Engoiboni* (female *Oloiboni*) in a dark hut. Fresh, green cow manure was used to curb bleeding on the girl who told me about her own circumcision, years later when she was a grown woman. Others used fat and ashes. I am told that Maasai female circumcision involves not only clitoridectomy but in addition, parts of the labia minora are cut off, which has a profoundly damaging effect on fertility. It leaves a gaping vulva into which germs pass much more readily to produce inflammatory pelvic diseases resulting in blocked fallopian tubes.

Back in the 1920s, the ceremony I knew about at Siyabei, began early one morning. The girls were led down the hill to the icy cold river, in which they sat all morning until they were numb. They were then rushed back to the hut where screaming women carried on a frenzied ritual to build up the girls' courage, but actually it was very frightening.

During many days of healing, the newly circumcised girls were kept in a separate group, bedecked with beads all over their faces, necks and arms. Vivid designs were painted on their faces with white lava dirt, black soot or with red ochre which was evidence that they had completed this traditional rite. It is proof that they have been able to withstand extreme pain honorably, and have earned the status of women. They were herded like sheep, kept in motion all day long, crawling about on hands and knees. They were not allowed to sit down and they just couldn't stand up yet.

They endured it, for not to go through circumcision would mark them as outcasts in Maasai society. When I saw this parade of girls crawling around, and was told why, I had to fight back nausea and tears.

When a girl was finally healed, her marriage ceremony was performed and she was led from her father's kraal to the kraal of the man who bought her. He usually already had other wives.

Circumcision causes so much scar tissue that few Maasai babies can survive birth alive and mothers often die in childbirth as well. I have seen both. The first time I witnessed this was when we were at the hospital in Kijabe with little Harry Daniel and his badly burned feet. Mrs. Davis asked me if I cared to see the results of female circumcision.

I went and saw a young, circumcised girl who had been in labor for several days and was about to deliver. Both the mother and the baby died. The mission doctor and nurse were grieved to lose her. The snow white uniforms of both Davises were ruined. They put on fresh ones and, though exhausted, turned to face the rest of the day's case load.

Massive scarring from circumcision made conception and delivery so difficult that the Maasai tribe has a very low birth rate. In fact, there are almost no pure Maasai left because for generations Maasai men have imported Kikuyu wives who, though also circumcised, were less mutilated than the Maasai girls were.

No inquiries I ever knew of, whether by mission, Maasai, or government, ever established reason for female circumcision. It did not accomplish what the Maasai claimed it was supposed to do, which was to keep a wife true to her husband. There was no such fidelity since free love continued throughout normal Maasai society. In fact, a man was duty-bound to hospitably share his wife with any visitor of his own age group. Wife-sharing was not looked upon as a sin as was, for example, losing one's temper.

We AIMers were divided on what approach to use against this deeply entrenched rite in the several local tribes which practiced it. Many of us felt that the Africans themselves would eventually call a halt to it. A campaign against people's beliefs—widespread in the Sudan, Somalia, Ethiopia and Egypt—that genital mutilation is essential to full womanhood was started by educated Sudanese women in 1979 and has attracted support from the United Nations Children's Fund.

As early as 1935 there were a few Maasai who wanted to stop, and over the years more and more girls have refused to submit to it. Education and observation have opened their eyes.

The constitution of the indigenous Africa Inland Church, formed many years later, prohibits parents from inflicting circumcision on their girls within church membership, at cost of exclusion from taking communion.

There came an evangelist named Justus Mumo wa Nzomo, from the Akamba tribe, to work among the Maasai, at God's command. Traditionally, the Akamba hated the Maasai, who throughout history had stolen their cattle. They called them *Wakwavi* (the enemy). The Maasai, in turn, called the Akamba *Iloongu* (they who stink).

But because Justus had many children, the Maasai began to admire him and to listen to him, for they would do anything to learn his magic of how to get so many children. They thought his powers of procreation might have a good influence on the area.

Justus' wife was not circumcised, and the Maasai took note of this. She bore twins; then four other children besides. She was a good wife and healthy mother, and the Maasai taking note of this were happy to have her in their midst. Then suddenly, she died of cerebral malaria. The whole community ate sorrow together!

Justus next married a widow named Fibi from his home in Ukambani. She had her own three children, so they now had eleven mouths eating around the fire at night. Fibi bore him other sons and daughters.

In his humble, wise way, Justus never argued with the Maasai about all their customs. He just lived among them and loved them in such a manner that, before long, many decided to break tradition and follow his pattern of life — even his *Yesu* (Jesus) — and the church grew.

The Maasai loved Pastor Justus and his family so much that they gave them land on which to build their own house, some milk cows and much else, for he learned their language quickly and became one of them in truth. But that gets far ahead of the story.

11 *Cowpen Crusades*

"WHAT IS YOUR PROCEDURE?" friends at home asked. "Do you have evangelistic crusades?"

Our Maasai were too sparsely populated for the gathering of any crowds.

"Do you appeal to the emotions?" they asked.

Far from any such. While the Maasai are not without emotion, they seldom display it. They reserve emotions for killing a lion, rescuing a cow, or fighting over a girl. As for the women, they get excited and all worked up dancing and making offerings around their sacred tree. Their living pattern prohibited our copying crowd-gathering methods and pressures for presenting Christ to our nomadic Maasai.

Instead, we simply went to them where they were, in isolated kraals on the windswept plains. You might say we had cowpen crusades.

The *engang*, a kraal lived in by an extended family unit, is a thornbush barrier roughly six to ten feet high and six to ten feet wide at the base, surrounding all the huts. It has as many openings as the number of heads of families living inside the kraal. Just inside this fence is the circle of low mud-and-manure huts shaped like oval igloos, each with its low, short, tunnel-like entrance. These huts are home to the Maasai.

Each wife has her own hut, which is respected as her domain. The open area surrounded by these huts is where the cattle, asses, sheep and goats stand all night, regardless of weather. Here they are safe from lions and leopards which prowl outside the fence all night.

So the term "cowpen crusades" is no joke; it is a reality.

Where else could we find Maasai if not in their cowpens? The *engang* takes the place of any hall, church, theater, or any building where crowds gather. Evening finds everybody at home. But this is a bad time to visit them for there is always much work at day's end for both men and women, including milking cows and caring for any sick lambs or other animals for the night.

Evenings, when the cows come home and low for their calves, the women bring out their small-mouthed gourds to milk the cows. After the calf brings down the milk, they can push the calf away and try to get a cup of milk from each cow before the calf gets it all. The cowpen becomes melodious as the herders whistle and call each cow by name, the women chatter as they milk, the cows low and the calves bawl, hunting their mothers. Each woman goes from cow to cow of her own herd — never another's, for they never steal from one another — hoping to gather enough milk for the needs of her own family for the night. She repeats the process in the morning. Men never milk the cows.

I recall my father sitting on a three-legged stool when he milked our one cow back home in Indian Territory. All the while he would talk to the cow gently saying, "So boss, so boss," and then come in with a bucket full of milk.

Maasai cattle are many in number but mongrel in breeding, mostly zebu humpback, and one cow does well if she gives two cups of milk daily. But the cream off Maasai milk is as thick as gravy and very rich. No Maasai woman uses a stool either. She just leans her head against her cow, stoops over to get the gourd's mouth as near the teat as possible and very adroitly catches every drop right in the tiny mouth of the gourd.

We habitually bought six wine bottles of milk daily from our nearest kraal. We boiled it all in one pot, then set it in a cool place overnight. In the morning we would pour out the milk from under the cream and set the bowl of accumulated cream aside until we had a quart or more. The cook then would take a spoon and stir a few minutes, and out would come a pound or more of rich butter, with almost no buttermilk left over. Our children preferred the thick cream and homemade brown sugar syrup on pancakes to any other kind of breakfast.

Young Maasai herdboys are usually hungry when they bring the herds home at night, for they go all day without eating or drinking. Should they really need nourishment during the day for any reason, they are permitted to suck the goats of their flocks which have milk.

They have names for each animal and each beast will respond when its name is spoken. This was hard for me to believe when they have so many, but the herder knows when even one is lost. He will go far and wide searching for it. Young herders are beaten with a stick if they lose any of the flock entrusted to them. Sheep and goats are herded together, calves by themselves, and asses with cattle. At age six, a herder-child will drive off a leopard, jackal, or hyena with only his sticks. Herders not yet fourteen years of age will drive away lions trying to steal from their herds.

Well before dark, after the herds are all in the kraal, every entrance to it is closed securely by pulling thorn bushes into it from the inside, with the long thorns pointing outward. Once the gates are closed, it is almost impossible to enter the kraal until dawn when they are reopened. Several of the fearless *ilmuran*, always carrying their gleaming spears, patrol inside all night, eager for hand-to-paw conflict with a lion.

If a lion is desperate, he will leap right over the "impenetrable" thorn barrier, grab an ox by the neck, toss its body onto his back and leap back over the fence with it. In such case it is the duty of the warriors on guard to go outside and try to retrieve the ox. So, all night long inside the kraal the warriors keep vigil, yelling, cursing and daring the wild animals to try to steal one of the herd. People inside the huts sleep better when they hear them yelling, keeping guard.

The evening meal of still-warm fresh milk is the only meal of the day. Some prefer sour, curded milk which they always have in certain gourds. After all the males get their fill of milk, the women and children get their share of what is left.

Maasai are born beggers, also free givers. No person of

any color or race who turns up at a Maasai kraal ever goes away hungry. They are offered milk immediately, either warm milk fresh from the cow, or curded, sour milk left over from yesterday.

They love meat but seldom have it, although they are reputed to live on meat and milk. The *ilmuran* do have the sanctioned right to a periodic *olpul*, a sort of bachelors' bash, when they will take an ox and go off into the bush to gorge on it for a few days all alone. Only a young girl or two can be allowed to share the *olpul*. In general, the Maasai hold their cattle more as wealth than as food.

When they do kill a cow or an ox there is rejoicing and merriment in anticipation of the feast. They always prefer the fat parts. They mix beef and sheep fat to make a gruel which they feed infants. I have seen the women forcing this fat down the mouths of their very young babies laying face up in the mother's lap. Sure, the baby cries and spits it out, but mother stuffs it right back into the infant's mouth with her fingers until the gruel is all in and baby is ready to pop.

They eat great quantities of fat, yet medical studies have not found among the Maasai any incidence of a high cholesterol level in the blood, or heart trouble. In later years our son Roy David, a medical doctor, was the liaison person for some significant research on cardiovascular disease among the Maasai. The question was: Why, on such a very high cholesterol diet, did the Maasai not suffer coronaries? There was no clear answer, but important factors seemed to be exercise, absence of hypertension, drinking milk sour much of the time, and maybe genetics.

Their diet includes fresh blood carefully drawn from the jugular vein of a healthy ox for a special treat, or for the ill, the aged, or the undernourished. I once watched as an ox was being bled in our back yard. A group of little children sat around a calabash of blood waiting for it to coagulate, which it did quickly in that cold climate. Very soon, they took out handfuls of the chunky blood the consistency of jello and ate it with great relish.

In their kraals there was just too much going on at the end of the day for Roy and me ever to do more than just stop by for a brief greeting on an evening's walk. We restricted our longer visits to daylight hours.

Only once did we venture to project our lantern slides inside a kraal at night, and never again. It was during another visit to Sendeyo's kraal. At his request, after all the cows had been milked by the women, all people and animals were safely inside the kraal, and the thorn gates all closed, Roy set up his slide projector and a sheet and began to show slides.

The people went wild over such sights appearing on the sheet. In turn, the people's excitement affected the stock. The bulls began to bellow, the cows to moo, the asses to bray, and finally the sheep and calves began to baa-baa, they knew not what for. Sendeyo had a human and animal riot on his hands. Roy rescued his projector and slides; Sendeyo ordered every woman and child back into the low huts. (I crawled in with them, inclined to be a little scared myself with all the confusion.)

The men gained control of the herds by whistling shrilly and calling the near-stampeding animals by name until they were lowing and mooing normally again. Fortunately, our three children had been put to bed in our closed truck just outside the thorn fence, with their nursemaid.

All the next day the Maasai wanted to know the explanation of the phenomenon they had seen. Had it been sent down from heaven? Or where? They were stumped.

"When did you talk to God for Him to give you these things that were seen on the big white piece of cloth?" they demanded. "When did God speak with you for Him to tell you to write down all the words in that little thing you call *embuku* (the Book)?"

During these questions, one woman was pulling at my stockings in amazement. "Everybody look how her skin stretches over the bones," she called out, laughing. Another woman put her hands all over my bosom to make sure that I was female, not a man. We had definitely started to get "closer" to the people.

Daytime visits to the kraals were far more satisfactory

and productive than evening visits. The herds and their herders had gone and when the morning work was finished the women and old men had free time during the day.

Since they build their kraals on open plains where the wind blows, it is often cold enough for a fire. Much of Kenya is low, hot and malarial, but our Maasai Reserve, four hundred miles long and one hundred miles wide, is mostly in the highlands at some six thousand feet altitude.

To keep warm, the older men built a brush windbreak outside the kraal. There we would find them all in the sun huddled behind the windbreak, wrapped up in their blankets or skins to keep warm. The Maasai men of that time wore either skins, neatly sewn together with gut, or blankets bought from the *duka* draped around the body and tied with a bark string over the left shoulder. The blanket was never washed. Its owner wore it day and night till it dropped off. However, after each of the World Wars, the Indians sold them military surplus overcoats and caps of wool, so that every man who had the price bought an Army coat and hat which he never took off, be the day hot or cold. An Army coat and hat became symbols of wealth and prestige.

If there were any brush or wood to spare, the men lit a fire behind their windbreak. There, they could sit and spit all day, literally until the cows came home, with a clear conscience. These men had finished their exciting warrior days and had served as responsible elders; they had earned the right to sit unmolested and sniff their snuff as an old man should, letting the women do the work. Men never sat on the women's side of the kraal, and vice versa.

The women sat just outside the kraal on the sunny side where it was warm. They would sit and chew and spit as professionally as the men but they would also do beadwork. Using an awl to poke holes, they would sew beads on gourds or skin skirts, or mend torn skin garments or gourds. Some used crude homemade needles made of metal forged by the *olgunoni* (blacksmith) who used solid, unbroken goatskins for bellows, and charcoal for fuel. The thread was usually gut or the sinews that are found parallel to the backbone of most animals. They deftly cut the sinew free from the meat and dried it into strings ranging from very fine to coarse in texture and very strong. I have watched them mend cracked gourds with this, incredible as it seemed.

The women also spent many daytime hours crafting beautiful seed bead necklaces and ear ornaments, a main part of their dress. They bought these beads at the *duka* at a high price for they are generally made in Czechoslovakia. They also use small cowrie shells with their beadwork. At this time of day was when they brought out their babies from the dark huts to toss and play with them, and to stuff them with fat.

I always went to the women on their side, and Roy went to the men out by their windbreak, or wherever they happened to be.

One day I went alone on my bike to a distant kraal.

"Entagwenya, Nagituak (Hello, all you women)," I called out as I approached.

"Igo," they responded, very quietly. After I admired all of their newly beaded gourds and beaded borders on their skin, wrap-around skirts, then the women began their exploration of my "stretchy ankles" (stockings), my whole torso, and my long hair, which I let down at their request. The head of every Maasai woman was shaved slick, regularly, with a crude piece of metal which had been sharpened on a certain stone. They used a bit of water, or spit, but certainly no soap. My long hair had them stumped.

After a period of awe-inspired discussion among themselves about the appearance of this white person sitting before them, they asked me what words I had brought to them.

"Where did you come from?"

"Where are you going?"

"When is it going to rain?"

"Have you ever borne any children?"

"How many wives does your husband have?"

"Are you his *Kirotet*?" (His first, oldest and favorite, as a rule. This word also applies to a favorite cow.)

They asked if we had any medicine for a cow that

couldn't give birth to her first calf, which was many days past due. Within ten feet of where we sat, there stood a cow with her head bent way down, in obvious distress. The women told me the medicine man had done all he could, then left with his goats (the fee for his services), but the calf was still not born. The elders and the women had done all they knew to do, but the calf was still in the cow. So they had called in the warriors for the final effort to save the cow's life. Two held her by the horns, one held her tail up high, and another reached into her vagina up to his elbow. After some time of strenuous effort he began to pull out fragments of the calf that had been dead some days, until all judged that everything was now out that should be. The poor cow never made a move nor gave resistance of any kind. She was too spent.

All the while, the women were carrying on a running commentary on the action, just as though they were giving a radio news report. They were so absorbed in this drama, they would not that day have been able to listen to anything I had to say. I have to admit, my stamina was really gone with the wind by then. I just had to give up plans for any songs, words, or prayers, and go home before they would have had to carry me there. They always rejoice over saving of a cow, especially one that might conceive another time and bear a calf.

Usually on visits to kraals, after all the introductory conversation they would offer me milk: "Do you prefer warm milk, or sour?" Warm meant fresh out of the cow. The Maasai usually preferred the sour milk, when large curds are formed, then the gourd is shaken vigorously to break them up. The small rawhide cap is removed and the huge, shining gourd is held up either to pour you a drink out of the cap, or so you can take your fill from the small mouth end of the long gourd (an art I never tried to learn, but Roy did and he enjoyed it). Roy loved their sour milk and could drink gallons of it. The inexperienced person will spill milk all over himself trying to drink from a Maasai gourd.

Milk has great meaning to any Maasai. Roy always did

the right thing in accepting all gifts of milk offered to him. I was a coward and would say, "No, thanks, I'm not hungry"; very poor taste, indeed, but I just couldn't overlook the Maasai method of washing gourds. Camping out among them as we did, we were always up early in the morning and witnessed how they milked cows, cared for calves and lambs, and went about many other morning duties. But I never should have watched them clean their milk gourds, for it prevented me from accepting future gifts of milk directly from the gourds.

It was the duty of tiny little girls who still lived at home to take the gourds out early when the young heifer calves came out of the huts, then stand around until the calves started to urinate, at which time the girls deftly caught the urine in the small mouth of the gourd. When they had enough of the warm urine, they took it to mother, who proceeded to rinse out yesterday's gourds. Following the urine rinse, the gourd was scrubbed vigorously for many minutes with the tail from a white cow stuck onto a long rod, or else with a wild olive "brush" and a little water. After that, red hot coals were put in and shaken around for a few minutes, then dumped out, actually leaving a fairly clean container. A visiting scientist once told us that the natural germs in sour milk will kill all other germs, so I needed not be afraid of drinking sour milk offered so graciously. Live and learn!

Whenever Roy sat down with a group of men at their windbreak, after formal greetings there might be a period of silence among the men when they would just sit and spit.

"Let us eat the news," one would say to Roy finally. "What are the words today?"

Roy always ate their news first, things about which they were concerned: perhaps a heifer that refused to give her first calf milk; or an ox stolen by a lion the night before; or a discussion of the dowry for the purchase of a man's third wife. After listening to their interests, Roy then had their ears to listen to his words found in the little black book, Tagi's New Testament.

Not many white people care to go inside a Maasai hut a

second time. If you can double over and squeeze through the small entrance, you have to immediately make a sharp turn to get into the room proper. After you squat down and sit on a cowhide a few inches off the ground, you will still wonder where you are, anyway, for it is pitch dark inside. There is no window and it is stiflingly hot, with a few red coals in the center of the small space.

The air is strong because wherever milk is used, it is usually spilled out of the gourd and when it is spilled, no one rushes to wash it off. Rather, it is massaged into the skin — whether on the face, arms or legs of woman or child — just as if it were skin cream. There are also the droppings of the lambs and calves which sleep in their section of the hut all night. Added to this is the odor of curded sour milk (which I eventually discovered is really delicious to drink when you are hungry). Then there are myriads of flies in any spot where there is manure and sour milk. Methinks you, too, will have a sudden desire to get up if you can, and crawl outside to where the wind blows!

Even outdoors the flies stick close. Toddlers' faces are usually blanketed with them. Adults sometimes shoo them away from their own faces but fly maggots in ears are a common medical problem. But in spite of all this, research into their general health reveals that Maasai kids are remarkably healthy considering their unhygienic dung-and-fly-ridden environment. Roy David pointed out that this research suggests that their good diet of milk is very compensatory.

Whenever I was invited inside a hut, we first ate their news, then I always asked to go outside so that I could read the words of the little black book, which they loved to hear. The women would always find a log for me to sit on for I could not sit flat on the ground, feet stretched out front, as they do.

Sometimes we held outdoor meetings in settled areas and on these occasions Roy's bugle calls were a tremendous attraction, drawing the people just as effectively as they had in Lincoln Park when we were at Bible School in Chicago.

We also often used the Baby Estey folding organ, and later my accordian.

But perhaps the most compelling drawing cards were our children, who spoke Maasai better than we could. We always took them with us while they were little.

"*Oi! iye engoshoke ai!* (O! you of my stomach!)" exclaimed the old women when they first heard any of our little ones speaking in Maasai to them. The seat of their affections is in the stomach, not the heart as we Westerns imagine, nor in the liver as other tribes consider it to be.

As we added one more, and again one more baby, we are sure that each of them bore fruit in the minds and hearts of the Africans because they loved the children. When Roy and I first went to Kenya in 1923, we had only Harry Daniel and Ruth Marie. By 1928, Roy David and Helen (although for only fourteen months) and Grace had come to bless our home, too. And as each of our children grew old enough, we took them to boarding school at Rift Valley Academy for three-month terms.

The first time we took Ruth Marie, when it came time for us to leave she went right off to play with other children, while Harry Daniel, who had been there alone before, stood by the car until the end, blinking back the tears but manfully bidding us goodbye. Only young parents know how hard it is to leave a child. Then how good it was at the end of every three-month term to have them back at home again for one month. In those short vacations they would once more turn back into little Maasai kids.

For some whites, it was a difficult hurdle to grasp the secret of thinking black and talking black. One new missionary who came to help with the Maasai work got it into his head that he didn't approve of the way the younger Maasai greeted their elders by butting their heads into the pit of the stomach of the one whom they were greeting. Their way is respected, a custom to be admired, not deprecated. We saw to it that all our own children always greeted Maasai adults in the proper manner, right on up into their teens, when one by one they went away to high school and college. The proper approach for a Maasai child or grownup who wishes to greet a respected older person is to step in silence close to that person, cast his eyes down and nudge him with bowed head. (A child's head usually only comes up to the stomach; an adult will nudge the heart.) In turn, the one being greeted will put his hand on the greeter's head, and then the usual words of greeting are exchanged.

Our Western custom of greeting, flashing teeth, grinning in the face and pumping hands, seems hypocritical and superfluous in comparison. The Maasai pattern reveals the deference the younger is offering to the older. It is also a form of blessing from the older to the younger.

Imagine us visiting government schools where over one hundred young lads awaited us, each wanting to greet us personally this way. They all came crowding around expecting us to touch each one's head as he pushed in close — or at least as close as he could in the crowd. We addressed all together after we'd touched each head:

"*Loiye*! (all of you!)"

"*O*! (Yes!)"

"*Endasoba*! (Hello!)"

"*Heba*! (Hello!)"

We enjoyed this encounter every time, and they responded with gusto.

When it was a group of girls, we'd use the feminine plural greeting and answer:

"*Entagwenya*" and "*Igo*."

If two adults met on the path and they wished to greet, they simply extended the open palm and brushed very lightly with the fingertips, nothing more, as they greeted.

It isn't only their greeting; there are other manners of the Maasai that we would do well to emulate. They live a life of kindness, friendliness, honesty, justice and hospitality. If I had to make a choice right now, I could so easily go back to live among them in the "back of beyond" not yet spoiled by the intrusion of the white man and his code of conduct, rather than staying in the USA.

We Nomads

Hunting our nomads, we became nomads. We seldom saw a white face for months on end. We spent most of our time camping wherever we found people, water and wood, or wherever sunset found us. We slept under the stars, in tents, in a truck, or later in the cozy house trailers Roy constructed from scratch. We loved the gypsy life out in the open air and, as Joyce Kilmer's song says, we "lived intimately with the rain." We taught our children to enjoy rather than be afraid of lightning and thunder.

Self-sufficiency for our roving life was as important as it was in the American West, where I was born.

For baking bread on safari, our cook dug a hole in the ground and filled it with a big fire for an hour. Meantime, I had put the dough into the bread tins and had it all raised and ready for him to put into the hot hole. Quickly, he pulled all the fire out and we put the bread in, covered the hole with a large sheet of metal and covered that with a foot of dirt.

After two hours, we took six beautiful loaves of bread out of our hole stove. We also baked cakes, stews, roasts and pies that way. And for our top-of-the-stove cooking, we just used a three-stone fire which both cooked our food and warmed us.

Indians operated a large sugarcane factory at Sultan Hamud, where we loved to buy brown sugar. With it we made syrup for our pancakes. We made our own vinegar in two-gallon crocks, using brown sugar, rain water and some mother from the last vinegar batch. For our yeast supply, we always kept a small cake of the last batch and mixed it with corn meal ground on our own mill. We bought rough rock salt, dug from the ground, then dissolved it in water and boiled it dry, producing our own refined table salt. When out of coffee, we burned some slices of bread to a black-brown, crumbled it and used it for coffee. It was very good, but then of course, when you are camping out, everything tastes good.

Chief Olegelisho and his retinue visited once when we were camped on the Loita. He was a handsome man, wearing his bead-edged skin garment; highly intelligent and highly respected by all. We always had visitors in camp and they were usually very curious. As was customary, they squatted around our nice big campfire, for it is always cold there after 4:00 p.m. I was taking pancakes from the skillet to feed my two little children their supper; they were very hungry.

"What is that you are feeding your children?" Olegelisho asked me.

"*Kekis* (cakes)," I answered. "With sugar — would you like some?" I offered him a plate of hot cakes with butter and brown syrup and a fork. He took the cakes with his fingers and ate.

"Umm," he said, "Umm, this is very good. Give me some more."

I did.

"How do you make them?" he asked, munching appreciatively.

"I use salt, flour, milk — "

"They're *very* good," he interrupted.

"—eggs, and —"

When I said "eggs," he stopped, spat out his last mouthful and tried to get rid of all he had eaten so far. This was how we found out that the Maasai eat no eggs!

But people change. All the educated Maasai now eat them as well as many other formerly forbidden, or unfamiliar foods.

Since the Indians were the only tradesmen in East Africa for many years, we nomadic missionaries found mutual friendship with them as we patronized their *dukas*. They lived right in their *dukas* far out in Maasailand. They were always very friendly and helpful to us. More than once have we been thankful for their highly spiced, red hot food that burned all the way down.

Once, up on the Mau at a well known stop, Kampi ya Chai, a good spot for a rest and a quick cup of tea (*chai*) on a long safari, our bearings burned out at sunset. We were expected at Siyabei that night. Along came an Indian lorry, as trucks are called by the British. It was Haji Aboo, a good friend. He stopped and set up camp for us all, complete with blankets and pillows in snow white pillow cases. Haji Aboo's grandson is still graciously caring for travelers in the area, but now with lodges and modern conveniences. The most common guests are tourists enroute to Mara National Park.

On safari, whenever we rolled up to a *duka*, all covered in dust, and thirsty, the proprieters always invited us in — at least for tea, and often for meals. These friendly folk were so deeply rooted in their own religions we did not go beyond telling them how much God loves them. Some were well versed in the Bible.

The Indian *duka*, a tiny building made of corrugated iron, was a story in itself. In there, they sold everything under the sun: cigarettes, matches, beads, blankets, salt, *posho* (finely ground cornmeal), yard goods, tinned goods, and almost anything made in Hong Kong.

Out in front of each *duka* was a petrol pump from which gasoline was sold. But in our early days, all petrol was sold in *debbies*, tall, square tins holding five imperial gallons each. It all came from Persia, as Iran was then called.

Debbies were very valuable, more so than the Tupperware found in most homes these days. We once had fifteen missionaries at our home for the opening of a new church. We cooked our oatmeal porridge in a *debby* and we boiled water for tea and coffee in *debbies*, as our old fashioned tea kettle was too small.

On safari, we used *debbies* for packing almost anything,

including eggs wrapped in paper, fresh bread, meat, *posho* and even lettuce.

I bathed babies in *debbies* each evening. We soaked our chiggered feet in *debbies* of salt solution. We boiled our white clothes in a *debby* down by the stream where Gashisha always washed our clothes until Roy piped our water in. Much of our house furniture was made of the wooden petrol boxes which originally held two debbies side-by-side in transport.

Airtight tins were also a great boon to safari packing. We made our own noodles, dried them in the sun, and kept them in biscuit tins. Other foods we dried for safari were sliced bananas, beans, figs, spinach, sliced onions, mint and sliced lemons. We kept fresh head lettuce from Roy's garden in airtight tins for two weeks or more, unrefrigerated of course.

Besides chop box self-sufficiency, we often had to exercise emergency quick-wittedness on safari. We had to ford the seasonally variable Athi River many times. When in flood, it was dangerous. One time when we were in our lorry crossing a ford on our way to visit the Nixons, we found the road almost three feet under water. The current was so strong that if we had not been fully loaded with over two tons of construction materials, we would not have considered attempting the crossing. Even so we were almost washed downstream into a deep pool below the concrete crossing.

Roy David was then fourteen years old and he was on the bank taking movies as the lorry started slipping downstream. His Dad stayed at the wheel. I climbed out of the cab and up on the loads in the back, to get a big rope. Roy took it and climbed on the hood, where he secured the rope to the front of the truck and then threw the other end to an anxious crowd of Africans watching on the far bank. They grabbed it and lined up on the rope for a real-life tug of war with the loaded lorry, using a time-honored chant:

"*Har-a-a-mbee!*" shouted the lead man.

"*Eh!*" shouted the ready pullers.

"*Har-a-ambee!*" repeated the leader.

"*Eh!*" they shouted even more ready.

"*Nguvu sawa sawa-a-a!*" he called out, and they all pulled together on the last phrase, roughly meaning "strength all together now." Jomo Kenyatta, in later years made "*Harambee!*" the slogan of national unity.

Slowly but steadily they drew our two-ton lorry up the steep bank, out of the turbulent water.

That evening, when we were safely dining with the Nixons at Machakos, what should be the *Daily Light* reading for the day but: "When thou passest through the waters, I will be with thee; and through the rivers, they shall not overflow thee."

13 *Moving . . . moving*

WE MAY HAVE THOUGHT we were pretty efficient at safari living, but we didn't hold a candle to the moveable way of life the Maasai had perfected over two, and perhaps more, centuries.

Sometimes we would go to a kraal we knew of, only to find it burned down to white ashes. Not a cow or goat or person in sight. Since the Maasai migrate so continuously in search of better grazing, the kraals they build are very temporary in structure and are apt to disappear overnight on an *enaidura* (a move).

This certainly puts an end to a lot of pollution, for on leaving a place they burn down the whole kraal, dung huts, thorn enclosure and all, destroying every vestige of human and animal life—lice, bed bugs, and all else.

They move up to high, forested areas for grazing during the dry season when there is no grass for their herds on the plains. Yearly, they go in large migrations up to some point on the Mau Range where they always find good grass and water which cattle must have to give milk.

If you can picture Abraham 4,000 years ago with his whole family and household, including countless herds of cattle, sheep, goats and asses, with tents of skins for nights, a few gourds of water, and all else they owned, tramping on foot from Ur of Chaldea to Haran through the heat of the day and cold of night — then you can see what the Maasai look like when they move. We have observed them passing our house through the years, moving ever in search of grass and water for their herds. It took half the morning for the long line of loaded asses and milk cows and calves and people of just one kraal to pass.

There is nothing quite like the asses, or donkeys, which the Maasai use as carriers of their loads when migrating. No other animal is so despicably stubborn and downright ugly. They appear to be good for nothing, always fighting each other and making the most blood-curdling noises with their screeching. They make the ordinary mule appear to be placid, genial, and even musical in comparison. Donkeys are very destructive to gardens, for they leap over or break down any fence that may be between them and food.

But when it is the season for *enaidura* to look for new grass, the donkeys come into use, for they are the only transport besides an ox or two. The Maasai place all of their hides, gourds, and the rest of their scanty possessions onto the backs of the donkeys and oxen in wicker bamboo structures tied with rawhide straps. They also let the very aged and those who are ill or not able to walk long distances ride in these baskets.

The donkey goes when he feels like it, and stands still when he feels like it, all morning even. He goes with alacrity once he decides to move, but no metal in his nose nor whip on his tail can persuade him to move one foot until he is of a mind to. It is real drama to see a Maasai woman pulling with all her might on the nose strap and another woman twisting the tail, both trying to get the animal to move on. It seems to literally go to sleep just then. The men pay no attention to the women in their troubles.

Men, women and children all help the warriors keep the herds moving and guarded as they pass slowly along through open, wild game country, grazing a bit when there is any grass to be had.

It was always time to say *Ashe Engai*, thank you God, when they finally arrived at the new grasslands after four or five days of hard walking across stony, dusty, barren soil. Even all the flocks would rejoice to be able to nibble shoots of grass again and drink the dew of the morning on the grass.

Not all Maasai were constantly on the move, of course. What we were on the lookout for were permanent, or even semi-permanent settlements where we might establish some sort of out-schools. In our earliest days, settlements were the exception rather than the rule.

The AIM had a wise policy that all missionaries, no matter how engrossed they became in their work, had to take a furlough as close to every five years as possible. We had come out in 1923, so in 1929 we boarded the steamship *Watussi* down at hot Mombasa and left for home on our own *enaidura*.

We had a week's wait in foggy London for our westbound ship to New York. This gave us some time to shift mental and emotional gears back into the pace of civilization as much as possible. We enjoyed the sights of London when the fog let us, but with four little ones it was not easy to gad about too much in London's traffic, tubes and buses. And there was no elevator to our room on the top floor of the hotel.

For warmth, we had to feed big brown coins into a tiny gas heater every half hour. It was quite a game, since drying non-disposable diapers was still a big part of our schedule.

One morning we put on our coats, opened the windows to the cold winter air and listened to the rousing, rhythmic sound of the drums and horns of a Salvation Army band down the street. This was a real tonic to our hearts.

Finally, we boarded the SS *President* to cross the Atlantic to New York. Roy was asked to take the Divine Services on Sunday. We ran into a violent storm in mid-Atlantic. How thankful we were when the long-awaited New York skyline appeared! But five days on an immaculate ship spoiled us for the shock of stepping onto the filth of New York's streets and warehouses. Debris littered the water surrounding the ship, the docks, the sheds and even the street where we stood waiting for a taxi — it was all depressing. We wanted to get right back on the ship and return to clean Kenya.

On Roy's mind was something more important, however. Before we reached New York, he had told me that after he had paid for all the costs, he had nothing left to tip the stewards. He didn't even have a dime for a candy bar for the kids. But we had learned to trust and not be afraid when in the dark financially, so Roy had a secure feeling that somehow our Commander-in-Chief would care for us as He had done so many times before.

I had sewed for many weeks to prepare clothes for our cold-weather arrival, yet we surely did look like six gypsies. Taxi drivers learn to read people like books. Ours read us, and our luggage didn't look like any he had ever seen. He was very kind and knew at once how to get this lost tribe to the address Roy gave to him for the AIM Home.

We had been in the African jungles, but the asphalt jungles of New York had our children guessing. Eight-year-old Harry asked Roy where all the people were marching to in such a hurry. He had lived all his life among wild game surging across the plains in living waves, but he had not seen hordes of white people running to and fro with "scared looks on all their faces."

Our cab pulled up with a jerk at 253 Henry Street, Brooklyn, the AIM Headquarters and Guest Home. Roy asked the driver to wait a few moments until he could go ring the doorbell and get some money. Mr. Fred Lanning, a former missionary himself, came to the door with a smile on his face. Only a person who has been in the heart of Africa for six years and comes home broke can know the feeling that flew like sparks between Roy and Mr. Lanning — the feeling of being a misfit, yet oh, so glad to be home again!

"Can you loan me the cost of the taxi?" Roy hesitantly asked after their greetings.

"So, you are penniless?"

Drooping, Roy said, "We sure are."

"No, you are not," Mr. Lanning said, casting a smiling

glance at the rest of us still by the taxi, "because last week $150.00 came in for you."

We wanted to break down and cry. Not only had a good friend in Chicago, Mr. Harry Wadham, sent in this money for us, but some smaller funds had also come in. We had enough to pay for the taxi as well as to cover all our expenses during our few days in New York.

First, Roy went hunting for a used car to take us home to Chicago. He found an almost-new Studebaker touring car with roll-up side curtains. It had been in storage all the six years we had been in Kenya. An elderly couple wanted to sell it but no one wanted roll-up canvass side curtains any longer as all the new cars had enclosed tops, with glass windows. The car was in such good condition that Roy promptly bought it with our precious $150.00. We didn't mind the lack of the latest rainproof top. To keep the children warm, we bought some chemical bags for them to hold in their hands and we used woolen blankets and coats. We really felt like aristocrats in the noisy, big, shiny Studebaker that looked like no other car on the road.

Roy was a bit nervous over the red, yellow and green traffic lights which were new since we had last been in the United States. To be safe, he hired a good driver to take us as far as Philadelphia, Pa., while he studied the unfamiliar lights and new road rules. They were all so different! Besides, we were used to driving on the left side of the road in British Kenya.

In Philadelphia, we met Emil Sywulka, a fellow missionary, who introduced us to Christ's Home, at Warminster, an institution of several ministries, one of which was sheltering transient missionaries. Here, Mr. and Mrs. F. J. Schwab created room for us and our four children at a time when there really was none. They were overcrowded, but limitless in love and compassion. In more ways than one, Christ's Home became our home that night.

The next day, Roy took the steering wheel of our car

and, observing the lights most religiously, he got us safely to West Virginia, where we visited his people.

After a few days, we drove on to Chicago, where my family lived and where Roy and I had first met, washing dishes at an evening job while we were attending Moody Bible Institute. Our two paths which met there wandered in from two very different pasts.

Family Roots

Roy Ellsworth Shaffer was a handsome youth, and ardent in his love for Christ. He had found Christ early, when he was about ten years old, at a little country revival meeting. He used to pray out loud, eyes wide open, walking out in the heavily forested Ohio hills which he loved. He had very few books to read so he read the Bible a lot. The elders of his United Brethren Church told him he knew his Bible so well that he didn't need any education; all he needed to do was open his mouth and God would fill it! So the United Brethren Conference ordained him and gave him a circuit of small, country churches to shepherd when he was just eighteen years old.

By that time he had already been out in the world on his own and knew what it was to work hard. This had been the case in his family the past three generations.

A hundred years ago only brave and hardy souls dared to cross the ocean to the New World seeking religious freedom and the right to build new lives and among them was a young couple named Shaffer, from Germany. They settled in Ohio and built a sod house just as did all of the rest of the immigrants in those days, as one of their descendants told me a few generations later at a family reunion of over two hundred Shaffers. They reared a large family, working hard at farming to survive and to help others survive.

As did many immigrants who were enamored with their new country, they named their firstborn George Washington Shaffer. George grew up before there were any schools in that area. He went off to fight in the Civil War when he came of age, and on his first furlough returned to marry a pretty little half-Indian girl he had fallen in love with, Abigail Yoho. Their son, Lewis, was the first of nineteen children. They settled down to farming after the war, at a time when there were neither grocery stores nor refrigerators and food was really from hand to mouth. With so many mouths to feed, they knew the value of even one bite. Each of the children grew up to be big and strong, and very hard workers at everything from hitching up the work horses to the plow to hoeing weeds to harvesting.

So did their grandchildren. It was not until the oldest grandson, Roy, left home that he learned that mealtime prayers ended with anything other than "Amen-boys-hitch-up!"

Roy had grown tired of having only one pair of overalls the year around, shoes only when the snow fell, and hoeing corn all summer to keep down the weeds. He ran away from home before he was fourteen, and briefly worked on a horse farm shovelling manure. Quickly disenchanted with that, he tried working in a pottery where he turned round and round all day, lifting trays of pottery from the kiln to drying racks. Finally, he found a much more satisfying situation at a dairy farm where he was given personal responsibility for the care of eleven cows after the English foreman noticed he was apt and energetic. Roy, in turn, was impressed by ambitious expansion plans underway at the dairy, including construction of sturdy, permanent buildings. He absorbed many ideas while he helped dig lakes and plant trees, storing up invaluable experience for a future which, though he could not yet know it, would put all this training to good use.

It was about this time that his overriding interest in God's Word led him into the ministry and he became a very young circuit preacher. He was also a very good one, but during this whole time he became increasingly obsessed with a hunger for more training. After only seven months on the circuit, he went back home to review the eighth grade, sitting beside his younger brother, George, in the country school. Almost immediately though, he received an urgent letter from the Church Conference asking him to come back because the preacher who had replaced him was found to be a crooked horse trader and had been run out of the country.

However, Roy was determined to get more schooling. The presiding elder of his church was of great help in getting Roy into Huntington Bible School and this made him very happy. With relish Roy scribbled in his diary, "This school life is *the* only life after all." But world events intervened.

America went to war. A fife and drum bugle corps parade stirred Roy's patriotism to such a high pitch that he joined the Army there and then. First he became a bugler in boot camp in Houston, Texas; then he found himself at the front line trenches in France, caring for the wounded and dying in the Meuse-Argonne drive. It was in this setting, through correspondence with friends back home, that he first heard of the Moody Bible Institute in Chicago, Illinois. He wrote at once for an application form, and on it he gave as his two reasons for applying: to prepare for foreign missionary service; and to find a wife who would go with him.

The following year, 1919, after the war ended, found Roy in Chicago at Moody. "In heaven," his diary called it, for it was such a contrast to the suffering and hell in the trenches in France.

Did Roy's immigrant ancestors float down the mighty Ohio River in company with my maternal ancestors, a family named Flanders from Holland? This intriguing possibility came to light when I read tombstones in an ancient cemetery in Marietta, Ohio, which gave names and concurrent dates for both families. There are also records in the Marietta Court House to establish that the two families settled there at the same time, all handwritten reports done with expert penmanship in the days when it was a real art to have a good hand.

Some years later, the Flanders family moved on west to Indiana, where the enthusiastic, talented Mertie Flanders, my mother, grew up. Here, where not everyone finished the eighth grade, least of all girls, Mertie not only finished it and taught school for two years, but she followed her impulses and joined the brave people migrating west into the "unknown."

Mertie was a clever teacher, so she easily got a job where her address this time was Marietta, I.T. (for Indian Territory, until 1908 when the territory was incorporated into the State of Oklahoma).

When she was twenty years old, Mertie met another teacher bitten by the bug of wanderlust, Harry Thiers, a graduate from Michigan State Agricultural College, where he had also been a bandleader before moving out among the Chickasaw, Choctaw, Cherokee and Cree Indians where Mertie was.

The whole world loves lovers and the usual gossip, giggles and good wishes were the order of the day when Harry and Mertie announced their betrothal. They were married in the frontier schoolhouse which they had helped to build and the entire population of two hundred souls turned out to see Mertie in her new fashioned dress with the latest bustle, puffed pillow sleeves and tight basque waist, with her short, curly hair and happy heart. Harry was nearly choked by his high, tight, stiff collar and was too tall for his suit, so he had very short coat tails, sleeves and pants cuffs. But his sideburns and mustache were curled just right for the occasion.

With schoolteaching, church and civic activities, and Harry serving as the town's postmaster — plus the advent of five children, one of whom died in childhood — one would think that Harry and Mertie were kept busy. But Mertie was not satisfied. Though it was not considered ladylike to engage in business, Mertie opened up a millinery shop, designing and making elaborate ladies' hats from scratch by sewing braids, floral decorations, beautiful dead birds, grass, beads and buckles onto frames she had designed and made with wire and covered with velvet, veils, silk, lace, or most anything that was considered artistic.

On one of her business trips to Oklahoma City for hat-making supplies, she encountered on the train a white-

haired traveler whom she discovered to be the president of
Friends University in Wichita, Kansas.

President Stanley was a Godfearing Quaker who could
effortlessly lead others into the very presence of Christ as he
spoke.

Always eager to grasp at something new and perhaps
better, Mertie felt a call when he told her about a need for a
married couple to take charge of the men's dormitory, North
Hall, at Friends University. She went home and told Harry.

At the end of the school year, the entire family moved to
Wichita and took over North Hall. Mertie lost no time book-
ing her two sons and two daughters for music lessons with a
splendid, talented, shy violinist named Wendell Hoss, who
lived in North Hall and studied at the Wichita College of
Music. In a short time we all liked him so well that, when
Mother presented us with a new baby brother, we named
him Wendell Hoss Thiers. Wendell Hoss gave the family a
superb violin for his namesake.

This excellent teacher soon shaped the four of us into a
string quartet: Pauline on the cello, Frank first violin, Alan
viola, and I carried second violin. Before long, we had many
calls to play for almost every kind of function, and we also
played in the Wichita Symphony Orchestra.

One year, Mother spent long hours working on an invention. None of us knew for sure what it was, but we did
our best to help her when she called for water pans, damp
cloth strips, rollers and strings to be used in her experimen-
tal models which we fitted into a window. Finally came the
day on which she called in some doubting professors from
Friends University to observe. With thermometers placed
both inside and outside the window, and a breeze coming
through her device, she showed them that it dropped the
room temperature by several degrees. Mother had invented
a primitive air conditioner. Though it was never sold, in
1916 she went to Washington, D.C. and successfully
patented it.

Mother never stopped learning and pushing ahead. Enroute
to Washington — wearing her finest black silk dress with a

fancy lace peplum in the rear, long, black kid gloves, and her most elaborate hat with lace, ostrich feathers, velvet and a stuffed bird on top — she met yet another white-haired gentleman on the train. This one told her about Moody Bible Institute, in Chicago.

Once again, Mertie was sure in her own mind that her family should migrate. She negotiated the purchase of a three-story rooming house in Chicago, located two blocks from Moody Bible Institute. The family occupied the first floor, and the rooms on the two top floors were rented out. We had scarcely ever ridden in a motor car, so it was a breath-taking pastime to sit out on our front steps, not twelve feet from the paved street and watch a steady stream of cars racing back and forth on LaSalle Street at twenty-five and even thirty miles an hour!

Mertie lost no time in enrolling Pauline and me in Moody, and that was when I got my evening job in the school restaurant washing dishes alongside Roy, the ex-soldier who liked to show us snapshots from Europe when we all sat down for a snack after the steamy evening's work. He didn't pay any attention to me, however.

Roy had started taking a pretty Norwegian girl who roomed on the second floor of our home to Moody Tabernacle. One Sunday evening when he came calling for her, I answered the doorbell with my kitchen apron on, for I had been washing supper dishes.

"She's just gone on with another fellow a few minutes ago," I had to tell him.

It was dark and I couldn't see his face, but he was glad I couldn't, because he was very embarrassed.

"Oh." He paused, then took a breath. "Well, would you like to come to church with me then?"

My apron was off in a flash. We walked over to the meeting at the Tabernacle and that was the end of his dating that girl. He later told me that my kitchen apron caught his eye and he said to himself, "Huh, there's a girl who is not ashamed to wear an apron — I'm going to find out who she is."

He started coming to Mother's prayer meetings in our

home. Mother was always quick to establish prayer meetings wherever we lived, inviting all our roomers and students as well. Her meetings were always to the point and never dragged out with gossip or daily news.

One day I invited Roy to a party at our house for Alan's nineteenth birthday. At the party, Pauline and I played cello and violin while Mother accompanied us on the organ. Months later, Roy told me it was the violin plus the apron that made him decide: "That is the gal for me."

Our family string quartet had closed down earlier when Frank went to Haverford College, then joined the Army, which sent him to New York City as a learner-instructor in the new science of radio at Columbia University. One day he wrote us that they, in New York, had just heard a voice in San Francisco "speaking clear as a bell" on the radio. He assured us that this marvel was here to stay and not just some gimmicky fad.

By now, Pauline and I had joined the Northwestern University Symphony Orchestra. We took an hour's ride on the elevated trains to get to the three-hour rehearsals on Wednesday nights. Since we arranged it so that we lost no time from our studies at Moody, we were permitted to continue playing there for three years. This required some careful scheduling, since each student at MBI was required to have three "practical work assignments" per week. This could include visiting jails, children's clubs, factory meetings, hospitals, churches, or any of the many rescue missions on Chicago's skid row sections of North Clark, West Madison, and South State Streets. The Pacific Garden Mission was the most famous, where "down and outers" swarmed around like flies in and out of cheap honky tonks and then into the Mission to get a hot cup of coffee to bolster them between drinks. My sister and I were sent out to these missions, Pauline lugging her cello and I my violin in the streetcars.

Very often by this time, Roy was able to wangle getting his practical work assignment at the Pacific Garden Mission, too, so he could join us for the streetcar ride there and back. He became very good at counselling wisely with poor, unfortunate, burned-out men in skid row, men so lost they couldn't see straight. Roy was used of God to lead some of them to Christ.

It didn't take me long to determine the exact time Roy went out to his jobs where he stoked furnaces and ran elevators in high rise buildings over on Lake Shore Drive. He walked right past our house with a quick, military step, and he was really something to look at, for he wore a bright blue and gold woolen sweater which you could see a mile away. I used to go to our heavy glass front door and peek through the lace curtain to watch him go by, and my heart would just go pitter-patter because he had such a stride—with his head held up high like a soldier—AND because he had asked me to marry him! But I had not immediately accepted his proposal. I did love him, but I didn't want to go to Africa, and this was what he planned to do.

"I've come here to be trained as a missionary," he said, "and I've come here also to find a wife. I've found it's heaven here and I have found my angel—it is you I want to take to Africa with me as a missionary."

Roy approached my father very bravely and confidently. They had the usual shy, wonderful talk between a lover and his prospective father-in-law, with Roy asking for my hand and showing Father the tiny solitaire diamond he wanted to give me. This was at Christmas and we had just met at the end of September.

Mother was happy, of course, that her daughter had a suitor and especially one who was interested in being a missionary.

"But you are both much too young," she stated flatly. "Ruth must first graduate from Moody, then get her RN or BA. Roy should finish both high school and college and then you will have my blessing."

Roy, on the other hand, felt he was old enough at twenty-five to get married right away. He had already had a hard life and he was eager to start in on his own plan for the future. But I vacillated.

I partially solved the dilemma by accepting the

diamond from him but not wearing it — at least not out in public. I would take it out of its box and enjoy carefully looking it all over, up in my room, then I would put it back into the box again.

The day he finally declared, "Well, I reckon I can find another gal who will wear the ring if you won't," I made up my mind right away. Blushing from head to foot, I promised him I would wear his ring in public, and we started to make plans for our wedding. Somehow we would have to take care of Africa later.

We married in my home the evening after my graduation from MBI. Roy still had a year to go before graduating. I had skimped and saved enough money to make my own white graduation dress. It was also my wedding dress. In every sense we got married on faith, hope and charity. We were penniless, for Roy had used his last dollar to buy our wedding rings.

His many friends over on Lake Shore Drive where he ran their elevators and warmed their expensive apartments came to his rescue and gave him money, the wedding cake and other niceties for our wedding — even my bridal bouquet. Consequently, we began our marriage free of debt and we have never gone into debt since.

We saw life together through the rosy glasses of newlyweds while Roy finished his final year at MBI. We both had jobs and saved our money. Our home was only a one-room kitchenette apartment, but there was real happiness.

Sundays we joined the young people of Moody Tabernacle, holding meetings on street corners and in Lincoln Park, with music provided by guitars, mandolins, my violin and a baby organ. Roy was always foremost, playing his trumpet.

"Hey Roy, give us some of those Army bugle calls," the leader would urge, and there would be no difficulty in getting a crowd gathered right where we wanted them.

One week, Rev. Lee H. Downing, a missionary from Africa with the Africa Inland Mission was a special speaker at Moody Tab. He accepted our invitation to eat dinner with us in our humble one-room home, where we basked in his

wisdom and kind, sweet manner. We followed his instructions and applied to the Africa Inland Mission.

To our great joy, our first son, Harry Daniel, arrived in
August of 1921, a few months before Roy was graduated.
That same term, besides acquiring a son, Roy was assigned
an interim pastorate in a little United Brethren church in
Greenfield, Ohio, where he had once preached. It was while
we were there that our second precious baby arrived, Ruth
Marie.

Now that we had two little ones, Roy's mother began to
have misgivings about our plans to go to Africa. In answer
to an anxious letter from her, Roy replied, "Mother, don't
worry about the kiddies being raised by the natives. . . .
No, I don't think the Lord gave us the children to keep us
from Africa, but rather that our testimony to the Lord might
be all the more effective when we get there."

Sure enough, when we returned on this first furlough,
we could tell her many tales of how the Maasai cherished
each one of our children. Not only had they thrived, but
they had also doubled in number!

Our first Sunday back home at Moody was overwhelming.
The dear old Tabernacle had been replaced by Moody
Memorial Church, a magnificent, modern edifice seating
4,400 people. The new pastor, Dr. Harry A. Ironside, was
a short, stout man who masterfully led that vast congregation. He was a man of God who expounded Scripture well
and was much beloved by all. He paraded our whole family up to the pulpit at the evening service. Roy and I had
to say words of greeting, whether we were emotionally
stable or not. The booming pipe organ, Dr. Ironside's
smile, and the sea of faces of dear friends who had been
supporting us for six years were awesome and thrilling.

As any mother would be, I was acutely conscious of the
fact that my children had on outdated clothes. Very soon,
kind ladies of Moody Church Thimble Club took speedy
action, so that our apparel began to look better after a few

sessions with them and their sewing machines and their missionary barrels.

After that royal welcome from the Moody Church, we got more calls for speaking engagements than we could fill. While I had some much-needed medical work done at Presbyterian Hospital, Roy went on with the deputation meetings and several good friends and relatives kept the children. Our year went by quickly, and soon we left for Africa again, this time on the *SS American Farmer*.

Roy wrote home: "Last night Harry Daniel was sitting with me on the top deck and he said, 'Daddy, do you know what I'm going to do?' I said, 'No, what?' and he said, 'Preach the Gospel. I can tell the little people while you and Mama tell the big ones.' "

Once out there, we were glad to be out of the United States, as the Depression closed in on everyone. Fortunately, we had checked out almost all our funds before our bank in Roy's hometown failed and closed along with so many others. Our generous support of $1,540.00 per year from Moody Church shrank when the church had to cut its missionary budget by twenty-five percent.

"So long as we can find enough to pay our school bills for the children ($500 per year for the three) and something to eat for ourselves, we are content," we wrote home. "Our last quarter's remittance is long past due. . . . The Moody Church is passing through deep waters these days." We were glad to be home in Africa.

15 *"Come to Kilimanjaro!"*

THESE WERE THE DAYS OF our Overland box-body safari car. Roy took a trip with Ndilai, our Maasai Bible Man, and his wife, Naiyolang, to Kajiado, the farthest south we'd ever been in the Reserve so far. It was a three-*duka* town.

They stopped directly in front of the middle *duka*. After greetings to a crowd which quickly gathered, Roy stood up at the rear of the car and read out of the little black book.

When he finished, a hefty, blanket-draped chief with a brass British lion insignia pinned on his U.S. Army hat and a wildebeest tail flyswitch in his hand stepped up to Roy.

"I have heard that there is a young white man who has talked with God in our language," he said. "I think you must be the man. Your words are good, something we have never heard before. Will you come down to my people and tell them all these words?"

This was Chief Kulale from Loitokitok speaking and the end of the matter was that Roy put him into the car and they all drove to where he lived, 120 miles south of Kajiado. Chief Kulale had planned on walking home, just as he came.

His kraal was in the foothills of Mt. Kilimanjaro, the ice-blue, glacier-clad peak we had seen from our railway carriage on arrival back in 1923. The top of the peak is a mile-wide crater, but was so heavily rimmed with glaciers it looked like a dome from below.

Roy wrote in our next newsletter:

> This area is beautiful beyond description. Arriving at Loitokitok, Kulale took us over the whole area and told me to choose a site where I would put a mission house. The Government School for 110 boys at Loitokitok presented a splen-

did opportunity for evangelism. There was an ideal site for a station on an elevated tableland with beautiful, large trees and a permanent spring of crystal clear, soft water. There were several other springs and irrigated gardens, the chief's included, and many semi-permanent kraals.

The springs are underground streams having their source way up in the snow-capped summit of Kibo, the highest of the mountain's two peaks. They flow underground to the foothills and then bubble forth and flow out across the plains.

A truly delightful country with abundant opportunity for missionary work. Here we left Ndilai and his wife to begin the work. Kulale gave them a hut to live in, a garden, and a banana thatch hut to conduct services in. Ten of the boys in the school expressed a desire to join the catechumen class right away.

As I drove away, there was a wistful look on the faces of the dear couple I was leaving behind, in what to them was almost a foreign country, but their determination was strong . . . they had set their hands to the plow and were determined not to look back. We can now better understand Paul's great love for his converts who labored with him; and for the infant churches he established.

The District Commissioner of the Southern Reserve has requested that, if we plan to develop the work to any extent there, we should make our headquarters there, for he feels that Siyabei is too far away to give necessary supervision. We have been told many times that the Masai do not believe a person on safari.

I had a message waiting for Roy when he rejoined Stauffachers and me back home at Siyabei. The elders at Kilgoris, far up at the north end of the Reserve where it borders two or three other tribes, had walked off a five-acre plot they wanted to give him for a school and a church! This is beautiful garden-like country with high trees and vast grasslands.

"We want a school for our good-for-nothing warriors," they pled. "They are causing much trouble stealing all the cattle of the Kipsigis and Nandi around here and they have nothing else to do."

Roy and I, with baby Grace, immediately left for Kilgoris. The older three children were in school at RVA. We

Roy and Ruth Shaffer were ready and eager to leave for Africa with Ruth Marie, 6 months, and Harry Daniel, 23 months. Soon after graduating from Moody Bible Institute in Chicago, they were sent out from the Moody Memorial Church under the Africa Inland Mission.

Ruth, 14, played violin in the Wichita (Kansas)
Symphony Orchestra while in high school.

Roy, 22, the Ohio farm boy and circuit preacher,
served in the U.S. Army in France during World War I.

Shaffers sailed from New York to London to Mombasa, Kenya, where they took a train inland to Kijabe, the Africa Inland Mission's main station. There they set out *(above)* to walk two days across the Great Rift Valley to Siyabei in the Maasai Reserve.

The "stick house" at Siyabei was their first home in Africa *(below)*. A 40-ox transport wagon came by with all their goods, including the U.S. Army field kitchen range.

New son Roy David arrived—here flanked by Harry Daniel, Roy, Ruth Marie and Ruth (*above*, left to right)—soon after Florence and John Stauffacher (*below*, right) furloughed in 1924 and turned Siyabei over to the Shaffers.

President Theodore Roosevelt (*below*, far left) secured permission in 1909 from King Albert of Belgium for the AIM to open stations in Belgian Congo. With him at Kijabe is Charles E. Hurlburt, successor to AIM Founder Peter Cameron Scott as Field Director.

Photo courtesy of Shirley Hurlburt

Roy very soon built this snug cedar log cabin where Roy David and Ruth Marie sit among the flowers *(above)*. Shaffers used a series of vehicles, starting with a cart *(below)*, a sidecar motorcycle in which Roy is taking Bessie Stevenson back to Kijabe after a holiday *(opposite, bottom)*, and the Muleobus *(opposite, middle)*.

Sunday services and weekday school on the station were held in the stone chapel *(opposite, top)*. Some cold days, School Teacher Milaun had to take his class, this day including Ruth Marie (under the hat), out into the sun.

The Maasai have been recognized worldwide for the
beaded ornamentation of their women *(opposite)* and the
distinctive hair style of their young warriors *(above)*.

About 200,000 Maasai lived in the Reserve straddling the Rift Valley from the eastern foothills of Mt. Kilimanjaro northwest almost to Lake Victoria. Most of them were still nomadic and lived in temporary kraals *(above)*. At dusk, the thorn bush enclosure's entrances *(below)* were closed securely with more thorns after all the cattle, sheep and goats had entered, to protect them from predators.

Cattle were wealth; his herd of humped zebu type cattle *(above)* gave meaning to life for a nomad Maasai, and his people moved with them to new pastures according to the season. In search of the people, Shaffers often camped on one of their favorite grazing grounds, the grassed-over extinct volcano, Mt. Suswa: Ruth Marie, Ruth, Roy David, Harry, and Roy *(below,* left to right).

This wife daubs her cracked hut with a fresh coat of cow manure, which repels the rain after it dries. Being part Kikuyu (a neighboring agricultural tribe), she has grown a garden and stored dried ears of corn nearby.

A visitor and Roy give some children the traditional touch-on-the-head Maasai children's greeting. A child will nudge your body with his head if you are distracted and don't notice he's waiting for a touch.

This *olmurani,* striking a pose from times when
warriors fought against other tribes during cattle raids,
wears the lion-mane headdress worn by one who has
killed a lion, and holds a buffalo hide shield, its designs
identifying his clan, subdivision and age group *(above)*.
Lion hunts gave these young men opportunity to prove
their bravery.

When a lion attacked the cattle which another
olmurani was guarding near a watering place and dragged
down a bull, he speared the lion. The spear pierced its
backbone, immobilizing the lower half of its body.

Ed Arensen

The lion dragged itself off into the bush, where it pulled the six-foot spear out of its body, leaving toothmarks on the metal and bending it in an arc *(left)*. The man had given the distress signal—*"U-u-uWI!!"*—and other warriors quickly showed up to finish off the old enemy.

In their dances which celebrate lion kills or battle victories the warriors take turns rhythmically leaping in place *(right)*. Each tries to jump higher than the others, while all chant a long account of the event in song.

During a two-year reassignment to the main station, Kijabe, Ruth organized the first orchestra at Rift Valley Academy. Practicing on the RVA verandah are *(above,* left to right) Ed Sywulka, Marjorie Bryson, who played organ, Roxanna Propst, Philip Davis, Charles Propst and Herman (Jim) Propst, who plucked the bass part on a guitar.

Helen Elizabeth was born on Ruth's birthday while there, and Eunice was her doting nursemaid *(lower, left).* But just when she was learning to talk, her life was snuffed out overnight by lienteric diarrhea.

In charge of Kijabe's Industrial Department those two years, Roy taught apprentices from several tribes stone masonry, sawmilling *(above)* and construction as he and Lawson Propst raised the walls and roof of the original, stone Moffat Memorial Bible School, open to all tribes.

Then Shaffers rejoined Stauffachers in the Maasai tribe, returning to live in the log cabin again between frequent safaris. Grace, with pups, welcomes Ruth Marie, Harry Daniel, and Roy David home from RVA for vacation *(below,* left to right).

Roy built a large box-body on a sturdy Overland car which let them travel to kraals much farther out in the Reserve. As always, the star attraction was little Grace *(opposite, bottom),* here warming up to a contemporary.

In addition to the Bible and Maasai Song Book, Shaffers carried with them a small medical kit. It included a pair of forceps donated by their Chicago dentist, with advice on their use after he found out Roy had been using pliers on teeth that would have been dug out by knife point. When the first aid requested was extraction of a painful loose tooth, Roy always had a sympathetic, if uncomfortable, audience *(opposite, middle).*

One day, far from home, Roy and Maasai Evangelist Ndilai presented the Good News at a 3-*duka* town named Kijiado. When they were finished, Chief Kulale from Loitokitok—seen here with his wife Ngoto Noondioli *(opposite, top)*—approached and asked if they would bring this news down to his people 200 miles away. They all got in the car and took Kulale home. When they arrived, Roy and Ndilai found themselves in the foothills of Mt. Kilimanjaro *(above).*

Kulale and the local elders donated a 44-acre site dotted with *lasit* trees (acacia) for a mission station, so it was named Lasit. Shaffers lived there in a tent *(opposite, top)* while they employed neighboring Chagga tribesmen to build a long, seven-room "mud-and-manure mansion" *(opposite, middle),* hastily completing one end before the other because the rainy season was coming on and they needed to move in. Kulale brought over all six of his wives to daub the walls. The Chagga advised them to use banana bark to thatch the roof as it was termite-proof, as were the red cedar poles in the walls.

When they completed the house, the glass in the windows attracted folks from miles around, especially the handsome young warriors who loved to spend hours watching themselves dance in the reflection. Women took to coming to "eat the news" with Ruth at the back door *(opposite, bottom)* near the kitchen.

Lasit was in the northeast foothills of Mt. Kilimanjaro where the nearer, lower of its two peaks, Mawenzi, 17,564 ft., appears as high as the distant, higher peak, Kibo, 19,340 ft. Here, gathered in the back yard are L. H. Downing, John Stauffacher, Roy, Grace, a visiting couple and Ruth *(below,* left to right).

A bubbling spring—one of hundreds in the foothills fed by glaciers up on Kilimanjaro—provided a pool for the first baptism at Lasit (*above*).

Sofi, the first Maasai girl to accept Christ at Lasit, her sister Mahoo, Nongota, and a friend (*opposite, top,* left to right) learned sewing and knitting along with school subjects in the little Lasit Girls School which Shaffers started because there was no government-provided education for girls. Among the many enthusiastic Government Boys School Christians was John Tombo Mpaayei (*opposite, middle,* second from left) in the Narok school.

Peter and Eunice Kasura, who first met as school children working for Shaffers, both went to Kijabe for training before joining in the mission work. After their wedding at Siyabei (*opposite, bottom*), Peter joined Roy as co-pastor of the Siyabei church.

The Rift Valley Academy *(above)* provided Shaffers'
children with formal education.

Harry Daniel, 14, proudly drives the Model T with his
cello strapped aboard leaving Lasit to catch the train for
school with back-seaters Grace, Roy David and Ruth
Marie, and Roy up front *(opposite, top,* left to right). At the
base of Mt. Kilimanjaro, the Shaffer household and the
visiting Harmon Nixon Family gather a month's supply of
wild olive firewood *(below).*

On an Atlantic crossing, Roy David, Jean Nixon, Betty
Sywulka and Grace *(opposite, bottom,* left to right) enjoy a
freighter's canvass pool.

Harry, in wool knickers *(opposite, top)*, with his school chum Phil Keller, Roy behind him, and Irma Brown, climbed to the saddle of Kilimanjaro.

Ruth Marie met this chimp on a trip to Belgian Congo *(opposite, bottom),* and Roy David encountered this friendly baby zebra at a trading post *(above, left).* Grace was the ace at snagging tilapia for supper *(above, right).* Esther enjoyed a swing *(below)* on the construction site of the original Narok church, the first of many Roy built during their years in Maasailand.

Joyce Johnson

Roy built many churches throughout the Reserve; this was the one at Kilgoris (*opposite, top*). Ruth spent years heavily involved in translation of the Scriptures, here with Joseph Leminjor ole Kanga (*opposite, middle*).

At retirement in 1958, Shaffers left the Loitokitok and Lasit churches with Pastor Justus Mumo, seen here with his family (*opposite, bottom*).

Seeing them off at the Nairobi Airport were AIM Field Director Eric Barnett, and Shaffers' grandchildren Dennis and Jennifer Johansen (*above*). Leaving meant parting with old friends such as Kanga, and Sitoya ("Baba") and Tabitha Sankan, here at the graduation of their son William Sankan from Scott Theological College (*below*, left to right).

Bea Noffsinger

Almost twenty years later, Ruth found herself in Africa again at a Remembrance Tea at Ngong. She is flanked by two sisters, Gredisi and Kasoni, also now grandmothers, who had been in her Lasit Girls School dorm in the 1930s (*above,* left to right). Her visit to many old friends throughout Maasailand was arranged by Roy David (*below*), who is with the African Medical and Research Foundation in Nairobi.

Holding the future in their arms: widely-beloved Pastor Paul Milia Magiroi shares a joke with Kristy Arensen, whose parents worked for a time at Siyabei *(above)*; Siyabei Elder Yohana Letoluo's wife, Mama Leah, and their youngest of nine children *(below, left)*; and Roy David Shaffer, Jr., and his daughter, Jessica, at the log cabin her great grandfather built *(below, right)*.

Roy and Ruth were always on the go. Here they attended a Keswick Conference in New Jersey *(above)* about ten years before his death. Now Ruth is settled down—though scarcely slowed down—in Christ's Home Retirement Center near Warminster, Pennsylvania.

set up camp where the Maasai directed us, and started construction.

Roy had the wooden framework of the first room up when we had a visit from a high-born German who owned a local creamery. He and his wife invited us to tea.

At tea, the Count politely explained that he was firmly opposed to our presence at Kilgoris. He was confident that Germany was about to take over Kenya from Britain and so he was investing heavily in an ambitious enterprise. He had placed cream separators all over the lush Kilgoris countryside among the Maasai, where, for a few cents per gourdful, he removed all the cream from their milk, then returned the skim milk to them. The cream he turned into butter and *ghee* (clarified butter, which keeps without refrigeration) from which he intended to make his fortune, he said. Quite simply, he did not want us working in the area.

"It is our land, not his!" said the local elders. "Ignore him."

But he was good friends with District Commissioner Dawson at Narok, and the DC told us we would have to leave.

We packed up and back home we went. Upon our arrival at Siyabei, we found a letter awaiting us from Loitokitok.

"We want you to come to us," it said. "Both of you." This time it was signed by the teachers Sendema, John Ndoiyai ole Mutury, and James Ngatia, and some of the lads there in the boys school. Ndilai and Naiyolang had begun a good work.

So we packed up again and took another safari to Loitokitok, camping in the "customized-by-Roy" one-ton lorry in which we lived while there. We felt our way a little more cautiously this time.

First of all, we checked with the District Commissioner, Leslie Whitehouse.

"Go on down the road toward Kulale's village," he told us. "I don't want you to build here at Loitokitok, as the school is all we need."

The AIM Field Council had assigned us to go and do

what we could in Southern Maasai, even though there was not one shilling available to begin the work. So we went down the road six miles and looked over the area, with Kulale and his sons showing us around.

Next, the Maasai called an *engigwana*, an elders' gathering at Kajiado where all business concerning any part of the Southern Reserve was conducted.

Representatives of the AIM who were invited with Roy were: Rev. Fred McKenrick, Dr. E.L. Davis, John Stauffacher and our visitor, Hans von Staden, from a mission in South Africa.

Samuel Karioki also was there, a Maasai Christian who, as a child, had been kept alive in Kikuyu country during a great famine. He married a Kikuyu girl when he grew up, and returned to his ancestral Maasai home at Ngong. He became a great help to us in arrangements for the opening of many centers. It was Karioki who had informed the Kajiado elders about Roy's wanting to accept Kulale's invitation to open a church school.

When the elders asked Roy how much land he wanted, faithful Samuel Karioki stood by Roy and kept punching him in the side to remind him to *ask boldly* and not let the whole thing flounder by asking for only a small plot.

Roy asked for ten acres, hoping to get five. The elders gave him forty-four acres, rent free, right where he specified, six miles down the road from Loitokitok. When he chose this place, Roy was completely unaware that this happened to be sacred ground to them, surrounding Engoitokitok Spring. This very plot was where the local elders held their regular *engigwanas* under high-spreading *lasit* trees, very tall, parasol-shaped acacias.

So we named the station Lasit.

Lasit was signed over to Roy without a word, and even twenty-five years later they told "Bwana Shefa" that this plot belonged to him and to his seed after him for as long as they wanted to live there among the Maasai. Many of these details completely broke custom, but the elders cast aside custom, for they did have the highest regard for "Shefa" as they called Roy. Roy wrote home:

We are hastening on to begin the new work at once. We do not plan to build up an elaborate station. Emma Mathys, a jovial friend who sailed back from furlough with Nixons and us, who works among the neighboring Kikuyu, says that the term "mission station" is a misnomer. "Mission" means go, and "station" means stop.

But at Kilimanjaro we feel we can both go and stop, for according to government statistics it is the most concentrated area in all Masailand, population-wise, for the people are not such frequent movers. This means we can carry on station work and go to kraals as well.

We expect to erect an inexpensive mud and wattle house with grass roof to live in for the present. There is no money for building, but we can be happy in a mud hut so long as we know we are where He wants us to be.

So began the building of our mud and manure mansion at Lasit in the foothills of Kilimanjaro. We knew well how to sleep under the stars, all right. At home the Depression was still on, and money was scarce everywhere. During an earlier period, when the American dollar rose in value from four shillings to six shillings to the dollar, we had made up our minds we were going to save those two extra shillings per dollar for a rainy day. Now we were sure that this was our "rainy day" so we took the savings and began our mud house. God certainly saw us through and we never went into debt, nor did we borrow. It was a case of hand to mouth; yes, from God's hand to our mouth. His arm was never short.

First, Roy got government permission to cut needed cedar and wild olive trees from the forest a mile away up the mountain, for uprights and roof supports for the house. Termites never touch red cedar nor wild olive. They quickly chew up, or rather down, houses made with other kinds of wood. On that same visit to the Forestry Department, Roy was given some *Grevillea robusta* oak saplings. That very evening in the rain, Roy and I went out and promptly planted them, six feet apart, as a windbreak on the southwest side of our plot. He was remembering the trees, lakes and buildings he helped put in at a dairy farm job back in his Ohio boyhood. There was already a pond at Siyabei, and Lasit's was soon to be dammed up.

Roy drew a twenty-foot by sixty-foot, seven-room house plan, with a twenty-foot-square central room and rounded end rooms. He added a detached kitchen and store room. He had to use Chagga workmen from around the mountain, for no Maasai will work and sweat (except for killing a lion). The Chagga dug a trench two feet deep in which they set heavy red cedar poles very closely, about every four inches, standing ten feet high. Then they wove cedar tree saplings horizontally on both sides of the uprights for walls, leaving spaces for doors and windows. After the walls were packed full of stones, they were ready to be daubed with a manure-mud-grass-water mixture.

The Chagga loved to sing and dance in rhythm as they puddled the mixture with their feet in a depression about six feet square. This method is as old as the nation of Egypt.

Kulale brought over all six of his wives to daub our walls, inside and out, gratis. I found it good sport to help them daub. Of course they laughed at me for my lack of expertise. There is an art to spreading deftly with the palm of the hand. The women made theirs as smooth as a board, but mine was full of rolling ruffles and ridges.

Spunky little Grace always got involved in everything going on, so of course she had muddied herself right along with the rest of us. She turned out to be such a good dauber that, in jest, Chief Kulale offered to buy her as his seventh wife.

"Daddy, you won't sell me, will you?" she asked that evening. Just checking.

We moved out of our inadequate tent into the first room some weeks before it was dry, for rains were on and we were grateful to get in out of the wind and cold rain.

To celebrate, we invited Mr. Whitehouse, the District Commissioner, to tea. He accepted, and came! This was the start of seven years of a wary but, on balance, cordial relationship with him.

When the walls were finally all daubed and dry, Roy took the truck four miles away and hauled back white volcanic ash, which he mixed with water. Then he painted the whole house white, inside and out, with a wide brush. The Maasai prized this same white dirt, in addition to red ochre, and soot from fire stones, to paint designs all over their bodies and faces on special occasions.

Our walls were really just eight-foot-tall partitions. The Chagga advised us to let them thatch our roof with banana bark, the dried layers of banana tree trunks, since the termites find it inedible too. This bark soon turned pearly white and the intricately woven pattern on the underside was so pretty we never put in ceilings to hide it. Later we added a layer of thatched grass on top of the roof.

We bought large mats which had been skillfully woven by prison inmates in Mombasa and Nairobi, to put over our dirt floors. These were made from those waving palm trees which dominated our first sight of the Kenya coastline from our ship in 1923. The outer bark, called *coir*, makes sturdy matting that lasts a lifetime. Our floor was made of rock pounded to a powder and, when kept damp, was as hard as concrete. We had to keep the floor damp to keep the chiggers from taking over, as we long ago had discovered in the little stick house at Siyabei. At last we could write home:

> September was a very busy month with packing and moving down here from Siyabei. We are very happy to be in our new home. The three warriors we left in charge here took good care of everything during our absence. There has been an endless procession of people to greet us since we arrived two days ago.

Over the years we also had many photographers from Europe visit our home, as it was what they expected to see in Africa: a mud house, walls a foot thick, with grass over banana bark roof. They always took many pictures, but only one ever sent any back to us. This one man was a scientist from Switzerland who spoke broken English. The warriors laughed their heads off when he asked them to pose for a mock battle. They wanted a real battle, not make-believe! They posed, though, and he got some good pictures even though the warriors' faces showed they were laughing as they held their long spears in combat position.

We found we had company in the house-building business. In a high *lasit* tree at one end of the house we had a most interesting display of two kinds of colored birds that seemed to whistle, scream and sing all day and way into the night. The larger bird was of irridescent blue all over. The smaller one was a rich yellow-gold weaver bird. The blues built their nests in the top of the tree while the weavers hung theirs from the lower branches. The weavers' entrances were on the underside, with the domed nests suspended on tiny strings they made themselves, tied securely to tiny branches. Each nest swayed back and forth with the wind all the time, yet no bird ever lost her balance, but kept right on building her home. I have watched two male birds get into real fights over a strand of grass or a fine feather. Each pair built its own nest.

We never did have time to sit back and relax to admire our work. The seasons began ordering our lives, just as they do the lives of the Maasai. Instead of the four seasons we were used to in the USA, however, the year was divided into the long rains and the short rains, separated by the long dry season and the short dry season. Now we wrote home:

> November and December have been very busy months here at Lasit . . . we were obliged to rush the work in order to have a roof over our heads by the time the rains came on, also that we might be able to give the people more time when they come back from the dry season pasture areas. The roof is now on . . . and so are the rains.
>
> Many come to our house every day . . . some for medicine . . . some to see the new, strange house, which causes them to think we are very rich. Some come to "eat the news."
>
> Our garden is doing well and many Kikuyu wives of Masai have taken courage to begin digging old gardens that

have lain idle for years because of the elephants. Chief Kulale came today and told about the elephants sleeping in his banana grove one night, doing a lot of damage. The next night they returned, but he was on the lookout for them with the rifle the Government had given him; so he put them to rout. Many Africans know how to shoot, having learned as King's African Rifles soldiers, when younger, during the war.

As a matter of fact, one of Kulale's daughters was named Noondiole, meaning "the of the gun," because a gunshot was heard when she was born.

After one year, Roy put glass in our windows to replace the cloth which had at least kept out the wind and rain. Now we had six large windows in the living room looking toward the majestic mountain. Right away, warriors and women began coming from far and near to spend hours dancing in front of our windows. The reflection enabled them to see themselves in all their gaudy paint, as they never had before.

During all this time, Kuyoni, in Bible School at Kijabe, had been studying and working hard. He completed the course and received his diploma after two years. Wambui completed her work at the hospital, learning first aid and general hospital training.

Then they were ready to be married. Kuyoni had, meanwhile, "made all the words" with her father, Mbae, and had started paying dowry for her. As a rule, friends and/or relatives will help a fellow out in times like this when he has nothing to go on. Since neither Peter Kuyoni nor Eunice Wambui had any money, and owned few clothes or possessions of any kind, we took them as our own children and came to their rescue, just as friends had done for us when we got married. We all went to Siyabei for a month to celebrate their wedding.

Stauffachers had to miss it because it came right at the time they went to Mombasa to meet Claudon, now 23, who was coming out as a brand new missionary, bound for Congo, as Zaire was then called. Two years later, Raymond was to follow him, with his new wife, Sara, also Congo-bound.

The day before Kuyoni's wedding in the chapel, Roy gave him the final fifty shillings ($7.50) he still owed Eunice's father for her purchase price.

Their wedding was the very first in the Siyabei chapel. By now we had our own family string quartet to play for them, since our children were home on vacation from school. They had loved Peter and Eunice from babyhood. Roy tied the knot securely; then, in our log cabin we gave them a feast of goat meat and rice, which they loved, and invited their special guests.

The father of the bride refused to attend the marriage in the chapel and the reception feast. Old Mbae was in hot water with the original suitor. He was supposed to have returned the goats paid in vain toward the purchase of Eunice, but he had already eaten them up.

We were so thankful to have Peter and Eunice trained and ready to go with us back to Kilimanjaro and our new work at Lasit. Their arrival freed Ndilai and Naiyolang for Kajiado, where they had been headed when sidetracked to Lasit.

Roy and Peter now turned to the building of the corrugated iron chapel at Lasit, sixty feet by thirty feet. Just at the right time when needed, Moody Church sent us a much appreciated gift of money; also a gift from the Moffat Memorial Fund, designated specifically for a chapel, came to us. How we did rejoice, for we had exhausted what small funds we had.

Now, if rain came during an *engigwana*, the elders just went inside the chapel to sit on the crude wood benches to continue their deliberations. Otherwise, they still preferred to sit out under the *lasit* trees on their sacred ground in the sun and wind. Of course, our coming had not necessitated their going elsewhere for the *engigwanas*.

When Peter and Eunice were married, they broke custom by taking in Eunice's young brother, Joshua, who was just a little pile of skin and bones. He had been cast out to die of hunger during a famine, but their tender love and care brought him back to health.

At Lasit, they built their own thatch-roofed, mud house and cultivated a garden very rapidly. In due time they were enjoying eating all the new foods Roy had taught them to plant. One was avocado pear trees that bore heavily after five years.

Another time Peter and Eunice broke custom, they rescued an old woman who had been cast out to die. The Maasai are no more shocked at putting their dying old people out on the windswept plain for the hyenas to devour than a westerner is of putting a dead person into a coffin to be eaten by worms, or an easterner is of burning one on a pyre, out in public view.

But Peter and Eunice found that this woman was very much alive. They took her home and brought her back to health. Although this broke custom, they were in such good favor with the local Maasai that their prestige did not suffer.

The time came when Peter Kuyoni's old father called him to come home "for words." Expecting additional curses, Peter went.

But when he arrived, his father turned and told his disinherited son that he now realized his mistake, and knew that of all his ten sons Kuyoni had followed the right path. In an almost Biblical ceremony, the old witch doctor gave Kuyoni the largest share of his estate, which included many herds.

On his dying day, when his sons were all there to hold his head according to custom, he told Kuyoni he now wanted to accept those words of God, if it were not too late!

Kuyoni returned to the work at Lasit with renewed faith, energy and zeal.

The mission work at Lasit grew, so we were indebted to anyone willing to do domestic work for us. Missionaries who tried to cut their own wood, build fires, cook food, clean house, do laundry on a wooden corrugated washboard, iron with heavy flatirons and tend their own gardens certainly had no time for the language study or the contact with the people which they came out to do at great expense to their supporters.

In our days we had the good fortune of having the best of relationships between our helpers and ourselves. We never thought of them as "servants" but as co-workers, for we depended upon them right and left. Never did we have to hire and fire one after another. They all seemed to become one of us, isolated as we were far from the rest of the world. They loved our children and would have gone through fire to protect them. Our children loved them in return.

Ngoso, a lean youth in a *shuka* carrying his spear, came bounding up like an antelope from the stream below Lasit one day early after our arrival.

"*Aiyeu esiai*! (I want work!)" he beamed.

He proved to be one of our best. With adequate instruction, in time he produced good meals all on his own, always smiling broadly. He would whistle and sing constantly as he went about his work. We paid him twenty shillings a month ($4.00) plus a daily measure of cornmeal in the 1930s.

Ngoso always looped his long, stretched ear lobes up in a knot on top of his ears, out of the way, when he kneaded the bread. Mischievious little Grace, loved to release them just as he got his strong black hands all floury up to the elbows, knowing well she was in for immediate retribution.

Ngoso became interested in our religious services, but his witch doctor father threatened to disown him if he joined the inquirer's class. He was the eldest, and in line to inherit his father's position. He attended all our meetings and loved to sing along, but never committed himself. Nevertheless, he became a permanent member of our Lasit family.

16 *Lasit*

ASIDE FROM OUR SPRING-FED "OASIS" at Lasit, the countryside all around was the picture of scorched earth during our first dry season there. There was no grass for cattle nor rain for the bushes and trees. All roads were dust pits. We often could not see the road for clouds of dust. Even the snow line on Kilimanjaro receded far up her slopes toward the glaciers.

Then for two days the mountain hid behind clouds. The third morning the clouds lifted and Kibo had on a beautiful new mantle of snow extending way down to the forest line.

The rains came on with a rush, and the land was transformed. The new grass was a beautiful green.

People who had migrated began returning. The hills and valleys were full of cattle again. It was a time of great contentment for man and beast, somewhat like a huge reunion. The cows came home evenings with full udders, so it was a time of feasting after months of hunger.

On Sundays when we pulled the rope that rang the bell up on a high pole, the long line of school boys in their white *shukas* could be seen coming down the road from Loitokitok to attend Sunday School and church service with us at Lasit. The wooden benches in the little tin chapel rapidly filled up with people. Those still in skins sought the back rows while those who had changed to dresses and shirts and pants, for Sunday at least, and who could maybe read the hymn book, crowded up to the front. But always in quiet silence, with no chattering as in civilized Sunday Schools.

By this time we began to realize that the very name of God runs through the warp and woof of the life of the unchurched Maasai. To them, rain is God, *Engai*. Grass is God, children are God — anything good is God. They are very free with *Ashe Engai* (thank you, God). Although He is acknowledged, yet they do not fear Him.

It is interesting that the word "Maasai" combines the word *maa* meaning "the people" and *sai*, the root of the word for "pray."

Any praying done is done by the women in sing-song groups, not personal prayers. Men seldom pray; that is the work of the women, and the women pray to the evening star, the moon when it is red, and to the sacred tree in season. Their prayers consist mostly of "God, give us rain, cattle, grass and children," repeating the same words over and over.

One evening I stood and listened to a group of women after the milking was all done and they sang, without too much attention to melody,

> To you, O star of the evening we always pray,
> Bless us —
> Give us children —
> Give us rain —
> Give us grass for our cattle.

Not much else.

The name for God is in the feminine gender and this in the face of how low women are rated. When it rains, they say *"Esha Engai, Ashe Engai,"* (God rains, thank you, God). When first new shoots of green grass appear they say this same pattern. When a new, living baby is safely born, they say the same. They know little about God but do give Him credit for all that is good that happens in their lives.

One day women came in single file from afar, all thoroughly greased in red ochre, and wearing their best, or newest skins and all their beads. All were jogging along chanting, "Here we come, our God, to worship you."

I asked Ngoso if I might join them, and he said to go along, so my three children and I joined them. I took my camera, but this offended them, so I put it into my pocket.

A mile from our house was the sacred tree called *Oljani Oreteti* (the helper tree). It is two trees in one: a wild fig choking an evergreen. The fig's aerial root tendrils grow earthward from horizontal branches, looking like fragile red strings until they reach the ground, where they take root and quickly grow thicker. Eventually, these support the tree which by then covers a large area. In the center of this wide growth is a natural opening.

The evening before the ceremony of worship, a goat is slaughtered and its blood is caught in a gourd, which is placed on the ground at this opening. It is put there so God can see it when He descends the tree and passes out this opening. This insures that He will forgive their sins. The women told me that they left the meat of the goat there also for a sacrifice to God, and that God would eat it when He came down. Anyone who lives in Africa knows who eats the goat and drinks the blood. The neighboring Chagga take the meat and the hyenas take the blood, quickly, almost before dark.

Each woman had brought her offering of milk to sprinkle on the tree, beads to tie in the tendrils, tobacco to spit upon the tree as a blessing, and very scarce tufts of new green grass to tie into the tendrils as their offerings to God the helper. None of these offerings were ever removed by anyone.

The women asked me why I did not join them in their jog-trotting around the tree, singing as they went and presenting their offerings as they danced around. They petted the tree and called it *Pasenai* (blessed) and said, "We bless you. Give us rain, cattle and children. Accept our offerings, we pray you." I could only tell them that we had a different form of worship, and they understood, for two of these women were very often in attendance at our services in the chapel, which they loved enough to always come back again.

I have never seen any American audience more in earnest and devout than were these women who spent most of the day dancing frantically around this tree. Some were old women who could hardly walk, ordinarily, but became agile at this tree worship. There was almost a frenzied intoxication in their fearful faith.

Once when our family went to see this tree (not during a worship ceremony), our children tied beads onto the tendrils for fun. Five years later, these knots had grown very large, so Harry cut one off the tree and took it to college with him, where it joined our other specimen in the museum there, a ten-foot-long tapeworm.

This worm was a relic from our efforts at medical work there in that back of beyond, where our little black medicine box was a very popular item. Right from the beginning at Lasit, we had twenty to thirty ailments brought to us daily. As soon as we had established ourselves, we saw that the medical work was expanding beyond our box which held eye drops, bandages, permanganate crystals, powdered sulphur, oils, and salt, which we dispensed right out of our back door, along with soap and hot water. Also, Roy extracted many teeth with a pair of dental forceps, following instructions given him by Dr. Harold Drumond, our dentist in Chicago.

Roy built a small two-room hut for a dispensary in hopes of our getting a nurse assigned to Lasit. A good deal of our patients came in with eye infections and wounds or broken limbs from encounters with a lion or an angry ox.

We also encountered many types of parasitic worms. We used an old fashioned oral liquid called "Male Fern" for tapeworm, but it was not very effective. A tapeworm lives in the intestines of its host's body and grows larger and larger, while the food-starved host wastes away. *Olmokotan*, the bark of a tree, is what the Maasai use for tapeworm. It is a very severe laxative.

One day Chief Kulale gave his own six-year-old daughter, Noondiole, too large a dose of this. Early next morning, a whole troop from Kulale's kraal hastened to our house, carrying Noondiole, now in a coma from the overdose. Roy took them all to our new little mud hut dispensary and we put her right into a warm bed, for it was cold. This was unlike her rawhide mat at home so we warned her mother and Kulale's five other wives who stuck right around, that by all means they were not to take the child out of the warm bed.

We went back home to finish breakfast and discuss what to do. Suddenly, we heard wailing. We rushed to the dispensary, to find the old women had taken Noondiole out of the bed, stood her on the cold dirt floor, holding her upright while one woman poured a gourd of cold water over her head and down onto her naked body.

Roy grabbed the woolen blanket, threw it around the child and took her to the kitchen by the fire we had built in the 44-gallon drum stove, away from the old women. He cried out to God for help and wisdom as he held the comatose child in his arms. We had never had a death yet in our work, and we didn't want one now.

Noondiole died in Roy's arms. Outside, sitting in the grass, the women wailed inconsolably. Warriors were poking dry grass straws up the noses of the wailing women, which they said was their way of keeping them from going into shock or unconsciousness from grief.

After the other five wives had gone home, I saw Noondiole's mother from the kitchen window, leaning against the garage and wailing, saying *"Naibirua, naibirua!!* (O! my too-soon departed one!)"

Next came the struggle over the disposal of the body.

"We will take her out to the plain," the warriors insisted, so hyenas could devour the body as was customary.

"No," said Peter and Ndilai. "We want to bury her."

"We will give her a Christian burial," offered Roy.

Kulale, her father, finally settled the matter, saying: "Since she was a member of the children's *kilasi* she belongs to Shefa, so let Bwana do as he wishes."

We had a short, but meaningful, reading of God's Word with the few Christians present. We buried her in our fenced yard near the dispensary, where the hyenas could not get at her.

Eating poorly cooked meat is the main cause of tapeworms of this type. Few Maasai did not have any worms. Our own little Grace, age five, once went out to the nearby village with her Maasai playmates, where she accepted meat offered her (for she was a pure Maasai when it comes to loving meat, especially meat roasted over an open fire) and a few weeks later, she began to have tapeworm symptoms. We gave her the usual medicine, but she retained the worm as is so often the case.

Months later, we went on furlough to Chicago. We went straight to Dr. Titus Johnson, also on furlough, who was famous for the work he was doing at the Ubangi Chari Mission in Congo, which included valuable experience with the African tapeworm. He gave Grace the newest medicine and very soon we got several phone calls from other doctors in Chicago, requesting us to please save them a "specimen" when she passed the worm. We were happy to promise them we would.

Of course we were on guard and watching for her relief. At this time we were all set to start out on our summer tour of deputation meetings that took us from Iowa to New York, to South Carolina. We travelled in our station wagon, with a house trailer and tent in which we all slept and ate the whole summer. Since we had our family string quartet, we had to have room to carry all the instruments, including Harry's big cello.

One day after we had stopped at a gas station and were nicely settled back into the car and started down the road, Grace yelled out, "Oh, I forgot to tell you, I think the worm came out."

It had. The eager doctors were cheated out of their specimen, for which we were sorry. But we were grateful for the effectiveness of the medication.

It should not have been any problem to get a specimen, since so many Maasai were infested, but even though we administered what was for then the best and newest medicines, we still had many losing fights with tapeworms. They are tenacious and we could never get the head to come out with the body, so it never ceased growing new body segments in the host's stomach.

I finally offered a reward of half a shilling ($.07 US) to anyone who would bring back his worm with its head on it after he had taken the new medicine. Some weeks later, one man came very proudly, with a fine "head-and-all" tapeworm in his hand — ten feet long! He got the money. I got the worm. We sent it, bottled in alcohol, to Wheaton College where Harry was by then a pre-med student. The Gordon Stephensons, going home on furlough, took it for us taking care of the legal authorization that was required.

In our medical work, the Maasai women always entered hastily into the more intimate circle of questions, woman-to-woman. The greatest desire in life is to bear children — yet their age-old customs made it very difficult for a woman to conceive. If she was fortunate enough to do so, however, the next step was to nearly starve her for nine months, hoping to insure that the fetus remained as diminutive as possible, and hoping for a safe delivery. For Maasai women, of course, it was almost impossible to expect a safe delivery free from complications.

The pattern of my productivity about every two years, was most interesting to them. They began to be concerned when there was a period of four unproductive years after Grace was born, and they asked me why had God cut off my bearing. But He had not. Shortly, number six was on the way. Grace, of course, had been born at Kijabe, before we ever went to Lasit, so these kraal people had never seen any of our children as babies. They waited with momentous anticipation.

Our own doctor, E. L. Davis, was away on furlough. Good friends from Friends University days, the Dr. Brian Micheners, from the Friends Mission at Kaimosi, five hundred miles away, were vacationing with us. They invited me to go home with them to his hospital for the needed watch care. We expected serious complications since I had had major surgery while on furlough, so I went up early to stay with them.

Roy kept himself mighty busy at home while he waited to be called. He wrote his folks of "enclosing our front veranda, building a long shed for the motor car, a wood shed, and a room for gasoline and oils. Then, there is some land to clear and plow, and oxen to train, and a dam to make for water power." He got it all done before the telegram came.

Baby Esther Aileen's delivery turned out to be my easiest of all, and she was my biggest one! When she was two weeks old, I bought a handmade rafia basket, put her into it, and caught a ride by truck to Kijabe. There I joined Roy and our four other children at RVA, where the baby in a basket caused quite a stir. Finally, we made it home to Lasit, new baby and all, well covered with volcanic dust since the dry season was on. All the Maasai, for miles around, came to see this new white baby with a bald head, whose mother cheated her by nursing her only every three hours. They all stood outside the back door and begged me to bring the baby out for them to see.

But first, I had to dicker with them to get them to promise not to spit in her face, which is their way of blessing a baby. None of them had ever seen a white baby, so all were keyed up and most anxious to see this one.

I went in and brought the baby out, well wrapped for it was cold, and held her up inside the half-screen door. It is well that I did, for some of the women forgot about their promise and tried to spit through the screen. Other women lifted their upper skin garment and spat upon their own breasts, as a sign of blessing to this colorless thing I held in my arms.

"Pasenai! Oi! iye engoshoki ai! (Bless you, you of my stomach!" they would call out. "Tubula (Grow up)," and they would spit lightly toward the baby. Many came to our little iron church on Sunday, just to see this white baby, for we always took our children to church. They named her "Nolasiti (the of the Lasit Tree)."

I always did my visiting with the women out in the

yard, rather than indoors, because generally each woman was covered with flies. They seldom, if ever, washed. If we let anyone indoors, not all her flies accompanied her when she went out. None of them ever bothered to drive the flies off their bodies, off the milk gourds they carried, or out of their eyes, nose or mouth.

We did ask Chief Kulale indoors whenever he came. Always a very gracious man, he observed white customs and would wash well and put on a clean blanket before he came to visit us. Sometimes he replaced it with an army overcoat plus an army hat with the British lion insignia on the front, and he carried his inevitable wildebeeste tail fly switch.

Kulale was esteemed highly by all the elders for his justice. He was honest and upright at freeing the innocent and punishing the guilty in civil cases. The white Government Officials valued him highly, which was not always true among the chiefs. He served his own people faithfully and could be depended upon by the District Commissioners.

We had never had a more supportive chief to work with. This, even though he never classified himself as a Christian, nor did he ever give up the ages-old Maasai elders' custom of drinking *enaisho* (liquor).

Throughout our years, both at Siyabei and south in the Kilimanjaro area, we met several of Kulale's cousins and brothers. All of them must have had a fine father, similar to John Tombo's father, Mbae, whom we considered superior among men. Their tone of voice, thinking processes, mannerisms, and moral sense of right and wrong were so markedly different.

Kulale had our co-worker Paul Lehrer's flavor of gentle speech and action. He never varied when he came and sat on our red, upholstered couch for afternoon tea. His concern for Roy's wishes always came first, for he knew and believed Roy was there for their welfare and all that is good, in cooperation with the good school programs offered by the government.

We deemed it an honor to work with him.

Kulale was among the first who came to see our new baby, number six.

One day when Kulale came a year or so later, as was our usual gesture for the chief of the area, we told Ngoso to make tea, which he brought in shortly. We were drinking it together when Sofi, our little nursemaid, one of Kulale's nieces, passed through the opposite end of the room carrying what Kulale took for a very big tea cup. It was actually Esther's potty. His eyes opened wide.

"Oh, that is the kind of a cup I would like to have my tea in, instead of these tiny little ones," he exclaimed. "Come closer, Sofi, let me see the cup."

"This cup is where the white baby girl puts her urine," Sofi honestly told him, in Maasai.

He was not at all embarrassed, but he did wonder why the white people would want to catch it in a cup. We all had a good laugh over it and, of course he was right. Dainty tea cups always do look ridiculous in men's big hands; they never do justice to the great amounts of tea they usually consumed at four o'clock tea time, one custom both Africans and Americans readily picked up from the British colonials.

When we first arrived home with our new baby Esther, I was thrilled to find that Roy had dammed up the Engoitokitok Spring and installed a Meyers hydraulic ram that pumped water up the steep hill, into our house just as at Siyabei. The dam became a beautiful pond, with canna and calla lilies growing all around it. The long branches of a Lasit tree reached out and covered one whole end of it with dappled shade.

Now we freely irrigated our garden, which gave us fresh fruits and vegetables almost the year around. Only those living a hundred miles from the nearest produce store can appreciate this. We grew head lettuce as fine as any in the USA. We planted several citrus fruits, as well as tropical fruits such as guavas, custard apples, loquats, mangoes, and papaya.

Besides the ram, Roy had installed a large, concrete bathtub, which he made big enough to let our three little girls all get in at the same time, and splash! He rigged up a 44-gallon petrol drum just outside the bathroom window over a firebox which heated the bath water almost too hot at times. This was a first!

All this meant a lot to us, living in a tribe who wouldn't carry water — not even downhill, let alone uphill. They are strictly nomads and we accepted it. Roy ran a two-inch pipe off the side of the ram where the Maasai women could fill up their small-mouthed gourds, and they used it most appreciatively.

We never wasted water. The kitchen drain went out into a bed of calla lilies, roses and nasturtiums. Same with the used bath water. As with our vegetables, the geraniums and nasturtiums grew to be twice the size of any I had seen at home. Nasturtium leaves were the size of dinner plates.

Along with our bounty, we did have pests. We shortly acquired a little engine to give us an electric light bulb to read by for an hour each evening. No more kerosene lanterns to carry around. But there were huge black moths that loved to spend their evenings hovering around our one precious electric light bulb, right when we ourselves wanted to hover around it. I admired them for their beauty but not for their persistent presence in seemingly taking over the whole house at night. The larger ones had a five-inch wingspread.

At Siyabei, the pests were snakes living in the cool air spaces under the house. But as long as we left them alone, they left us alone.

Our worst pests were the wasps at Lasit. Our children had been stung by wasps often, so one noontime when Roy and the two boys had gone to Moshi for supplies, the girls and I took a long pole with a firebrand on the end, and burned out some wasp nests up under the three-foot banana bark eaves of the roof. Banana bark is fire resistant, like asbestos. The whole roof was banana bark. On the front side, where the roof had begun to leak a bit, a thick, tight layer of grass had been thatched, up on top of the bark.

Grace, age 7, Ruth Marie, age 12, and I, burned wasp nests for some forty feet around the rounded end of our house, to the iron-roofed veranda in front. We then went back to the start to see how many nests had failed to burn, for they were all big nests.

When we got back to the veranda, we saw a bluish-yellow flame creeping up over the grass-thatched area, clear to the comb of the roof. We never figured out how fire could get from underneath the bark eaves up onto the grass, but it did. Had the grass not been packed so tightly, it would have burned up furiously in no time.

We rushed into the house just in time to catch our Maasai helpers who were ready to go home.

"Fire is eating our house!" I yelled in Maasai. "All of you bring blankets, ladder, water in the pails and potties out of the bathroom," (where we had a water tap), "and water in *debbies* out of the kitchen!" (where we had a second tap).

Ngasotu, the new cook, who was usually slow, nevertheless was first to hear me call in anguish for the ladder. He acted fast and followed me back out to the fire.

Sofi, the nursemaid who had just put the baby to her nap, ran out to the brow of the hill and in her shrill voice screamed the distress call non-stop.

"U-WI! U-WI!" she wailed, and was heard within a radius of four miles, for it was an unusually calm day with no wind at all, and her voice traveled far and wide.

Naiyolang ran into the bedroom and grabbed the sleeping, two-year-old Esther out of her bed, and took her outside, then returned to the bedroom to grab the bed mattresses to take them out.

Eunice, Ruth Marie and Grace all joined the water brigade, climbing up the ladder, giving Ngasotu and me the potties full of water. We were by now on the roof's comb, straddling it, laying the full length of our bodies on blankets brought up to us, spread over the comb to cut off the air from the blaze.

We kept calling on God to help us, which He surely did. Soon there was quite a brigade carrying water to the top, where the blaze was worst. We were a sight, some six adults all fighting fire on the roof, choking on the smoke and dust and filthy from beating the black burnt grass with boards.

If anyone hears a distress call and fails to go at once to answer it, he is a marked man and no one will ever go to his distress call if he ever cries out. From the top of the roof I could see Maasai and Chagga merging from all directions, coming speedily to our house, for the call and the smell of fire had gone far. Suji, who was another of our workers, Ngasotu and other men stayed up on the roof but told me to go down and take a rest. They could see I was not doing very well. They knew they could control it now, without me. They stayed over an hour, beating the roof all over, inch-by-inch with the boards, to play safe against hidden pockets of fire. This is another reason why I know God answers prayer, for normally, the whole front roof could have gone up in a cloud of black and blue smoke, but He heard our cries and came to our rescue. The fire burned only the top layer of grass on the side toward the road.

When I climbed down the ladder, there was Chief Kulale and a crowd of elders and warriors all milling around, all wanting to help.

"Did you do it on purpose?" Kulale asked me.

"No!" I cried.

"Then stop crying, for I will tell your husband not to beat you when he comes home," he said, as he laid his hand on my shoulder.

After getting down off the roof, I was so exhausted and ready to collapse that I felt the need of help from above, so I took my girls into the house, sat down on the homemade settee with them, and asked Ruth Marie to read me some Psalm out of the Bible to calm my heart, which she did. I shall never forget this balm from above, when she prayed so sweetly. Kuyoni, Ndilai and Eunice stayed close by me until Roy came home that evening.

True to his word, Kulale sent a delegation out to the main road to meet Roy when he neared home four hours later, to tell him not to beat me for my accident, which I had not done on purpose. Roy could see the burned roof section and the people still standing around; but the elders and warriors would not let him come on home until he promised not to beat me.

A new thatch of grass on top of the burned roof soon made it look like new. The Chagga are clever workmen in grass and banana bark for houses, and much else. This fire was another demonstration of how and when even the non-Christian Maasai turn to God. For any deliverance from calamity they are quick to say, "*Ashe Engai* (Thank you, God)." They thanked Him repeatedly for not letting our house burn down.

We had come to the aid of the Maasai for their sick bodies, and they were not slow to come to our aid at this time. We were beginning to belong to each other. They needed us, and we certainly needed them for survival in this back of beyond.

17 *Dini and Girls School*

It was about 1939, when I was a young boy of about six, that I came to know this tall, huge white man. On Sundays we heard the bell ringing in this missionary's place and so we rushed to see what was happening.

O! Memsaab is standing outside the church holding the *kinanda* (accordion) which produces a wonderful and strange sound, while this tall white man is saying, "Come in and sing, you boys."

We got in and enjoyed these wonderful songs, not that we knew what they meant but we like to hear the *kinanda*, and so we continued coming every Sunday and I got slowly acquainted with Bwana and Memsaab "Shepa," which means "happy" in Maasai.

(A letter from Gabriel Ndetia, 1958)

THE MAASAI WERE UTTERLY CONTENT with their self-sufficiency, living largely on meat and milk, and dressing in the skins of their animals. But in the early '20s, the British Government decided to open schools for Maasai boys and introduce change. The first schools were at Narok and Kajiado, later at Loitokitok and other centers. Heavy fines were levied on any chief who failed to furnish his quota of lads to attend this free schooling. The first mud structures soon gave way to more permanent stone ones. Each hut for six lads was allowed its tiny brazier of red hot coals for the cold evenings.

Besides studying the three R's, the boys were required to learn the use of soap and water. Carpentry and gardening were taught where possible and time for religious instruction was also scheduled into the day. These religious instruction classes with these eager schoolboys have been one of our most productive approaches to the tribe with the Good News of the Gospel of Jesus Christ.

Being the only mission in the whole Reserve, the AIM had the privilege of giving this tri-weekly class in religion. With music, pictures and Tagi's New Testament, we had an enthusiastic class, for without exception every lad eagerly awaited these periods of instruction called *dini*.

We always arrived early. This meant we usually found them at their morning wash-up at an outdoor faucet, lathering their arms and feet and shaven heads with soap, then rinsing and letting the wind dry them. There was one bucket of water to serve every four lads when water was scarce. They literally danced jigs to keep warm in the cold wind, too.

Once inside the classroom, they sang lustily, which soon warmed them up as they sat close together. Their only garment was a little white *shuka* knotted on one shoulder. Eventually, the uniform for all schools was khaki shirts and shorts and they got real bathhouses with hot showers and towels!

Maasai are dramatists. We loved to attend the shows put on by the schoolboys. They enacted the real tragedy of an African officer pulling a lad away from his weeping mother and taking him to school; the ever-present lion on the path as the officer and lad walked forty miles to school; the anguish of a chief heavily fined for sending no lads to school; and the attempt of a lad to escape and run back home, with the dire consequences of re-encountering the lion. The climax came when an actor, well tied up in one of our large lion skins, roared onto the stage. The house was convulsed with laughter, while visiting warriors who had never seen this show before had to be restrained, for it was all so realistic to them that they started to dash up to the front with their poised spears to kill the lion!

The boys excelled in our tri-weekly *dini* classes at their school, for most of them enjoyed this more than arithmetic. They could not get enough singing, it seemed.

One of our many delights over the years was the parade

of school lads whom we could clearly see in their snow white *shukas* far up on the path as they descended the mountain, coming down to Lasit from Loitokitok, or at Siyabei coming down the road from Narok, to attend Sunday services in our chapel.

Every one of them entered the catechism class, passed the examination and requested baptism after two years. Each one had to be sure of what he was doing before he could be baptized, of course.

One evening at Siyabei, back in 1923, some travelers stopped at our back door for a drink of water from our tank. They turned out to be the man named Mbae, his three wives and their children, and this was our first meeting. They were all tired out for they had carried all their loads on their backs about thirty miles from Nairagie Engare to Siyabei, where they were moving to live, having left Kijabe. They had come from Kijabe by Indian lorry as far as Nairagie Engare. Among the children was a tiny boy not yet three, paddling along in the dust with his little bag on his head the same as the rest. His mother was his father's favorite wife although she had borne him only two children. The other wives, one of whom was Wambui's mother, had borne him several — almost a Rachel and Leah story. Next Sunday in Sunday School, we saw a tiny little pair of pants, not seven inches long, on this same little lad with his big brown eyes and a smile from east to west. He had been named John Tombo when born. Time came when John Tombo entered the little mission school, where he zipped through his classes, then went to the Government School at Narok for grades 6 to 8.

At this point, he and several of the progressive lads came to our camp up on the hill where Roy was starting to build the Narok Church. They asked me to teach them singing and leading in music. I recall it was always Tombo who was first to catch and absorb it all. We felt *he* would make his mark in the world.

In 1964, when Kenya became independent, it was this group of lads who had been forced to school when young

who now became leaders. In the end, each lad had reason
to be thankful he was forced into school.

Two years after we got started at Kilimanjaro, the Maasai
elders at the *engigwana* out under the huge Lasit trees decided to entrust some little girls into our care for schooling.
The schoolboys had decided they wanted to marry educated, Christian girls and, more importantly, several parents wanted to keep their girls out of the *manyatta*. So in
1933 we opened the first Maasai Girls School, with the
sanction and blessing of the Maasai. Peter and Eunice were
our main help in this work.

Our girls' dorm was a round mud hut with banana bark
roof, dirt floor and grass on board bunk beds well up off the
ground. We had eight girls who came daily from nearby
kraals and eight who lived in our little dorm, including
Dora.

Now Roy put thirteen more acres under cultivation, for
even Maasai girls must eat. They got so they loved all our
foods which they had never tasted before. The soil was so
fertile, all the food grew fast. Our largest sweet potato
weighed nine pounds. All little Maasai girls are skinny, but
these skinny ones who came to us soon began to fill out into
healthy, sturdy bodies.

I worked out my own method of teaching them to read.
First, I hung up a white sheet on the wall, on which I had
written vowels, consonants and syllables. We had no
blackboard but we did have pencil and paper after they had
outgrown slate and slate pencil.

The method I used is similar to what is called the
Laubach "each one teach one" method. Each girl took her
turn to stand up at the big white sheet and "teach the class."
They took great delight in jumping all over the chart, lest
someone learn by rote, and they loved this better than the
writing game.

Then I cut out colored pictures of objects familiar to
them and their culture and wrote in Maasai each object's
name below. Syllable-by-syllable they learned these until

each one could read a five-syllable word as easily as a child in the United States could read about Dick or Jane. In Maasai there are not five sounds for the letter "a" as in English, nor are vowels neutralized. Maasai adheres closely to the International Phonetic Alphabet in spelling and pronunciation.

The children were as thrilled as I was when, after three months, they were reading excerpts from the New Testament. I also wrote up original little readers for them as we went along.

In sewing class, each girl learned to make her own panties, slip and dress, and also a baby dress. Before we went on our next furlough they learned to knit.

We selected and bought the raw wool right off the sheep backs up at Nakuru because not all sheep have the kind of wool needed for knitting. I taught them to tease the wool into thin lines, twist it into strings without a spinning wheel by means of constantly twisting a small weight at the bottom of the thread. They would then tie it into skeins, wash it, dye it in colors, using leaves, bark or roots of certain trees, dry it in the sun and roll it into balls. Then it was ready for knitting. Our own daughters, of course, learned to knit right along with the Maasai girls. Proper needles were not to be had at first, so Roy gave me all the eight-inch nails I wanted and they made a good substitute. Maasai girls loved to knit, even as they sat in their skins and beads at first, before they acquired dresses.

When our Maasai became Christians, they were eager to exchange their *shukas* or skins and beads for something more encompassing.

By then, they were building more permanent homes near the school and church, and beginning to have more things in the home than a cowhide to sleep on.

They were not just "trying to be like the white man." It was a far deeper-reaching outward evidence of turning away from the old life patterns and superstitions, to a new life.

But whether they wore cloth clothes or were in skins, we felt close kinship with every Maasai we met. Our lives had become intertwined as we sank our roots deeper into this good land that Kulale had beckoned us to.

"But what about your own children?" was a familiar unspoken question we often read in the anxious eyes of friends when we went home on furloughs. Weren't they missing out on a normal life?

18 *MKs at Large*

PITY FOR CHILDREN OF MISSIONARIES was misplaced concern. Few children on earth were as privileged as the MKs (missionary kids) who travel on ships (those days), planes (these days), trains and safari vehicles in strange countries, seeing many different places and cultures enroute. Some kids in the U.S. never see beyond their own county or state line, and never know the salty tang of the ocean.

Colleges have found that the MK is often a better student because he has had to meet and cope with unusual experiences and opportunities, not the least of which is the culture shock of reentering U.S. life when he comes home for college. Most MKs pick up at least one foreign language with some fluency. Not so the kid who has been brought up on TV, radio, drive-ins, fast foods and other pressures of civilization.

Meeting diverse people was one of the most educational parts of our trips. Once, just before we embarked on the *SS Wasukuma* to sail out of Port Said for London, a fine-looking, dark-skinned passenger was brought on board and introduced to Roy. The officer asked Roy if he minded this new passenger sharing the cabin with our eldest son, Harry, then age fourteen. There was, of course, no question.

The young man's name was Mohamed Said Morad, and he was the son of an Egyptian military officer. He was about eighteen years of age and going to university in Sheffield, England. Harry told us about how, daily, this young man spread his prayer mat on the floor of his cabin and prayed toward Mecca most ardently. Up on deck, he attached himself to our family every day. He even asked if he might sit and listen during our own family devotions, which we held at the very bow of the ship where we could sing, read and pray as was our family custom. He was delightful company and we welcomed him each day. He said he loved to hear us sing in four-part harmony as we did. It was our desire that some tiny seed might filter through to his heart. We enjoyed his companionship as much as he seemed to enjoy ours.

Once, in Chicago, our problem was a place to live and call home — the same song of all missionaries on furlough who have children. Finally, we found a basement room near Moody Church. How thankful and happy we were.

"Just you two?" the man asked as Roy handed him the rent money.

"No, we have four children."

"Oh, my God, git out!" the man yelled, throwing up his hands. We got out as he shut the door on us. If we had had four dogs instead of children, we would have been welcome. All along the street, window signs said "Rooms for Rent — Pets Welcome."

On our second Sunday, the Assistant Pastor, Dr. Charles Porter, told us that a widow lady, coincidentally also named Shaffer, who had to give up her apartment, was in need of somewhere to store her furniture. When she heard in her Sunday School class of this family just back from Africa in need of a home, she said she would loan us the furniture if we could find a place for it.

We couldn't find an apartment, but God did, through Reverend Bill Fox, a dear pal from our MBI days. Just around the corner from his home, it was on the second floor, with two tiny bedrooms and a large open veranda. Only a returned missionary with four children and no place to sleep or eat can fully appreciate our thrill when Roy found a truck to haul Mrs. Shaffer's furniture to this apartment on Seeley Avenue. We verily sang the Doxology and meant every word of it when we and our four ducklings were settled. It seemed too good to be true! Roy and I had to sleep on the cold, wide-open back porch, but we had brought with us from Kenya a large fur *koros*, a robe the size of a blanket, which I had made of rock rabbit skins, tanning them in our back yard and stitching them myself with Eunice and my other Maasai girls helping.

During that whole year-long furlough we frequently traveled to deputation meetings in many different churches telling about our work. We soon found that Roy seemed to be able to give the people just what they wanted to hear: not sermons and preaching, but stories of actual happenings in our field of service.

Roy also worked wherever he could get a job, at painting, construction, or just anything to stretch our funds. We had not only to eat but also to save toward our fare back to Kenya, so we surely did watch our pennies. We bought day-old bread at the factory for half price and always watched out for all bargains. We never ate steak.

Once, when we had pigs' feet and sauerkraut for dinner, Harry had invited a neighbor lad to eat with us. He was glad to do so until he found out we were having pigs' feet; then he went home fast.

On board ship was where our kids had the most fun and learned a great deal, especially when we went by freighter. One of our captains planned games for the children; but mostly just nosing around all the activity involved in running a freighter filled their time.

Returning from our second furlough, Roy David at age twelve wangled himself into helping the paint gang painting the outside hull of the ship. He had the enthusiasm of a real man at swinging the brush — until discovered. Dad soon had him put on some other gang where there was less risk of falling into the briny deep.

One favorite, but questionably educational, aspect of a freighter trip was the "guli-guli" man, a magician who came on board at dockside wearing his "white" gown (which was last washed no one knew when). He carried an equally dirty bag. He muttered words, songs, prayers — anything to get your attention — then held out his hand for *bakshish* (a tip) before he began his show. His tricks were clever, especially the time he pulled a live baby chick out of Roy David's nose.

On the freighter *The West Cawthon* we were only twelve passengers. Besides a settler from Rhodesia, we were five Shaffers, four Nixons, Emma Mathys and Betty Sywulka, all going to Kenya. We had a grand time. Our cabins were on the top deck and we ate at the captain's table, so we were much too well fed. The canvas swimming pool was the most popular place on the ship.

The officers and crew made quite a festival when we crossed the Equator. "King Neptune" held sway and our five-year-old Esther was his tiny attendant. The ship's radio operator was the biggest tease on board, so he came in for a lot of rough treatment from the crew. They painted him all over with tar, covered him with feathers, then threw him into the pool. It took five or six men to handle him.

One crew member held up field glasses for any greenhorns to "see the Equator as we were crossing!"

"Do you see the camel on the equator?" he asked.

He had pulled a hair out of his head, and held it before the field glasses, a standard joke on these occasions.

We spent eight weeks on this freighter, going from New York to Mombasa by way of Cape Town, South Africa. The ports between Cape Town and Mombasa were all clean and well ordered. There were beautiful flower gardens at Port Elizabeth and tall, modern buildings at Durban even in 1939. At Beira, Mozambique, we roasted for five days while the ship took on a full load of what seemed to be dirt, but was very valuable chrome ore, well worth transporting all the way back to the United States.

The most beautiful port we ever saw was Zanzibar. In its unbelievably clear water, colored fish came right up to the dock. While the ship loaded up with cloves, we took a walk through nearby clove groves.

Getting back and forth to Africa was always restful in those early days on ships.

Later on, flying became no more expensive and far more practical. But Roy never liked to fly. Even at the cost of a little seasickness the first day out on every ship we ever took, he preferred the vast blue ocean, the sea gulls, the throb of the ship and the calls at various ports.

Being such roamers at heart, we always worked in whatever interesting side trip experience we could at minimal expense. Once the MacIntosh family, AIM missionaries from California with three children, arrived at Kijabe wanting to return to their station in Belgian Congo (Zaire), but they had no car.

At the same time, Quaker friends of ours, the Chilsons at Kitega, Urundi, had written asking us to bring a grist mill to their station, adding that the Biglow family, needed a way out of Congo to get to a ship at Mombasa for their furlough.

So we put this all together with our own desire to let Ruth Marie, 13, and Harry, 14½, see Congo and the pygmies before we left on our second furlough. We decided to go, leaving Roy David and Grace in school at RVA, and Esther with the Otto Kellers, close friends in the Friends Mission.

The nine-hundred-ninety-mile safari with no motels enroute took us through Jinja, Uganda, where Lake Victoria spilled its lovely blue water over Ripon Falls at the beginning of the great Nile, and where now it flows through great turbines generating electricity which is sent out all over East Africa. We also passed through beautiful Kampala, built on seven hills like Rome. From there we drove on to the AIM station at Oicha in the fantasyland of the cathedral-like Ituri Forest which covers much of Zaire. This was where Claudon Stauffacher was working, at the threshold of a long colorful career that was to rival his parents' in scope. He was a quiet young man, exemplifying the saying "still water runs deep."

With him as our guide, we gingerly hiked through dense undergrowth and fallen logs under huge, sky-reaching trees for an unforgettable day with a pygmy clan in the green heart of the Ituri Forest. It was obvious that the several years Claudon had spent gaining the confidence of these tiny brown people had produced an enormous mutual esteem.

After a few moments of sharing their day's activities

with us, they asked if we would like to see a dance. Then they all disappeared.

Suddenly, there appeared from the black forest, a swarm of men, women and children like bronze leaves blown into sight by the wind. They were chanting antiphonally in their own rhythmics and melodics, quite different from ours.

They danced in lines, then circles, bowing, jumping, gesticulating with arms and hands, at the same time singing, first on a low bass note, then in a crescendo reaching up to a high, clear, flute-like pitch. After stomping the ground in perfect unison then clapping loudly, they disappeared as suddenly into the forest as they had come — clear out of sight and sound.

Reluctantly, we left Oicha to complete our journey, still thinking of the pygmies.

After we deposited the MacIntosh family in the Congo, we took the grist mill to the Chilsons at the Friends Mission Station at Kivimba, down in Burundi. Here, we saw a fabulous Watusi Dance Festival.

Then we went to Goma and Sake, to pick up the Biglows who were heading for Mombasa, and started home.

One year after we were there, the town of Sake disappeared completely. Molten lava poured out from a volcano nearby until it reached the top of the church walls.

Enroute back to Kenya, we stopped at the AIM school for missionaries' children at Rethy, Congo, where we found warm hospitality and real cow's milk for the first time in Congo. Rethy is high, where cattle can live. Most Congo stations have to depend upon powdered milk, for cows can't survive in many low tropical areas due to the prevalence of the Tsetse fly.

Rethy, like our Rift Valley Academy in Kenya, is a very fine school and children from many missions attend. We enjoyed several evenings of good music when Ruth Marie and I with our violins and Harry on his cello joined the Rethy orchestra.

All too soon, the time came for us to pack the truck and head back to Kilimanjaro a thousand miles away.

19 *MKs at Home*

WHENEVER WE RETURNED TO LASIT, we were almost cut off from the world. There was a weekly paper published in Nairobi, the *East African Standard*, but by the time we got it, it was two weeks old. Then most of the space was taken up with advertisements for liquor and other stuff we were not interested in, so we cancelled our subscription.

We had a tiny little electric generator powered by a gasoline engine that was given to us by Art Burnett, of Waukegan, Illinois, which kept our radio battery charged. We followed the approaching World War II by listening to the BBC News from London one hour each evening. After the war, when petrol was no longer rationed, we could run the engine all evening and enjoy classical music programs from BBC on our little Philco Radio. But much of the time, this was our only touch with the outside world other than our weekly mail bag.

We took Christmas as it came. Gifts and eats had to be what was on hand and we kept happy even if we went without. Once, all we had for gifts were the clothes we had stored for the kids to grow into, and fish from the pond. We still played our Victrola and had all the carols and other good music we could make for ourselves. I baked an eggless cake but had to tell the gang there would be no boiled icing, for we had no egg whites and of course no confectioners sugar.

Next day an African brought us a gift of a live chicken, which we kept tied overnight on the dirt floor of our cold storeroom. Next morning when I went in for her, the chicken had laid an egg, so we had icing on our cake after all!

Our little folding Estey organ was a big blessing in our

home. I loved to play it while our little ones sang. As pre-schoolers they stood close when I played. We sang from memory all sorts of songs suitable for children. One time four-year-old Roy David was singing "In the Garden" with me and after we had finished all the verses of the hymn he got closer to me and asked, "Mother, who is Andy?" We had a dog named Andy, but I was stumped until he reminded me that I was teaching him to sing, "Andy walks with me, Andy talks with me, Andy tells me I am his own," which is how he heard, "And He . . ." in "In The Garden."

Years later, in an old basement in Philadelphia we found a used piano to take back to Kenya with us. It cost us $100.00 but proved worth it many times over. It had a metal sounding box, so was eminently suitable for the tropics. Esther, then age three, loved to sit alongside me on the piano bench and sing her whole list of songs: a repertoire of "Sunshine Mountain," "When He Cometh," "He Loves Me Too" and a lot more. She had a voice clear as a bell.

One time music took the place of medicine for me. On the whole we had excellent health in Kenya, but one time a bad case of eczema overtook me covering much of my body. We were at Lasit and after all our attempts to find relief came to naught, Roy took me and our two girls to Nairobi, hoping to get some help. Enroute from Lasit, having stopped at Simba on the railway line to get water and wash our dust-covered faces, I was very low down in the dumps because of extreme discomfort. The nonstop burning, itching pain all over was driving me beyond tears, when suddenly I heard ten-year-old Grace singing in her high soprano voice (not to me but to the wind) with all her heart. This was like oil on troubled waters, and a balm on my chafing skin; it soothed my soul, my mind and my body as well.

Besides her beautiful singing voice, Grace also had a definite artistic talent which was discovered and encouraged by Rev. David Jester, a missionary from Tanganyika, when he taught a term at Rift Valley Academy. Today, Grace is one of the top draftsmen of an engineering firm.

Chugging along on safari we always sang together. Roy

would carry the melody and the rest of us sang alto, tenor and bass parts. We always had four part harmony and we knew all the words from memory of the dear old hymns: "Trust and Obey," "His Eye Is on the Sparrow," "I Will Sing the Wondrous Story," "Power in the Blood," "My Anchor Holds," "Wonderful Words of Life," and many more.

Africa's brilliant, flaming golden sunsets always inspired us to sing:

> Day is dying in the west,
>> Heaven is touching earth with rest.
> Wait and worship while the night,
>> Sets her evening lamps alight. . . .

Then of course there were Roy's raucous Army songs shouted out gleefully, like "Mademoiselle from Armentierre, Parlez-vous? . . . Hinky dinky parlez-vous." And during World War II our girls taught us a few British soldier songs like "We're going to hang out the washing on the Siegfried Line," or "Run Hitler, Run Hitler, Run, Run, Run."

A highlight of my life was one Christmas when the children came home from RVA, jubilant as usual. I was in the kitchen, giving Ngoso the menu for dinner when I heard music on our baby organ. Quickly, I went and found Harry Daniel and Ruth Marie (ages twelve and ten) playing a duet Mrs. Emma Farnsworth had taught them at RVA. I cried with delight. They remembered this number for years, and later played it on the old piano we brought from Philadelphia.

That piano served our own family for years, then when we left Kenya, we gave it to RVA where it served many more years before it was finally worn out. On our first furlough back to the States, my sister Pauline, with whom I had played music when we were young, had just returned to Chicago from a missionary tour in China. She had bought a Russian cello in Hong Kong, which she gave to Harry Daniel! This was the real start of the Shaffer family orchestra. Harry was nine when he started on the cello, on shipboard returning to Africa. Ruth Marie was put on the violin at the same time, when she was seven, and shortly thereafter I started Roy David on the violin, too, when he turned seven. Before long we had our own string quartet, with the sheet music partly from the Thiers family orchestra, and some written out by hand on the spot. The cello was actually bigger than Harry Daniel on his learning voyage, and it was quite a job for Roy to carry it up and down from the hold. We had to keep it in our tiny cabin and it almost took up the space of another person. By the time they arrived at Kijabe for school, the two older children joined the same RVA orchestra I had started seven years previously.

It was an Herculean task getting all the clothes sewn or repaired for four children; khaki-covered pith helmets had to be scrubbed, trunks packed and contents double checked to assure nothing was left out which they would need during the ensuing three-month school term at RVA. It gets cold at Kijabe, so long stockings were required and stockings always wore out first at the knees, which meant lots of darning. After the knees, toes and heels wore thin. We always got together and had a "darning time"; boys and girls all helped. We never dreamed of throwing a pair of stockings away just because it had holes. We darned them all, even putting patches on the worst holes. The same was true with our clothes, which were sometimes patch-upon-patch. But we never owed anyone a cent!

Some of our greatest blessings in the line of earthly goods were the supplies sent to us by Christ's Home, in Warminster, Pennsylvania.

Wealthy homes in Philadelphia kept this Home well supplied with all their cast-off clothing and household goods, which were most of the time usable items needed to maintain the Home. Very soon they were acquiring so much they began to share with others all over the world. They shipped missionary boxes to Turkey, China, Africa, Europe, and wherever they heard of a need. More than a few good old humpbacked trunks were packed with pots, pans, pencils, paper, tools, mirrors, blankets, pillows, clothes and much else, then tightly bound with strap iron and shipped to us in Kenya. Contrary to all the jokes about missionary barrels, the donations dispensed by Christ's Home were not only usable but were also a blessing to the Lord's work at the right time and in the right place.

Christ's Home is exactly what the name implies. It is a home started in 1903 by Dr. and Mrs. A. Oettinger and "Mother Krausslach" who picked up orphaned, unwanted babies and children in Philadelphia and brought them "home." They soon outgrew their few rooms in the city and moved to the countryside where they could farm acres of food for the growing orphanage and unsalaried staff.

Now Christ's Home is a large, Christ-centered institution caring for and educating children from broken homes; caring for old folk; and caring for transient missionaries (including the Shaffer family at least once during every furlough to the United States). Dr. Oettinger was head of the Philadelphia Council of the Africa Inland Mission when it was founded in 1895.

One year our children spent part of a school year in Christ's Home Grade School before returning to Kenya. Reams could be written about the splendid group of Christian people serving Christ without salary, caring for other people at Christ's Home.

Back at Lasit, we usually sent the children to RVA by train. We were sixty-five miles from the nearest railway stop, Simba. "Simba" means lion, and the place was so named when the railway was built because it was in a semi-desert and the lions always came to drink out of the railway water tank for the engines. The town of Simba consisted of the water tank, a tiny waiting room made of corrugated iron (later replaced with burnt brick) and two tiny outhouses a few yards away.

The boat train from Mombasa to Nairobi always reached Simba at five o'clock in the morning, and arrived at Kijabe late in the afternoon. For our kids to catch this train back to school, we would get up at midnight, get all the gang dressed and feed them a good, hot breakfast of pancakes with thick cream and brown syrup with sweet pickled figs. Then, with trunks all loaded on the Model T, violins, cornet and cello tied on the runningboards, and the kids sitting on top of the four trunks inside, they were off into the dark of night. The children were growing such long legs that by now it had become a geometrical problem fitting them all into the tiny car. They loved to watch for the fiery eyes of animals that glowed in the early morning darkness, reflecting the headlights of the car, as they drove along. The road was either a succession of ruts and rocks, or deep, volcanic sand that billowed like fine dust before, behind, and into the car. Visibility was very poor. Speeding it up to twenty-five miles per hour did help them keep ahead of the dust somewhat but it still poured in because our Model T's top had to be folded back to make room for the big load.

Once when Roy had deposited the kids safely on the train and then started back home before dawn, this time with Suji our cook, he suddenly came upon a pride of lions lying right in the middle of the road, rolling in the deep dust. Grass on each side of the road was three feet high. Roy froze in bewilderment, not knowing what to do.

"Bwana, shall I shoot?" asked a very frightened Suji at Roy's side, holding the gun in a trembling grip.

"No!" Roy answered, as he abruptly stopped the car to avoid bumping into the lions, but kept the motor running.

The lions blinked at the glaring headlights, then got up, approached in growing curiosity, and came alongside the car. Roy could have reached out and touched them since the top was down. All the time Roy was wondering why he could not get the car to move. The motor just raced when he accelerated and the car remained stopped, right in the middle of the sniffing lions. Roy yelled at them and Suji banged on the side of the car, cursing them in Maasai.

Suddenly, Roy realized that he had pulled up the emergency brake in stopping so quickly, and had forgotten to release it. So, holding his breath, he released the brake, once more pushed the "low" pedal on the Model T and accelerated. The car lurched forward and then quickly they left the lions behind in the darkness. Roy still seemed to be very pale, even through the dust, when he got home about 10:00 a.m. Our kids never tired of hearing him recite this episode, far more exciting than "The Three Bears," and they were only sorry it didn't happen when they were in the car with him!

Oling Kijabe was the Maasai name for Kijabe, for it was their territory when they were the paramount tribe over all that area. The words mean "much cold wind." When RVA was in session, the students were taken on all sorts of hikes and picnics. They were toughened to the cold and they loved to climb the steep escarpment. It was covered with a dense, black forest of age-old cedar, wild olive and other trees which are home to troops of colobus monkeys. Further up toward the top was the large bamboo forest, where the elephants lived at an altitude of over eight thousand feet.

Students and staff of RVA often climb and camp on the two extinct volcanos in the Kidong Valley, Mt. Longonot, and Mt. Suswa, seven and nine thousand feet high. These are now highly advertised tourist attractions.

The Maasai live down in Suswa's large crater where grass is green and water is ample, just as in the more famous and vastly larger Ngorongoro Crater. We have been up both Longonot and Suswa, hunting our Maasai. They live right in the midst of all the wild game which also needs green grass and water.

Another favorite recreation for the RVA children is the hike down the escarpment and out onto the Kidong Valley to a small hill called Mt. Margaret, named after the deceased daughter of a government service worker about 1904. Near the base of Mt. Margaret today is a satellite tracking station through which telephone conversations from the United States come through clearer than local calls.

All five of our children were the recipients of wonderful training at RVA, where they lived with houseparents who were as beloved as family: Paul and Elizabeth Lehrer, affectionately dubbed "Ma and Pa Lehrer." The school remained closed for the months of May, September and January, while all the children were home with their own parents.

When ours came home, we always managed several picnics, hunts, fishing trips and of course lots of swimming. At Lasit we also took hikes up the slopes of Mt. Kilimanjaro, whose foothills rose right up in our front yard. We enjoyed the bracing climate there, at 6,500 feet.

We hauled many tons of good, solid, rocky soil down from the mountainside, rolled it flat and made a tennis court. We also had evenings of croquet to finish off a perfect day.

All five children, after Roy drilled them on gun handling safety, enjoyed hiking off into the bush to hunt for meat, especially the wild guinea fowl or the tastier dik dik, a tiny antelope the size of a hare, with long, spindly legs and two-inch horns.

On safari we would never stop to disturb the wild game since we lived in the midst of the Game Reserve. The zebra loved to gallop ahead of our car. They were determined to veer across the road immediately in front of us, then gallop away. No two zebra are striped exactly alike, and they all run differently, too. Just what the unending attraction is between the smelly petrol of cars and trucks and wild animals (at night especially) is yet to be unravelled and explained. The same would happen with the eland and the ostrich, too. Large groups of them will be far off the road, and yet they will make a bee line for a point of convergence with the car, then race alongside, trying to cross over the road directly in front of the car at the last second, risking our crashing right into them. Actually, we could never go fast enough to hit any of them on the run; the ostrich are so long-legged they could outrace any car we drove. We had to keep down to thirty-five or forty miles per hour because of rutty roads that would tear our old car to pieces if we didn't. The children and I liked to bang on the car door and sides, whooping at the racers as if we were at a football game and winning.

Our big old dining table saw many happy hours as we

often invited Peter and Eunice and our house help in on Saturday evenings for "Pick-Up-Sticks" and other games. Once, playing ping pong by blowing instead of with paddles and net, Roy's dentures fell out on the table when he blew violently. Mulei was so alarmed that he crawled under the table, yelling, "Oi! Oi! what shall we do?" His horror was redoubled when he saw Roy pick them up and put them back in his mouth.

Mulei was a bright Mukamba lad who had learned cooking easily. Obviously, he had never realized Roy's teeth were false.

One vacation when Harmon and Clara Nixon and their children, Paul and Jean, were with us, we decided to go fishing. Driving the truck and stopping on the way so we could gather a supply of wild olive firewood for our stove and fireplaces, we went three miles east of Lasit, downgrade to the clear, cold Oldukai Stream which gushes right out of a rock. *Oldukai* means palm. The spring was surrounded by a young forest of palms, besides other trees and dense bush.

This Oldukai Spring is so plentiful that the government in later years harnessed a fraction of the flow in an eight-inch pipe at the source. It went downgrade all the way to Mombasa, providing an abundant water supply all along the railroad line through the desert. The water was pure and clean and needed no treatment of any kind.

We soon caught several of the large white fish which inhabit that stream and started cooking them over the fire, looking forward to some good eating. Jean, Grace and Esther were wading, climbing trees and behaving like noisy monkeys. (Our three older children were not home.) Paul went exploring with the men while we mothers were getting a fire and food for the famished families.

We had all the food set out on a blanket on the ground when Paul came running back through the bush, breathless, white as a sheet and thoroughly cut and bruised by briers and thorns. He shouted that a rhino had just been disturbed from his sleep and was charging around toward our camp. Harmon was close behind him. In no time at all we corralled the kids, crammed the food all back into the debbies, grabbed up the blankets, threw water onto the fire and raced back to the truck.

Roy puffed in at last, long after everybody else. He was scratched and hatless, having dropped his hat while scrambling up a thorn tree in the stream when the near-sighted rhino picked him out to chase from among the gang of humans that had broken in on his privacy. Not until Roy was up the tree and watching his hat float downstream did he realize he had picked a thorn tree for sanctuary! He got down, very carefully, after the disgruntled and now confused, myopic rhino had ambled off.

On our arrival home, we ate our food in the back yard with a nice big fire on which to roast our potatoes and onions, and finish frying the fish.

That very night, September 1, 1939, we heard on the radio that war had been declared between Britain and Germany, and it was rumored that some Germans from Tanganyika were coming to blow up the railroad line. The Nixons packed right up and quickly went back home to Ukambani.

District Commissioner Whitehouse at Loitokitok told us we should leave, too, since we had the only isolated house between Moshi, in Tanganyika, and the railroad line at Simba. We packed up everything, including the piano and all canned food, thinking this was the end of Lasit. We left the house keys with Whitehouse.

He also sent all the government school boys from Loitokitok and their teachers up to the Government Boys School at Narok.

Roy drove our truck, taking Peter with him, and I somehow drove the Model T, never having driven one before. With me were Eunice, Joshua, Grace and Esther. We were stopped at many military roadblocks but made it to Nairobi by a back way through a farm. From there, we went on to the Nixons.

On arrival, I sat down on some bricks, still shaking like liver from driving the "Tin Lizzie." After a few days, we went on to Siyabei where we rejoined the Stauffachers. At least there we had swings and swims to distract the children until school started. The large Siyabei pond was good for deep swimming and it was also stocked with tilapia fish. The little pier Roy and John had built was clearly visible from the house just over a hundred yards up the hill.

We also swam and fished at a spectacular waterfall on the Siyabei River five miles from our home. After hiking across hot, dry thornbrush country, unexpectedly you came upon a drop in the earth where the cold, brown river dropped down about seventy feet in a powerful, foaming falls which was over thirty feet wide. The noise was deafening. When we jumped into the cold, swirling pool at its base, we had to yell to be heard over the noise of the falls and swim fast to keep warm. We caught catfish a little farther downstream, among islands thick with cattails.

At Narok, we set up camp at one end of the grassy Sports Ground in the shade of some high acacias. At the invitation and instigation of the fine young Maasai teachers at the Narok Government School who had come from Loitokitok, we began a little Narok church. With their moral and material help, the stone chapel went up on the bluff above our camp. The school lads and all the local men and women helped with their hands, from clearing the sage brush to chinking the stone walls with cement. Yes, we kept their hands well healed with Vaseline.

The final day of dedication came and we all rejoiced. However, to tell the truth, we were risking the displeasure of John Stauffacher in this whole venture, for he feared the Siyabei work, eight miles away, was threatened by it. In the end, he went along, and Siyabei did not suffer at all.

When the Christians at Kilgoris heard that the new church had gone up at Narok, they let us know right away that they were still waiting patiently for one, too.

20 *Cerebral Malaria*

ROY BUILT A TEMPORARY LITTLE mud hut at Kilgoris for us to live in while he built the long-delayed chapel, early in 1942.

World War II had turned the tables on the German Count who had kept us out of there. Once more the Maasai elders paced out the plot on which they wanted a mission constructed, and, with the approval of a new District Commissioner, Roy started building.

But suddenly Roy became sick. Typically, he kept on working, thinking it would soon pass away as an old-fashioned stomach ache.

The weather was cold, windy and rainy, which is why Roy had put up the hut for us to sleep in instead of sleeping under the stars as we so often did.

For the chapel, Roy had already cut trees and sawed them up into lumber to make brick molds. Our Watende workmen from an adjoining tribe danced and sang as they puddled mud for the bricks with their feet in a hole six feet square and two feep deep. Mixing just the right proportions of clay and water gave good mush, which they threw into the molds with force, packing it in to prevent air bubbles, levelling it off and turning it upside down on the ground to dry. Then they covered the rows of these moist bricks with grass against the midday sun so they would not dry too fast, turning them over every other day.

When the bricks were dry enough (and much lighter in weight) the men built them into a large kiln, approximately ten feet by six feet by six feet, sloping inward toward the top. They left a very small air space between the bricks for circulation of the heat, then they plastered the entire outside of the kiln with a thick layer of mud to hold the heat in.

The fire box was a space left inside the full length of the kiln, where long, dry tree trunks were inserted through a small opening at the front, day and night, keeping a steady, hot fire for several days. The last two days, they increased the fire, then closed it up tightly, completely sealing it with more mud all over, and left it for several days. When the top bricks have a certain "ring" when tapped, they are properly cured. The soil used determined the color of the brick. Beige, brown or red are all possible.

Right in the midst of this kiln process Roy finally had to admit that he was not well, for he couldn't even walk from our hut to the outhouse sixty feet away, he was so weak from simultaneous vomiting and diarrhea. So I kept on the run with the little white pail, day and night. I fixed him rice water, barley water, milk and nutmeg. It was all in vain.

When I saw his lips turning dark, that was enough. I sent a letter by barefoot runner fifty miles to the nearest white settler who happened not to care much for these missionaries. In my letter, I begged him to phone to Litein over the only telephone line in existence from the settlers to the main box. At Litein, AIM had a station maintained by Earl and Esther Anderson, Earl's widowed mother, Mrs. A. M. Anderson, and a nurse, Veda Nicodemus, known to everybody as "Nicky."

My letter urgently requested a nurse and a man to help me get Roy to Litein for medical help. He was in a coma much of the time by now.

Miraculously, the settler made the phone call. Then after thirty hours, here came Earl in his Model A car with Nicky, the nurse, and Mr. L. Adkins from the Holiness Mission, the father of Grace's best friend at RVA.

While the two men put away Roy's tools, the tiny but tough Nicky prepared Roy for the long, bad road back to Litein. Earl drove as fast as the little car could go, but we had to stop when Roy had a bad spell and needed relief. I was so grateful for these dear folks coming to us in our time of need.

Nicky weighed only ninety-eight pounds, but she knew how to handle even a big, strong man professionally. For our arrival at Litein, Mother Anderson had a nice room ready in the little, brick one-room guest house her husband had built before he died three years before. She had real beds for us, a far cry from our stick and straw bunks in the mud hut. Nicky saw to it that Roy had a good sleep, but she was still bewildered to know what medicine to give him.

Word came in as she worked with Roy of one more death in her Infirmary, with Roy's symptoms. Many had died with these, already. Nicky had lived with this for over two weeks, unable to stem the tide of what seemed to be striking all over Kenya among black and white, WWII military troops and civilian personnel. Government medical services were stumped as well as mission hospitals, for no case responded to any medication. It was an epidemic of cerebral malaria.

The next day, Sunday, Nicky had made Roy as comfortable as possible and then left for a much-needed few minutes of rest herself, for the first time, at 3:00 p.m. I, too, had just lain down.

"Ruth, I'm sorry, but I need your help to get on the pail this time," Roy said.

I helped him. Then suddenly he began to shudder, turned black in the face and was about to fall off the pail when I caught him. That was the hour when everybody was down at the big church having a convention, singing loudly.

For some unknown reason, Amos, an elder of the church, had chosen that time to go to the phone booth by the Anderson house to get a book he had left there. He heard my screaming. I was overcome with fright and was screaming at the top of my voice.

"Please come and help us — anyone! Just anyone!" I cried.

Just then Nicky turned over on her bed, which let her one good ear catch the sound, so she also heard my call and came on the run. She took one look at Roy then rushed out the door to her office.

I told Amos, who had come at once, to help me lift Roy back onto the bed and rub his feet and legs while I rubbed his arms and chest, for he was very cold. His eyes were set and he was in coma. I piled on the blankets, then Nicky came back in and gave him a shot of digitalis in the arm.

She then pushed me out the door into the arms of Esther Anderson, who took me by force down to her house nearby. I resisted. I didn't want to leave Roy. She made me promise to stop crying and wailing and hindering Nicky's efforts to help him. Then she led me back and we sat on the grass just outside his room. Soon I was again allowed to go inside and be near him.

Roy was so still. Both his breath and pulse had stopped. For thirty minutes, tiny Nicky used artificial respiration on his big, strong body. God was pleased to intervene and let his breath return, also his pulse, though it was slow.

Earl Anderson drove twenty-five miles to Kericho to get the government post doctor, who was playing tennis with his wife. Earl begged him to come at once.

He came. His diagnosis: "This is a dying man and his family should be prepared for it." (He didn't know I was the wife, standing right there.)

No, I did not start wailing all over again, for God gave me whatever it took to keep control and keep my mouth shut. I had received unseen and unknown strength to hold my mind and heart under control.

The doctor injected a heavy dose of old-fashioned quinine in one leg and told Nicky to do the same in the other leg two hours later if he were still alive, and to continue to do this through the night, if he lived. He asked her to let him know in the morning if the patient were still alive, then he left.

We four adults stayed with Nicky on and off through the night, for Roy was perspiring profusely from head to foot, growing weaker. We kept towelling him off. Nicky didn't always wait for two hours, for he always revived right after each shot of quinine.

Morning came and he was still alive, but he stayed in a coma for three days. His whole mouth became one huge blister from the fever. He could hardly open it to receive the liquids Nicky wanted him to take.

At this time, Trudy Shryock arrived, a fine nurse also from the Holiness Mission (later renamed World Gospel Mission) a hundred miles away. She graciously relieved Nicky of this great burden she had carried so bravely for five days and nights nonstop. The next day, the coma left Roy and he knew me and others for the first time. He even tried to smile with his ulcerated mouth. It was not so easy.

Trudy's coming illustrates how, in Kenya, we missionaries did not harp on denominational differences. We helped each other in as many ways as we could when needed.

The Sunday night when Roy was so near death's door, I asked Earl to send a wire to Grace and Esther, our little girls at RVA. By then the older three children were in school in the United States. Roy and I never believed it was right to hide from our children the real issues of life, whether sadness, gladness, death or misfortune, for they were old enough and mature enough to know right from wrong and to accept the Grace of God given for any occasion of joy or sorrow.

Dear Mr. Lee H. Downing received the wire, then went to our Grace and Esther and told them the message. He prayed with them, asking God to comfort their hearts for anything that might come later; but he told them he felt strongly that this was not a sickness unto death and that their Daddy would get well.

Everyone, black and white, loved Mr. Downing. If any human being ever talked with or had seen God, surely Lee H. Downing had. We saw this that day when he first visited us in our one-room apartment back in Chicago twenty years earlier.

And indeed, Roy did pull through. We brought the girls to Litein to be with us during their school vacation while

Roy convalesced. The gracious, tender, loving care of all the Litein folks and friends can never be forgotten. The many weeks of uphill recovery seemed so slow. Litein is in high, cool country where it rains every afternoon at four o'clock in season.

After a long period of recuperation, Roy and I rejoiced when he was fit enough to go back to Kilgoris. He finished burning those bricks, then turned to building the chapel! The Maasai there had patiently waited many years since they first asked us to build at Kilgoris long before World War II and now we looked forward eagerly to the completion.

One night in our Kilgoris mud hut we hung up a five-pound piece of meat we had just bought, high inside the mosquito net over my bunk, where no predators could get at it (so we thought). Mosquitoes were so bad during the wet rainy season that we had to use nets over our bunks or else be eaten up all night by the anopheles, which give malaria.

During the dark night I kept scratching my head, then neck, then ears and eyes. I finally turned on my flashlight and saw ants dripping in clusters from the meat above me. It was covered with a layer of ants two inches thick. My net was covered with them. I never knew how they got in. They didn't bite me — all they wanted was the meat! I got up and awakened Roy.

After a good laugh, we lifted the net to let the ants clear out of my bed and I had to spend the rest of the night with Roy in his twenty-four inch bunk, under his net. Our bunks were just a framework of sticks covered with straw, with our bedding on top.

Next morning, we found that our five-pound roast was reduced to a two-pound one. No, we would never throw it away. We cooked it and ate it gladly, with thanks to the ants for leaving some to us. Setbacks meant nothing to us by now.

Finally, the day came when we finished the chapel and the people poured into it.

The Kilgoris work developed so well after we went back

home to Siyabei that the little chapel soon proved too small, and Earl Anderson (who had the oversight of Kilgoris) enlarged it. Later, the Field Council saw that Kilgoris was still growing, so assigned Arnold and Marilyn Newman there, full time.

The Maasai called Arnie *Bwana Shefa Kidogo* (Little Mr. Shaffer) because he looked and acted so much like Roy, they said. I gave the Newmans their lessons in the Maasai language and they passed easily — but that, too, gets ahead of our story. A new direction for our work was shaping up.

One day while holding a service in the new little chapel, Roy read I Peter 2:1-2 out of Tagi's New Testament. When he read "As newborn babes, desire the sincere milk of the Word, that ye may grow thereby," the word "milk" was not there. Milk is life to the Maasai, but somehow that word did not even appear in the translation. When Roy put it in, the passage leaped to life for them.

Just how "milk" could have been left out of that translation is a mystery, but there were similar problems all through the book. One vowel or one consonant can change the entire meaning of a word, so printers' errors plus translators' errors can completely spoil any book. This was compounded by the fact that the Maasai manuscript Tagi and Bertha Simpson had sent off to the British and Foreign Bible Society was never thoroughly proofread before printing. Gradually, the growing ranks of educated Maasai were noticing errors in their New Testament and asking about changing them. At last we heard that the much-needed revision of the New Testament was in the offing. The Church of Scotland Mission was now also doing some work among the Maasai.

While at Kilgoris, I began picking up new Maasai words I had never caught before, and whenever I heard one, I would immediately scratch it down. There were lists everywhere—on the back of envelopes, in fly leaves of my Bible and song books, and on odd scraps of paper. We hoped to hear more definite word about a new translation next time we went to Kijabe, and I was keenly interested in helping out.

Translation Work

KIJABE WAS CROWDED. Roy and I joined the throng of folks who came for the wedding of Claudon Stauffacher and his bride, Gladys Taylor, in October of 1942. We found her as beautiful and talkative as he was handsome and silent.

At the reception, we sat down with old friends from our earliest days in Kenya, the Blaikies. Mr. Blaikie leaned over and said, "Say, you folks are going to be called in to the special meeting of the British and Foreign Bible Society, in Nairobi, to discuss the revision of the Maasai New Testament."

The next week we received an invitation from Bishop Leonard Beecher, the Chairman of the BFBS in East Africa, to attend the meeting. Those present were Mr. Charles Richards, of the East African Literature Bureau; Will Blaikie, now with the Church of Scotland Mission; Charles Teasdale, still head of the Bible School at Kijabe; John Stauffacher; and us. Florence and John had recently moved to the Congo in semi-retirement where they could be near both Claudon's and Raymond's stations.

At the BFBS meeting, Bishop Beecher explained that the society had instituted a new policy that no further translation work would be accepted unless done by a team composed of one or more African translators and the white translator working together side by side in joint discussions on the project. Then he turned to Roy.

"Mr. Shaffer, will you take over this revision project?" he asked.

Roy was completely caught by surprise.

"Ah . . . Well, I don't feel I have the command of the

language needed for the job," he protested. "But I think Ruth might. She has always scored higher than I on language exams. Besides, she is always correcting my mistakes." After the laughter died down, the Bishop turned to me.

"Would you be willing to undertake this work, Mrs. Shaffer?" he asked.

Now it was my turn to be totally taken by surprise. I had only foreseen helping from the sidelines. My mouth went dry, and I was barely able to whisper: "I feel inadequate, but I can only try to do my best."

"You will be expected to sit down together with your Maasai collaborators and work in conference with them," he explained.

It was BFBS policy that all Scriptures should be revised periodically, so it was time to get started. Tagi's translation was a marvel for its time but it had been printed mistakes and all. The entire book was full of obscure passages.

For the new revision, Bishop Beecher asked me to use all available manuscripts, as well as plenty of Maasai informants and assessors. By now there were also missionaries working among the Maasai from the Lutheran Church, the Church of England, the Bible Church Missionary Society and the Church of Scotland Mission, and all were working on their own translations of both Old and New Testaments. So Reverend Beecher said to consult all of these and make an entirely new translation, starting on the book of John, then Genesis, as trial sections, to see if we could meet the needs of all the various areas that would use it.

Because of the Second World War, we were now living at Siyabei, which was deemed safer than Lasit. Jacobo Parmale ole Nakola, who was among the first to be baptized at Siyabei, was chosen by the Siyabei Church Elders to be my informant and translator. He proved to be expert at it, being fluent in three languages. As we worked together at our round dining room table, we constantly called in all the teachers, including ones from the Government School at

Narok, and all the leading elders of the community, for consultation and criticism.

The war was raging in Europe but we were oblivious to it, plunged deep in the process of hunting the precise words to adequately put into Maasai both the content and the intent of the original. Translation work certainly meant getting to know the Maasai in even deeper perspective than ever before. Their own pastoral, nomadic pattern of life made it easy for them to translate Genesis so that it sparkled with life. Abraham was a natural.

We completed John and Genesis just about the time the BFBS Bible House and printing plant in London were bombed. All production ceased for the duration of the war, and our work lay dormant.

We had been on the field for seven years, and even though the war was still on, we decided, if possible, to go on furlough in 1943. We yearned to see our growing teenagers who were at school in the USA. On our second furlough in 1936, we had left Harry and Ruth Marie at Westervelt's Home for Missionary Children at Batesburg, South Carolina, and returned to Kenya with just Roy David, Grace and Esther.

After Harry graduated from high school at Westervelt's, he studied pre med at Wheaton College, Wheaton, Illinois; following graduation he joined the Navy, which provided him medical training at Northwestern Medical School, in Chicago.

Ruth Marie, meanwhile, had gone through Moody Bible Institute after Westervelt's, and then went to Wheaton, where she majored in Home Economics.

Roy David had gone back to the United States, traveling with the Bill Mundy family, when he turned fourteen. He went briefly to Westervelt's, then after graduation from Wheaton High School he was drafted into the Army, which put him through one academic year at the University of Michigan. When we decided to go home, he was stationed in South Carolina, awaiting overseas service which was eventually to take him to the Meuse-Argonne, the very area of France where his father served in World War I.

Wartime seemed to close all doors to our taking a furlough, but we were determined to try.

John and Florence Stauffacher were now living near the "Mountains of the Moon," in Belgian Congo, at Ruwenzori, a paradise of a station, and they invited us to come see their place. Here, John could roam up the mountain paths to the content of his Swiss heart. They most efficiently operated a rest home open to weary missionaries from all missions, an opportunity especially welcome during the war when furloughs home were long deferred. So we spent several happy weeks with them, enjoying lots of pork, strawberries, bananas, enormous roses, good company and fresh, cool mountain air as the first part of our furlough.

Evenings when work was done, John cranked up the gramophone just as he had in the old days, and often put on Grieg's "In the Hall of the Mountain King." As always, family and guests had to be quiet!

Using parts from the junkyards in Nairobi, Roy had created a Model A car which we called "Little Yaller Doggie" because, due to wartime shortages, the only paint he could find in Nairobi was mustard yellow. "Little Yaller Doggie" got us to the Congo.

A paddle steamer, the "Reine Astrid," took us down the wide Congo River, reminding Roy of his paddle steamer days on the Ohio River. At the mouth of the Congo, which was seven miles wide, we caught a ship to Lisbon, Portugal. Here, after an anxious three-week search, Roy secured bookings for us on a Portuguese ship. It took us eighteen days to cross the Atlantic, fully lit up at night, being the ship of a neutral country. Both Germany and the Allies had mined the highways of the ocean. With much zigzagging, our captain went just where he was ordered and we made it undisturbed to Philadelphia.

Then we were arrested. The Coast Guard took our ship

under custody far out in the bay. The entire passenger list was categorized as possible spies with stolen missionary passports, for many of us had German-American names, "Shaffer," meaning "shepherd" in German, being one of them. Our ship was escorted to a side dock, where for five days we were rigidly questioned by the FBI, and the Immigration, Health, and War Departments, and our luggage was searched. (We were only glad that our country was taking proper precautions, of course.)

Ruth Marie was on the dock to meet us when we were finally released from custody and got off the ship. Such a feast to have her in our arms again! She took us to Christ's Home for a thankful reunion with the dear folks there, the girls and I wearing some new dresses Ruth Marie had sewn for us.

Then she took us by train to Chicago, where Mrs. Mortimer Lane met us in her big car and drove us all to their lovely home in Wheaton, Illinois. Mrs. Lane had maneuvered getting Roy David from his Army camp in South Carolina, and Harry Daniel from Northwestern in Chicago, so we could all be together after seven years apart. What a dinner! We feasted around the enormous Lane table, which provided a banquet of food and love for twenty hungry people.

Mortimer B. Lane was a professor of political science at Wheaton College. He and Mary Lane were parents of Betty Lane, whom Roy David had chosen as his beloved for life. And it was to be at a friend's wedding in the Lane home where Harry would later meet and fall in love with Dorothy Guindon, the Quaker girl from Ohio who became Harry's own bride.

Next, the Lanes took us over to the upstairs apartment of a house named "Little Africa" which they had prepared for us to live in during our furlough. It was the first time we ever arrived back on furlough and weren't stranded for a place to call home. They had the beds made, a refrigerator full of food, flowers on the piano, and a full winter's supply of coal for the furnace—plus a new station wagon named "Zambezi" parked out front for us. All we had to do was tuck in!

Downstairs lived Mary Grimshaw from AIM work in Congo and her two teenage daughters. They had made the hazardous Atlantic crossing by sailing ship, one of the last of the tall ships to do it commercially.

That year, Grace finished high school at Wheaton Academy, and the next Fall entered nurses training at West Suburban Hospital. I enrolled at Wheaton for a semester of anthropology and phonetics, under Dr. Fred Gerstung. This proved invaluable for my next term in Kenya.

We returned in 1946 to find that Rev. Frank Bedford had succeeded Bishop Beecher as Chairman of the British and Foreign Bible Society for East Africa. Rev. Bedford called a meeting at our home for representatives from all missions working among the Maasai, to resume the revision of the Scriptures which we had begun in 1942. Those present were: Chief Sefania Sumlei and Dr. R. Reusch, from the Lutheran Mission in Tanganyika; Edith Webster and Ruby Grindley, of the Bible Church Missionary Society; Joseph Kango, of the Presbyterian Church, East Africa; Charles Richmond, of the Church Missionary Society; and Rev. Bedford, as chairman. Joseph Kango and I were chosen to resume the revision at once, starting with the New Testament.

Joseph was one of our first converts at Kajiado, eighteen years before. Fluent in English, he proved to be keen, capable and easy to work with. He was Head Teacher at the Ngong government school until he was assigned to this translation work. He cherished a well-marked Bible I gave him which had belonged to a former missionary named Old Bill Harrison, who had gone on to his reward.

Old Bill was the beloved grandfather of our son-in-law, Gordon Johansen, who grew up with our children at RVA and asked Ruth Marie to marry him after she went back out as a missionary and taught at RVA two years. Gordon was by then the Government District Officer on the Yatta Plateau.

One day Joseph told me that Old Bill's marked Bible, plus our work in translating it, was a Bible School course in itself. He sat with his aged father around the fire evenings and searched out old, good, pure Maasai words for us to use.

We also had Esther's help, for, being born and reared among the Maasai, just as the other four, she was as fluent in that language as in English. She had just finished high school at RVA, where she learned to be a fast typist. She could type as fast as we could write a rough draft, meanwhile spotting errors, for inevitably we did have errors.

Esther later went to Wheaton College, then subsequently took her M.A. in journalism at Syracuse University. One of her early jobs was with *Houston Magazine*, in Houston, Texas, where she met and married a geologist, Ronald Wilcox. Ron is from Des Moines, Iowa, and received his Ph.D. at Columbia University. Their three daughters grew up in Houston, picnicking often at beautiful Memorial Park where, fifty years previously, their grandfather, Roy Shaffer, had sounded his bugle through the pines playing reveille, mess call and taps when his World War I army camp was bivouacked there.

During the Maasai translation work, Esther and I camped in a new little house trailer which Roy had created from scratch. Roy was away, finishing up some construction work at Machakos, but first he had settled us in, parking the trailer right next to James Ngatia's kraal at Ololua, Ngong, only a mile from Joseph Kango's home. James was a teacher at the government boys school when we first went to Lasit, and we had a close bond.

At night, Esther and I proofed each day's work by kerosene lantern light. We worked five to eight hours daily. Our trailer was stuffed with reference books and Bibles in Kikuyu, Swahili and English, for Joseph knew them all. We had several versions of the Bible in English, also commentaries, encyclopedias, several dictionaries and Wuest's complete set of *Greek for the English Reader*, which Mr. Wuest had given me at Wheaton. For purity of text, we diligently solicited help and criticism from the teachers and the intelligentsia among the Maasai, near and far.

I have a beaded belt a Maasai woman gave me forty years ago while Roy was building the Narok Church. It is solidly decorated with beads of blue, red, white and yellow in their *isirit* pattern, all sewn with sturdy sinew, as strong as nylon. The zig-zag pattern is such as you see in American Indian designs. The Maasai always use the same pattern when decorating their cheeks, arms, bellies, thighs, legs and shields with red ochre paint. Our Maasai verb for writing was taken from this word, *isirit*, by Sir Claud Hollis, when he reduced the language to writing in 1902, for this was what his helper, Justin Olomeni, gave him for the verb "to write." The root of the word is *-sir*. So the noun for Scriptures or The Writings today is *Isirit*.

We had many real treasure hunts tracking down the exact Maasai words to use. For example, it was with pleasure we tore apart the misleading account of the gifts of the Magi visiting the two-year-old Jesus. It said they brought him a wineskin of *enaisho* (a fermented brew of bananas or honey, high in alcoholic content). Instead, we found just the right Maasai words for gold, frankincense and myrrh.

But of course some words have no exact Maasai equivalent. When we came to Revelation, speaking of the twelve precious stones in the foundation of the walls of New Jerusalem, we decided to use the English words, adapting them to African orthography, or spelling.

After many months, we completed the revision of Tagi's New Testament as requested by the BFBS. Miss Grindley, working among the Samburu Maasai under the BCMS, typed five copies of our work and sent one to each of the missions working among the Maasai for their criticisms, comments and suggestions.

A language expert from London University had come out on his own to our camp near Ngong as we were working on the revision of Tagi's New Testament. He asked to see our manuscript. He had just spent ten days among the Maasai, he told us, and he strongly disagreed with the Hollis orthography we were using. Joseph and I were quite amazed over all his words.

Some of the Maasai accepted his radical changes in spelling but at that time many did not. However, publication of the work in Kenya was stopped because a firm policy of the BFBS was that where there is any lack of agreement, such as we had over this, the Society will not publish the work until the differences are resolved. We were at an impasse.

The Lutheran Mission in Tanzania eventually published their own Arusha Maasai New Testament in Germany in the early sixties, under the direction of one of my Maasai students, Rev. David Simonson, stationed at Ilboru, near Arusha, Tanzania. They used our manuscript with appropriate modifications to adapt it to Arusha Maasai usage, which, for example has a different word for "disciple" than the one used in Kenya.

But again, that gets ahead of the story.

22 *Near Call*

THE INDUSTRIOUS AGRICULTURAL ARUSHA MAASAI on the other side of the mountain in Tanganyika (now Tanzania) did not have much to do with the truly nomadic Maasai in Kenya, whose roving herds were their only delight. In fact, each disdained the other's occupation.

But many years ago, two adventuresome lads of ours, Kamau ole Ndiati and Mbalosi ole Kulale, the Chief's son, had gone around the mountain to visit the Lutheran school among the Arusha Maasai. In turn, some lads from Arusha came around to visit our mission station, which was about four days of travel on foot. They saw our song book and Tagi's New Testament, which they found so easy to read that they were delighted, and took copies home.

By 1953, the Tanzania Maasai Christians at the Lutheran Mission asked our AIM to send someone to help revise their books to conform to the Hollis orthography, and I agreed to go.

They had a hymnal, a liturgy, and the *Luther Catechism*, all of which they found hard to read. Why? Because the German Leipzig Lutheran missionaries who came in 1904 used German orthography in spelling Maasai words. For example, "Kilimanjaro" was spelled *Kilimantscharo*; "papa" was spelled *vava*; and "spear," *mbere*, became *mvere*.

So Roy took me around the mountain. After a quick stop for a visit with the Ludwig Lanys at Marangu Hotel, we went on to Ilboru, the Lutheran station where the Bill Budkes, just out from the USA, were my hosts. Pastor Lazaro, Chief Simioni, and Church Elders Eliahu and Eliezar came to greet us, and made us very welcome. Then Roy had to go back around the mountain to his current construction project, the Bisil church.

The next morning was Sunday. Their worship service was held in a grove of trees, since the church, built in 1904, was far too small to hold the crowd that came. It was a collection of Western-dressed people, warriors, tribal elders, mothers in skins with babies on backs, herders with goats not far away, and a few dogs.

At the front, the tall khaki-clad song leader did an excellent job as they sang in four-part harmony without any instrument nor even a pitch pipe. How I wanted to record this on tape and film, but I had neither. When this was German East Africa, the German missionaries had trained the people to sing in parts and, though they had left twenty-three years previously, their training had lasted.

As we drew near, the congregation arose en masse to stand on their feet until we four had been seated on the narrow little bench behind the altar-table. They had no seats but were packed in close lines, sitting on the ground. On the altar was a huge brass crucifix, some three feet tall, which they carried in real pomp from church to grove. Budkes told me this was a German custom they liked.

After many songs of ten to fifteen verses each, rituals, liturgy and long prayers, the offering was taken in gourds. Uganda, Kenya and Tanganyika all had the same currency in shillings and cents, one hundred cents to a shilling, which was worth about fifteen cents of American money in those days. If the gourd was not large enough, the offerings of eggs, ears of corn, or any other garden produce was taken up to the altar by the giver. It was not unusual for a skinny goat to be led up the aisle as an offering (maybe the only goat the man had and he was giving his all). God keeps the books.

Time came for Lazaro to announce the speaker of the morning.

"*Endasati nairo engutuk ang nairo irorei le Ngai taata* (the old lady who speaks our mouth speaks the words of God now)," he said.

Except for a dog's bark or a baby's cry, an African audience is always quiet and respectful, especially in church. But this morning the hush and stillness was even more pronounced, for they had waited almost an hour already, to find out who that white woman on the front bench was (where no woman ever sits, but only men in authority). When Lazaro said this woman was going to speak about God in their language, their mouths began to open, for few of them had ever seen a white woman who spoke their language and few ever saw a white-headed white woman. So, she was quite a curiosity, yet highly respected in African culture for her age and white hair.

In Maasai fashion, I said all the greetings, expecting a reply. Instead, pandemonium set in. It seemed like a rushing wind caused the crowd to rise up off their haunches and move forward, the front ones pressing up to touch my feet and skirt.

I heard many whispers of *"Ai! Oi!"* and exclamations of awe and wonder; but I went right on. For a moment, I thought the crowd would crush me, it was all so quick and almost alarming, so I turned to Lazaro to get some clue as to what was going on.

He was laughing and enjoying the excitement. I didn't know whether to stop or go on. He quickly stood up and shouted for them all to sit back on their haunches, stop the noise and listen so the white-headed old lady could go on with her words. It took a few seconds to get them all down again. Then I went on, all the while my words being punctuated with audible grunts of approval and understanding which is good Maasai courtesy.

At the close of the meeting I was swamped by the women who wanted to feel me, to see if I were real or fake.

The next day at 8:00 a.m., Lazaro, Eliahu and Simioni met me in the big school building where for six weeks we worked together until noon daily, revising first the hymnal, then the liturgy, then the *Luther Catechism*. Afternoons, I typed up the morning's work. They were delighted to be able to read their own language and understand it all easily at last.

My hosts, the Budkes, lived in a small teacher's house

with one bedroom, complete with outside sanitation. They had a small storeroom with a cot, which I called home. I loved my work, also the food Mrs. Budke prepared for us, for she did all her own cooking. I enjoyed my kerosene lantern at night when I could read some of their books on the shelves in the storeroom after going to bed.

One Saturday after working hard all week, I decided to go to town with Budkes and another couple, the Karvonans, in their new Jeep. Enroute home at 8:00 p.m., going around a curve, a truck with only one light and no brakes, loaded with five tons of wheat in sacks and going 70 miles per hour, curved over onto our side of the road and crashed head on into our Jeep. The impact spun us around and pushed us back forty yards before both vehicles came to a halt, tipped half over into the gutter. Both vehicles were badly damaged and all occupants knocked unconscious except the truck driver, who ran for his life and was never seen again.

"Bill," I said during the crash, "let's get out of here before something happens!" But already something was happening. Being in the front seat on the passenger side, I was flung out the door and into the wet grassy gutter.

I felt neither dead nor alive. I could hear far in the distance the crowd of Arusha-Maasai gathering around, talking excitedly.

"The old lady is dead!"

"No, she is not."

"She is still breathing!"

"No, she is dead."

At this time I had a vision of Christ standing beside me, as real as if I were fully awake.

"Now is the time for you to come to me." He spoke to me in Maasai, and He seemed to move up closer, beckoning with His hand in Maasai fashion, for me to follow Him.

"I can't possibly come now," I said, "for I'm so busy with this translation work — nor could I think of leaving our class of five little uncircumcised Maasai girls back at Lasit— nor do I want to leave my own five children and husband at this time—so I don't see how I can go and follow You." (How I ever dared to answer Him so, I will never know.)

"You are not indispensable," He said to me as plain as day. "I have others who can do the work better than you. I can also take care of all these children."

As I gazed on His beauty, glory and magnetism, my heart was suddenly captivated and I became totally willing to go with Him.

"All right, Jesus. I'll go with you right now!"

Just then, someone in a group of Greek businessmen who had come over from a club across the street where they were drinking, was putting a coat over me, for it was cold. They had covered me all up but my head and arms.

He stooped over me, laying it gently over my neck and arms, trembling.

"She is still breathing. She is still alive!" he exclaimed, exhaling his breath with force into my face.

Abruptly I regained consciousness and, to my great sorrow, left the presence of Christ. If I ever had a great disappointment in life, this was it, for I didn't want to come back from the presence of Christ.

We were all taken to the African hospital which had a little x-ray machine, operated by a fine Goanese doctor.

The two missionary couples I was with got minor bruises and cuts, and were able to go home after treatment, but I suffered subluxation of the fifth and sixth vertebrae, which kept me in a critical state for several days.

Although I was feeling very sick, he had me walk to the x-ray room. He took films which showed my displaced vertebrae, and ordered me put on a stretcher in a horizontal position, between sand bags, at once. They carried me out on the stretcher.

A professional nurse, Mrs. Mary Manning, was called in to care for me. I sure needed the confidence this nurse gave me just from knowing she was there, for I seemed to slip away and die periodically. It was pressure on the spinal cord, she told me, hence the sand bags, which were to hold my head in one position, immovable. The Goanese doctor called an English doctor to look at the x-ray and check me over. He found a tensity in my shoulders and paralysis in my left arm and right leg and foot.

I asked Bill Budke to send a telegram to my husband. After two days and nights, going around the mountain through inefficient offices and a police walkie-talkie, the telegram finally reached the radio box at Loitokitok, where an African was listening in.

In this office was a friend visiting the radio operator, who also knew quite a bit of English. As messages came in English, this friend heard the name "Shaffer" so he paid attention. The operator did not know Shaffer, as he was a new man from Akamba. His friend was a Mkamba also, being our very own local pastor-missionary, Reverend Justus Mumo Nzomo. Alerted, he got on his feet quickly, took the telegram down six miles to Lasit, where Roy was in the act of getting the truck loaded with building supplies for the Bisil Church. Roy at once got into our small car with Justus and drove like Jehu to Arusha, where I lay in the hospital.

The young English doctor told Roy he had two problems. One was how to get me to Nairobi when it was as though I were now in two pieces. He wanted to put me in a cast, but feared to move me. It was Saturday afternoon and most of the *dukas* and stores were closed, but Roy scouted around and found one *duka* still open, where he bought three leather belts. Then he found a board, some cotton and bandages, and he fixed up a brace for my head and spine to keep me immobile, so I could be flown to Nairobi.

The second problem was that the weekly plane had not yet returned from London because it was coming via Dar es Salaam, which would make it late. It was bringing back several chiefs of Tanzania who had been flown to a special convention in London. One of them was the good Chief Sefania Sumlei, who had been in our home a year before, attending the BFBS meeting concerning translation work. The Ilboru Church had a great welcome planned for his arrival at the airfield. Their band of ancient horns, tuba, trombone and cornet, practiced hymns right on the airstrip before the plane arrived.

As the makeshift ambulance brought Roy and me to the

airfield, which was only a wide space on the plain with a white wind sock flying, we could hear the tooting of horns. It sounded good to me, just what I needed in my soul.

We didn't know they were there to meet the chief, and they didn't know we were to be flown to Nairobi. Finally the roaring little plane touched down.

Everyone was curious, of course, especially the chief, as to who was on this hospital stretcher going up the steps of the plane he had just come home in. It soon filtered through that it was *Gokoo* (Grandma) Shaffer, the white-haired old lady who was doing language work at Ilboru, and had been in a car wreck three days before.

Chief Sumlei bounded back up the steps, three at a time, and into the plane to where my stretcher was on the floor after seats had been removed to make room for it.

"O, my mother, what has happened to harm you?" he exclaimed when he saw me.

I was rational and could talk, but I let Roy say all the words. Sefania stood there and wept. All of the Maasai thought I was dead, or soon would be.

Our plane took off for Nairobi. The pilot apologized for all the tossing about, which he could not avoid as Nairobi was only forty minutes away so he had no time to climb higher where it was calm and smoother. Meanwhile, I felt sorry for Roy, who was just as airsick as I was. We both made use of the little paper bags supplied for just such a contingency. We were struggling together to survive all the air bumps, knocks and holes. Below us slipped the Maasai plains where we had bumped along together for so many years behind our mules and later in trucks and trailers, hunting our elusive nomads and telling them *Irorei Le Ngai*, the Words of God. Those were happy, rich, work-filled years. Here we were up in the sky, covering in forty minutes the distance that used to take up to four days.

Flying along low, right over Bisil where Roy was headed when he got the radio telegram about my accident, we wondered: Was our work to be prematurely concluded by this errant driver who lost control of his truck?

Soon we were right over beautiful Nairobi. Our son Roy, and his little son Danny, and others were at the airport waiting to help get us out of the plane into what was called an ambulance. Nairobi may have had a good ambulance, but this was not it. It was like the rear of a truck body, with nothing to fasten to nor hold onto. So the fast drive over the rough dirt road to town, with us six bobbing about in the rear of the truck, was a little different from what one thinks of when he hears the term "ambulance ride." It was so rough the leather strap holding my head broke loose, causing my head to toss about. Roy grabbed my head to stabilize me as much as possible.

We finally got to the hospital and were taken into the emergency entrance. I was still very nauseated and wanted to pass out all the time. A nurse quickly took x-rays and then showed them to the doctor. He came out and told us he saw nothing unusual on the film and asked what the trouble was.

Roy then handed him the Arusha Hospital x-rays showing the subluxation clearly. Now the doctor was stumped and unable to explain it.

We were told later by our Mission doctor that it must have been the turmoil of the plane, the broken leather strap, and the rough ride in the Nairobi ambulance all put together that caused the two vertebrae to slip back into proper position! This was certainly a case of divine intervention, for God let me breathe freely again.

I had to spend ten days in the Nairobi Hospital to get over the shock and to learn how to hold my head up properly without fainting. I had received a whopper of a whiplash which still, thirty years later, tells me I do not have perfect balance.

After spending a month at home resting, I was able to have Roy take me back around the mountain to the Lutheran Mission to complete the work. My fingers refused to type properly and my head and neck were stiff, but we managed to complete the work just before Christmas. Roy came and took me home for a quiet, peaceful celebration. The Lutheran Mission lost no time getting our revisions printed and into the hands of the Ilboru Maasai.

Six months later, the Lutheran Mission again asked our AIM to send me back to teach the Maasai language to four new seminary graduates, including Dave Simonson, of Il-boru, who became instrumental in getting their new New Testament published. So Roy took me around Kilimanjaro again.

The next day was Sunday. After the worship service outside, my hands and arms were gently grabbed. Once more the arms of women and girls were about me, all trying to hug me.

"Oh! you are the old lady who changed our books of God," they joyfully exclaimed. "Now we can read them and know what they are saying."

All I could do was laugh and cry with them.

In a few months, the four new missionaries were speaking Maasai and it was time for us to head for home again, back around the mountain. It's no wonder we felt like we owned that mountain, we've taken so many safaris around it. Up it, too—always with Chagga porters, to the mystification of our flat-plains Maasai who could not fathom why anyone would ever want to venture so high on purpose.

23 *Mount Kilimanjaro*

THE MAASAI CALL ICE-CAPPED Kilimanjaro *Oldoinyo Oibor* (the mountain which is white).

During our earliest years at Lasit, we often saw Kibo, the higher of the two peaks, robed in snow clear down to the saddle between the two peaks. Our house was in the north-east foothills of the mountain, so it seemed to loom right up from our front yard. Before daybreak, while it was still dark around the house, we would see the golden glory of dawn already covering Kibo.

Every vacation, the magic of Kibo lured us to try to climb it. In our first attempt, the party included Dr. Bryan Michener, his wife Edith, and Irma Brown (all from the Friends Mission) W. Phillip Keller, a teenage pal of Harry's at RVA and the son of dear friends, and Roy and Harry. Mountain sickness turned them back at the saddle that time.

However, Phillip is now the author of over thirty books, one of them being *Mountain Splendor*, subtitled "This is My Father's World," lavishly illustrated with his own superb photography shot in both Africa and North America. One of his best known books is *A Shepherd Looks at Psalm 23.*

A few years after that first assault on Kibo, we again had guests who wanted to climb it. This time we packed up all the food and bedding and the umbrella tent into forty-pound loads and hired some Chagga porters to carry them for us. The party included Bob Lichty and Bob Griffith, each of whom had a great sense of humor, Roy, Roy David, who was 14, and me. We went by truck ten miles up to a forest station, then climbed the rest of the way.

Weather was good and we started with a song, with the

two Bobs in top joke-cracking form. We were all feeling fit and good.

When we got up into the snow above timberline, I was concerned to see the Chagga porters walking in the snow with only sandals to protect their feet. However, they never wear shoes and they all have a very thick layer of callous on the bottom of their feet. Each porter carried his load on top of his head, walking along with steady rhythm and poise. They didn't stop to rest as often as we white folks had to.

Our route took us down and up, then down and up, traversing deep ravines cut by fast-flowing ice cold water from the glaciers far above.

This part of the climb tended to cut down on our hilarity as we panted along, far behind the porters. However, it was beautiful up there! Neither man nor beast had polluted this water and we drank freely, without first boiling it, every time we crossed the bottom of a ravine.

We had given our porters warm coats, caps and blankets. Blizzards at the top are every bit as bitter as any midwinter storms in the States. Before we left home, food for everybody was measured out very accurately. Our second and third night stops were above the forest and stream line where tiny drops of water disappeared underground as quickly as they had appeared out of rock or shale, so we had only the water we had brought along. It was very precious and each cup was measured and used carefully. We spent those two nights in shallow, cold caves. This sobered us up a lot. In fact, the men were very quiet.

On the third night, all five of us slept in our umbrella tent. We were on the saddle, among huge boulders and in three inches of snow. We had sent our porters back down after they brought our necessary loads to that point at the saddle. So they slept below the snow line, in a cave, using the only firewood they had which was tiny bits of scrub cedar, more like weeds, but they kept warm and cooked their food.

We had a primus stove with us, for there is no wood up there among the shale and rock to cook with. But we did no cooking that night, as we had already-prepared food to eat for that supper. Besides, we were all so tired, cold and in a state of "don't care what" that all we wanted was to crawl into our blankets inside the umbrella tent — all five of us on the ground, packed in like fish in a tin — and try to get warm and quiet.

Even the next morning no one wanted food, for during the night all four men had succumbed to an attack of malaria with the accompanying chattering teeth and chills, obviously brought on by fatigue. In addition, the malaria was complicated by every known symptom of mountain sickness. This was one morning we went without smiles and jokes. No one loved anybody. Only those who have had malaria will know the feeling.

So that morning I was all alone, wandering around outside, enjoying the grandeur of the new layer of snow that fell during the night, and the indescribable cloud formations below me, and the glorious sunrise bursting forth in the east through white cumulus clouds. I was so eager to go on to the top and sign my name in the book in a tin box there (about which I had heard so much), but it was not for me, because to go without a guide would be a plain act of foolishness if not suicide. It is a nine-hour endurance test even for real climbers. There, they say the gravelly shale, called "scree," makes climbing very difficult. It seems almost vertical, and one takes three steps up and slides back two. Beyond the scree are the glaciers to cross, crevasses and all.

I was dressed warmly and was at least comfortable but it was more than I could accomplish to get Bob and Bob and Roy and Roy to drink some hot tea. They refused. They were all so sick with fever and chills that all they wanted was to get going back down the rocky path home. As soon as they could get out of the tent and stand up, they stumbled around in the snow, laboriously picking up the bedding, the chop box and finally the wet tent. We carried the loads down to where the porters were hugging a nice, warm fire of brush. They saw us plodding along, far off, so had hot tea and food ready for us when we arrived, which helped.

In spite of it all, it was funny to see our four strong men who had left in such high gear, each bragging that he would be the first up, fail to get to the top at all. With the porters we all laughed until we wept, over our failure.

We were a sorry looking bunch, but began to recover quickly, the lower down we got, where the air was not so rarified. We descended so fast that I got a bad pain in my side. Roy pulled off his broad belt, and fastened it around my waist, which helped a lot. We were thankful to get down past the cold, slippery shale into the scrub cedar, rocky belt, then into the forest where we began to warm up.

Many people can't see the sense in climbing mountains. I just loved this, my first and last climb. The beauty, still-ness, clean air and almost sacredness of being up so near to God was something I will never forget. We do have to pay a price to get close to God. Salvation is free, but discipleship costs dearly. To one who truly loves God and His ordi-nances, the cost of discipleship is not counted.

We traveled from the saddle back home in one day, for it is largely downhill. None of us wanted to, nor could we, walk one unnecessary step for the next two days, we were so foot-weary and physically spent. We walked to the table to eat, but crookedly I assure you, on our blistered feet.

John Stauffacher, being of Swiss descent, loved Kilimanjaro. Before we left on furlough in 1936 the Field Council asked the Stauffachers to move to Lasit and take over our girls work, which was thriving by this time. They were glad to do so, for John loved to sit out in the yard with field glasses and study Kibo and Mawenzi, which are so different from each other. He would also go off, all alone, and climb the slopes, which is really not safe. But John was an expert as well as an enthusiast. In 1928 he had climbed Kibo with Reverend W. J. Roome of the British and Foreign Bible Society. They placed a copy of the Bible in a small tin locker at Gilman's Point.

Roy and our son Roy David have been guides to several parties ascending Kibo from our house at Lasit, six miles south of Loitokitok. Roy David, while a teacher at RVA, initiated "senior safaris" up Kilimanjaro for the senior class. They always got at least as far as the frozen leopard which wasn't there anymore and some made it to the top. Some absent-minded people had long since brought back all the pieces of that frozen leopard, just to prove they had climbed that far. The frozen leopard had been there for years and no one ever had any explanation as to how it got there, for absolutely nothing lives up there. There is no life whatsoever under any stone you may overturn though climbing parties are doing their share of polluting this magnificent creation of God in leaving their tin cans, boxes, clothes and refuse of all kinds for the next party to see. No scavenger birds fly that high to clean up the earth, as they do at lower altitudes. No wild goats climb up there either.

Climbing Kibo calls for tough endurance, rather than mountaineering skills. However, boots with crampons are necessary, especially on the crater rim beyond Gilman's Point where the ice crevasses are dangerous without a guide who knows every step of the way and has been up there dozens of times guiding climbers. The Chagga are excellent guides and indispensable to a successful climb.

Fourteen years after our attempt, our daughter Esther and Bob Lichty's daughter Mary wanted to make the climb. I insisted on their doing it with proper equipment and trained guides. Bob, going along for his second try, agreed heartily. Their climb was organized by good Czechoslovakian friends, the Ludwig Lanys, who own Marangu Hotel on the other side of the mountain from Lasit. They took two guides instead of one, which proved to be wise.

The whole party of six, made it clear up past the scree, to Gilman's Point on the rim of Kibo's crater.

Then Esther and one guide, Kimatari, started off around the rim toward the true summit, while all the others with the second guide started back down as fast as their wobbly legs and stomachs would allow.

Esther, on the way around the rim, became so utterly spent that she went to sleep each time they sat down in the snow to rest. But she was bent on reaching the very highest point — Kaiser Wilhelm Spitz, 19,340 feet. Kimatari was a wise old Chagga who had been up there dozens of times. He would let her have a good snooze for just a few minutes, then he would nudge her and say, "Let's go."

On one of these awakening occasions Esther answered, "You go on to the top, alone. I will stay right here and wait for you and sleep." (They were speaking in Swahili.)

"No!" he replied. "There are open crevasses hidden here under the snow. I can't leave you! In fact, from here on, you must put your feet exactly into the footprints I make."

Now startled fully awake, although still sluggish as though drugged, she was more than ready to follow him closely the rest of the way. She stumbled along, endlessly it seemed. Suddenly he whirled around, grabbed her mittened hand and pumped it vigorously, congratulating her for making it!

Aroused from her stupor, she realized they were on bare, wind-swept rock and this was, indeed, Kaiser Wilhelm Spitz. This high point was subsequently renamed "*Uhuru* (Freedom) Point" when Tanganyika gained its independence in 1961. (Tanganyika was renamed Tanzania in 1964.)

To her right was the yawning crater a mile across. To her left was the glacier-draped mountainside plunging down to the plains thousands of feet lower.

She was too groggy to eat more than one section of an orange that Kimatari offered her out of his knapsack, so she gave it back and he ate the rest with relish. He then pulled the tin box holding the registration book out of a crevice under one of the larger boulders where it was kept sheltered. He unlocked the box and they signed their names and the date (which was about a week after Esther's sixteenth birthday). She suffered a blistered face, for she forgot to smear vaseline heavily on her face to protect it against the sun glare reflected from the ice and snow — but she made it!

Their descent was a lot speedier than their ascent. Once they reached the loose scree again, each step downward carried them twenty feet or more at a time. The downright fun of their bounding descent matched their exhilaration at having conquered the highest point in Africa.

Whenever Kilimanjaro is mentioned, many Americans think of Ernest Hemingway. This gets far ahead of the story, but once in the early 1950's Dennis Zaphiro, the Maasai Reserve Game Scout, took it upon himself to introduce us to the Hemingways. Dennis was a frequent visitor in our home, so one day he invited us to meet him down at the Kimana stream to go to the Hemingway camp in the foot-hills of the mountain.

We took along a good supply of vegetables from our garden including huge tomatoes and cucumbers, which won Hemingway's admiration. Miss Mary, his wife, in all colors of paint on cheeks, eyes, fingernails and toenails, hopped about as lady of the tent, being hospitable. All the while, Ernest sat at the end of a long table, scribbling notes when not asking us questions. Mary commented, "This is how he always writes his books." He had just published *The Old Man and the Sea*.

When it developed that Hemingway and I were born near each other in Indian Territory, he observed that now we had both ended up near each other with the Maasai in Kenya — I to lift up and he to tear down. His camp was literally barricaded with cartons of liquor, and drunk Maasai were all around his big tent where we ate.

Soon after the meal, we all walked out to their parked plane which Dennis was piloting for them that day. They got in, waved goodbye, and up they flew to photograph herds of elephant, zebra and whatever else Dennis had scouted out for them. Roy shot a guinea fowl for supper on our way home to Lasit.

24 *Retrospect*

W HEN I TURNED OVER THE completed manuscripts of the re-vision of the New Testament and Genesis to the British and Foreign Bible Society and finished up the Lutheran Mission's translation work, and Roy completed the chapel at Bisil, it seemed it was our time to go home. The accident at Arusha had dealt me a more severe blow physically than I wanted to admit. We had been in Kenya thirty-five years and had always believed strongly that, in most cases, old-sters should step out of the way when there are others to take over.

In spite of the rugged life we'd had to live, we enjoyed it, living intimately with the wind, the rain and the hail, the sun, the cold and the heat. We slept on all kinds of beds, from bare ground to grass pads, leaves, kapok, on boards, air mattresses that never held air and many other kinds.

Yet we had nothing to complain about really, for the ship under whose flag we sailed had a Commander who gave us all good health, strong bodies and a joy in serving Him. We slept under the stars, under the cart, in the Muleobus with canvas top, in tents, in a home-made house trailer, in a big truck, then in later days in the end room of the latest church Roy had built.

It pleased God to let us watch many groups of adherents develop, starting as early as 1928 when we first went to Kajiado behind our mules, the year there was an historic locust plague. All our wandering around let us see the open-ing of the work at Narok, Rotian, Olololonga, Kilgoris,

Ngararu, Narosora, Ngong, Ilbisil, Mashuru, Lasit, Loitokitok, Rombo and Kimana.

Through the years, God has caused His work to go ahead all over Maasailand, so that many of the little churches are now replaced by larger ones to accommodate the larger crowds who come.

At Narok, the church was built of rough rubble stone; at Rotian, red cedar; at Kilgoris it was burned brick; and at Lasit it was corrugated iron. At Ilbisil, Loitokitok and Kajiado, the chapels were built of concrete blocks, generally using sand out of river beds close by.

By 1950 the many young *Grevillea robusta* seedlings we had planted at Lasit in 1932 were fully grown to huge trees. Roy installed a bench saw in our back yard and sawed some of them up to make beautiful new church benches.

As I look back, each center we opened was at the request of the local people. Never did we have to beg or scheme to get a plot. Twice, government officials tried to block us, refusing a permit for the plot the Maasai had specified for our use, but the Maasai won the case on both occasions and we entered.

Over the years, starting way back with our first kraal visits, many lives were definitely changed, which is not a small thing in Maasailand. Our evangelistic crusades were not to the countless throngs, but person-to-person, one-by-one, each one is won. We have never counted raised hands as most "hit and run" traveling evangelists or eager missionaries have done then written glowing reports back home claiming large numbers of conversions to make themselves feel good. This kind of conduct seems to be the ground for the statement that there are three kinds of lies: black lies, white lies, and missionary statistics.

The Spirit of God does break through here and there, and lives are changed completely. One of our finest Maasai men was Sitoya Ole Sankan, one of these little but mighty men, and one of our first converts at Siyabei. He passed rapidly out of four years of schooling and went to Bible School at Kijabe for a term. He became skillful at taking an

English song and translating it into Maasai, which made Florence Stauffacher very happy in her Sunday School work. He did a translation of the entire Psalms, in addition to his work on the rest of the Scriptures with John Stauffacher, and later with me. Sitoya was shy and silent as the hills, but brilliant.

After he served as a tax clerk eight years, the Government took Sitoya on as President of the African Court of Law at Narok. He was fearless in his stand for all that was right, and never wavered in front of the medicine men, nor the ungodly elders who would bribe if they could, nor any white officer who misjudged. He refused all the liquors offered him by both white and black who knew nothing else all their adulthood. He soon had a powerful influence over them all and they highly respected him.

Sitoya's wife, Noolmusheni (the of the mission), was one of the little girls who tried to stand against female circumcision when Eunice did, at a time when otherwise staunch Christians nevertheless found it impossible to break with that particular Maasai custom. Noolmusheni's father, Olduboi, the schoolteacher, beat her until all thought she would die. Sitoya, who had already spoken for her, was helpless. She was circumcised.

Then they were married. God must have been pleased with them, for He blessed them with many fine children in spite of such persecution. Noolmusheni was a staunch leader of the women at church. At baptism, she took the name Tabitha when Sitoya took the name Stephen. When he died in 1981, they had five sons, five daughters, and over sixty grandchildren.

Sitoya was an excellent speaker each time he gave the message at church on Sunday. After decades of faithful ministry to the church he was officially ordained a pastor in 1979 at eighty years of age. He wrote a compilation of Maasai customs entitled *The Maasai*, published in paperback by the East African Literature Bureau, Nairobi, 1971, in both English and Maasai.

He was truly one Maasai who was born again. Jesus told

Nicodemus that the new birth of one's soul is like the wind, you don't know where it comes from nor where it goes. So to be born again is a great mystery, known only by God. No man can bring this about.

How I wish my friends in the USA might meet Rev. John Tombo ole Mpaayei, Eunice's half-brother, and his lovely wife, Martha. After government boys school at Narok, John was admitted to the prestigious Alliance High School, which was operated jointly by all the missions in Kenya. Then he went to Makerere College, in Kampala, Uganda, and finally to Cambridge University in England for his BA in education.

Throughout his intensive training, John never grew weak in his faith in Christ. He had magnetic influence over all who knew him, from tiny lads to top leaders, African and white, in government circles in Nairobi. We loved his noble father, Mbae, and his mother, Ana, very much ever since that hot day back in 1923 when the whole family walked down the dusty Siyabei road and into our lives.

John succeeded Rev. Bedford as the East African representative of the British and Foreign Bible Society.

After many years with the Society, he took a leave so that he might work on compiling the Maasai Bible at last, after it had been so many years in manuscript form. Although John and I have honest differences of opinion on the correct Maasai orthography question, this has not broken the bond of love between the Mbae, Mpaayei and Shaffer families. John is held in high esteem throughout Kenya. He served on the Governing Council of the University of Nairobi, and, working in collaboration with World Vision's Nairobi office, rejoices over a burgeoning of new Christian Centers throughout Maasailand.

I wish you could meet another of John's sisters, Mary Sialo ene Ndipilit, who is an excellent teacher, counselor, wife and mother of five fine children. She is the widow of Joseph Masaa, who worked with us as an evangelist for a time. Mary is a favorite leader among the women at Loitokitok.

John Mark, the son of Samuel Karioki who helped us get

Lasit as a mission station, was an outstanding Christian teacher for many years and was appointed Provincial Education Officer in Kenya.

How I wish my inquiring friends might hear these Maasai tell of their love for, and trust in, *Engai*, and in *Yesu*, their only Mediator between them and *Engai*. It is not a mathematical nor a scientific, nor a social question. It is nothing but the mystery of a new birth that the Spirit of God gives to any soul who seeks Him and invites Him into his heart.

In addition to others mentioned specifically, some of the leaders who chose to join the march of progress for their people have included: Geoffrey Kanyakua; Christopher Kipaata; Godfrey Njau; Solitei; Gwitu; Jason Kiruta ole Sein; Melton Njaro; Livingston Takona; Peter Nakola; Josia Shaidi; and Rev. Paulo Milia and many of their offspring.

Paulo Milia ole Magiroi, who did not receive much formal education, has become the senior pastor in Maasailand, loved throughout the tribe for his dedication to the people and respected by even the Maasai out in the bush.

As is to be expected, we hear continually of more young leaders, whose names are new to me, emerging among our Maasai, who are following in the footsteps of Tagi Oloiposioki, who dared to step out, embrace and propagate Christ, and be true to all that the love of Christ constrained him to be. It brings to mind Isaiah 55:11: " . . . my word . . . shall accomplish that which I please and it shall prosper in the thing whereunto I sent it."

Now in my old age, I stop and salute the parade of young Maasai who are emerging and carrying out Tagi's conviction that "My Maasai people must hear the Word."

All of Kenya has rapidly, completely changed from what it was like when we first lived there. There have been both catastrophes and giant leaps of progress. Following World War II there was Kenya's internal struggle for independence, known around the world as Mau Mau. The Mau Mau uprising convulsed the country with blood baths beyond description, largely within the Kikuyu tribe. Since our Maasai had for generations bought Kikuyu wives, the two tribes are intertwined, so the crisis was not easy to cope with and it split whole families down the very center.

The Christian Kikuyu elders led in taking an indomitable stand, refusing to take and execute the awful oaths to annihilate the white man and reject the Christ he brought to Kenya. It is recorded that this is what broke the back of Mau Mau — not guns and swords.

After the Mau Mau came the unprecedented drought, floods, and famine of the late 1950's, all of which left scars on the Maasai along with all the other tribes.

Independence did finally come to Kenya in 1963. The British Government had done a thorough job of training the Africans how to administer their own affairs. Nairobi and each town of any size has its own city council.

Years after we had retired in the United States, son Roy who, after the Army, went through Wheaton College and Albany Medical School, and was by then a medical doctor working with the African Medical Research Foundation as a Flying Doctor, wrote us in 1961:

> "The Maasai Council Meetings are on and it has been fun to sit in on some of them. They are at a crisis time when the old reactionary way of thinking and acting must give way to the 20th Century. One big thing is voting by ballot. I have tried to point out to the Maasai that their own *empukunoto*, way of voting, is very democratic in itself. So they are not being asked to accept anything fundamentally new. The ballot is traditional with them; *t'olngejep*, by the tongue, and *t'olkimojino*, by the finger. All that is new, is the paper to indicate their choice.

Kenya is governed by an elected Parliament, and headed now by President Daniel Arap Moi, the second President of Kenya.

The first President, Jomo Kenyatta, was elected President for Life when Kenya became a republic in 1963. For 15 years he successfully led the land as one of the most stable countries on the whole continent.

When Kenyatta was elected he showed such a firm sense of fairness and direction that it was not hard for him to introduce his slogan *Harambee!* (Now let's all pull together!)

Though he experienced controversey endemic to politics, he was respectfully called *Mzee* (the Old Man), as well as "Father of the Country," much as we Americans speak of George Washington. He died in August, 1978.

Of the fourteen African members elected to Parliament following Independence, at least eight of them were mission-educated men. Since there are over 20 major tribes with as many cultures, plus other smaller dialects, it is no small job to keep peace in the family. Having mission-trained men in Parliament seems to have a great influence for stability. One thinks of the verse that says:

> Blessed is the nation whose God is the
> Lord . . .
> > Righteousness exalteth a nation,
> > But sin is a reproach to any people.

The African church emerged on its own so that it is now out from under the canopy of various missions — a goal which began in the minds of the very first missionaries who came to Kenya. Recently I read Bishop Alfred Tucker's two volumes on his eighteen years in Uganda and East Africa, where he wrote in 1895:

> The African church must be so trained from the start to stand on its own and the white man only to act in advisory capacity.

The Africa Inland Church (AIC) is now in full charge of and propagated by the Africans themselves; not departed from, but working alongside the parent group, the Africa Inland Mission. This is the desired goal of many years' labor of the AIM in six provinces of East Africa. The Africa Inland Church is autonomous and now has full responsibility for the churches and schools. Our colleague Peter Kuyoni ole Kasura is one of the Maasai leaders in the new inter-tribal Africa Inland Church.

The first President of the AIC was Andrew Wambari Gichuhu, whom we first knew as a fine lad at Kijabe. He became a chief in his own Kikuyu tribe, for he was a gracious, intelligent and unusually capable administrator. Either of these two jobs was enough to tax any strong man. After the hard years of bringing the AIC to birth, his health failed.

He had to retire shortly before his death, which was a great shock and sorrow to all, for none could match his sweet spirit and skill.

Daniel Arap Moi, who was first Vice-President and is now President of Kenya, was one of Gichuhu's close associates during those hard years.

25 *Farewell*

ABOVE ALL TRIBES, WE LOVED the Maasai. We never ceased to enjoy our work with them. And when it was time for us to go, we felt confident about leaving Loitokitok under Miss Lorna Eglin, a new worker from South Africa, and Rev. Justus Mumo wa Nzomo, the beloved Akamba pastor called of God to serve among the Maasai. Lorna ran a very fine Girls School and the church work was growing fast under Justus' leadership.

As Lorna's work grew and prospered, she became affectionately known as *Ngoto Ndoiye* (Mother of the Girls). At Kajiado, she started a home for crippled children in addition to another girls school. Then, in recent years she and a new colleague, Betty Alcock, who became known as *Kokoo Lmurran* (Grandmother of the Warriors), developed a school for evangelists, which sends eager young Christian men to witness throughout the tribe.

We were pleased when the Field Council sent to Kajiado MBI-trained Paul and Elizabeth Lehrer, who had been beloved houseparents to our children at Rift Valley Academy. Paul was now Field Treasurer of the AIM. They bravely entered the work at Kajiado even though they had to start out living in the tiny tool shed where we had lived, on the cold, windy plain among the animals, while Roy was making concrete blocks in preparation for building a house and a church. The Maasai loved the Lehrers at first sight and forever after.

Siyabei, Narok and Kilgoris were also staffed by

couples who had met, fallen in love and were married at Moody Bible Institute just as we were. James and Charlotte Bisset, stationed at Siyabei, were beginning to enlarge the work at Narok; Arnie and Marilyn Newman's work was prospering at Kilgoris.

The day I wrapped up my translation work with the Lutheran Mission, Rev. Milan Lany and his son, Viki, drove me from the Lany's Hotel at Marangu, around the mountain to Lasit. Here, we picked up Roy and went on to Loitokitok. Kibo was snowy white, and crystal clear that day.

There, a large crowd had gathered for a Farewell Tea for us. It was organized by Pastor Justus, John Mpaayei, Lorna Eglin, Mary Sialo, and Chief Kulale. The people all came: the warriors, the elders, the women, the school teachers and students, all of the church women and children, and the Indian merchants from the *dukas*, including the Sikhs in their white turbans. A most colorful gathering.

A few tables were arranged in a U-shape on the grass near the church, with cloths on them and a vase of flowers in the center of each one. There were a few chairs and benches, but most of the guests preferred to sit on the ground, Maasai fashion.

It was very moving, with Kibo so majestically in full view above us, the dark green forest up close to the church, the clear blue sky overhead studded with rolling white clouds, and all those beautiful bronze brothers and sisters sitting on the ground quietly, waiting for the ceremony to start. Maasai elders stood around the perimeter in their army overcoats or blankets and army hats, holding their wildebeest tail fly switches, knob sticks and short spears denoting their station in life.

Painted warriors in their red ochred *shukas* with their six-foot spears and their eternal grunting like lions, completed the setting. It was unforgettable.

Wild, noisy hilarity found at such occasions in civilized countries was absent. It was replaced by quiet dignity, poise and sobriety such as only a Maasai group can produce.

First were the refreshments. Miss Eglin with Mary Sialo and the schoolgirls had made a lot of cookies over the open three-stone fireplace, and they made plenty for all. They had a balanced, 44-gallon drum of water boiling on an open fire which produced plenty of hot, very sweet tea served in enamel cups borrowed from the boys school. No one was not well filled. All smacked their lips with satisfaction and delight. They did not make such a feast very often.

Everyone became quiet when Gabriel Ndetia ole Meoli, whom we first met as a six-year-old schoolboy in 1939, stood up as master of ceremonies.

"I greet you all," he said.

They all returned the greeting.

Then with quiet dignity that would compete with the solemnity of any courtroom, he said:

"This is the *Shai o Sere* (farewell tea) for Bwana and Bibi Shaffer on February 22, 1958.

"Now first, we thank all of you who have come to this 'goodbye' for Bwana and Bibi Shaffer.

"The Church of Loitokitok has prepared this Tea for the Shaffers, for the time has arrived for them to go to their country in the month of March, 1958. They will not return to Loitokitok and all of Maasai country and we see that it should be so. We have arranged this occasion so we can all say goodbye together, all you who know of the big help which they gave us.

"For thirty-five years, Bwana Shaffer and his wife worked in the land of the Maasai." Gabriel then traced our work over the years, recalling the many safaris to remote areas, the opening of Lasit station, the programs with the school boys and girls, the translation work, and the list of churches Roy put up, one after the other. He continued:

"We now return thanks to the leaders of Government for their help from those times up to now. We return also thanks to our Chief, Kulale, for his help from 1932 until now.

"Now to express our gratitude to Bwana Shaffer and his wife, we wish to give a few small gifts of Maasai things, along with a picture of the people of the Loitokitok Church so that they may think of us when they are in their country, all the days of their lives."

To my surprise and delight, Ngoto Lois, Molungit's wife, called me up to the front where she, in sweet dignity presented gifts to me. She was one of my closest pals my age when we first lived in Siyabei. She had her babies when I had mine and we had much in common. She was a highly respected leader of the women.

In typically shy, Maasai woman fashion, with suitable sweet words, she first handed me a long, new, bead-trimmed milk gourd with beaded cap. Then a three-inch-wide rawhide belt, covered with beads in the *isirit* pattern, with triangles of blue, then red, then white — all sewn by hand with sinew, not thread. It was so pretty I put it right on.

Next, she pulled over my head a shoulder-to-shoulder bead necklace.

Then she added several more simpler necklaces. These were the choicest gifts they could give me. They all knew that I loved and appreciated these ornaments. This was a precious moment which can't be put on paper adequately.

Now Gabriel Ndetia asked Roy to stand to receive his gifts. The first was a new six-foot warrior spear, which Gabriel handed to him saying:

"You came to us many years ago with your first wife; you were a fearless warrior. You were not afraid of lions nor leopards, but you helped us destroy them because they ate our cattle, sheep and goats.

"Here, take this spear and think of us when you go home to your people."

The second gift was a new, sharp, two-edged sword, an *olalem*, 16 inches long, in its new scabbard of rawhide, sewn by hand, and painted with the traditional red dye. It was fastened securely to its beaded belt. No warrior is well dressed without the *olalem*.

"This is to remind you of your youth and vigor. You established your home in our midst as a proper *olbarnoti* (newly shaven, married man). You worked very hard all the time. We know because we watched you."

The third gift was a small snuff pouch, made of highly polished cow horn, with a heavily beaded rawhide lid and a long rawhide strap to go around the neck. He put it around Roy's neck.

"Now that you are an old man, it is time for you to go and sit down and sniff your snuff like an old man should," he said, to everyone's amusement.

The fourth gift was the *olkuuma*, the Maasai scepter of authority, the equivalent of the royal scepter which King Ahasuerus held out to Queen Esther bidding her approach him freely. This *olkuuma* was a special one because it was made of rhino horn, not of wood as ordinary ones are. It was 24 inches long with a round knob on one end and a point on the other. Such an object is held and owned exclusively by the head chief, or man of authority. Gabriel told us that only three other white people had ever been given an *olkuuma* made of rhino horn, because they were admired by the Maasai. The three were: Queen Elizabeth, Major Grant, before he was killed, and Mr. Windley, another highly respected District Commissioner.

"You have proven your love for us by learning our language, so we can hear you and you can hear us when we talk," he said. "You have won our confidence and our trust so we now declare you to be our *Olkitok* (chief); we give to you this *olkuuma* for you are our *Oloingoni* (prize bull of the herd) and you have acted strongly like a rhino."

Icy Kibo was sending down cold air. The sun wanted to set and the wind was astir; still the crowd stayed on and wanted to sing hymns, so we all sang and sang to the end. It was a precious farewell. The very end of the Tea was a mass chatter of "*Ashe . . . Ashe . . . Ashe* (thanks)."

"You went to your country five times before," Chief Kulale had once said to us, "and always came back to us — so we know you will return again to us for we love you and you love us."

Two days before our plane left Nairobi, we went to Bisil

where we had been invited to their Farewell Tea at their brand new concrete block chapel. The emcee, Gideon Saina, now School Supervisor, was one of our fine first converts when we went to Lasit twenty-six years before.

The preparation, attendance, gifts and dignified presentation were nearly a duplication of the Loitokitok experience. Roy and I were again, greatly moved.

In addition to the gifts they gave us, most precious were the thoughts spoken from their hearts. It was not easy to leave; but we had to say goodbye and return to Kajiado where Roy wound up loose ends of mission matters with Paul Lehrer.

Our last night in Maasailand, we pitched our umbrella tent next to their tool-shed home, even as we had spent our first night in a borrowed tent down on the Kidong Valley among the wild animals, 35 years before.

Next morning it was cold, foggy and cheerless as Paul Lehrer drove us to Nairobi Airport in his International pick-up. He had to drive cautiously because of the fog.

Suddenly there were zebra dancing back and forth across the road; hundreds of them were frolicking after a good night's rain which had moistened and sweetened the grass for them.

We laughed out loud as they treated us to a dizzying display of their black and white stripes — racing with us, crazily crossing and recrossing directly in front of us — just as though they were trying to keep us right there, on the road to Kilimanjaro.

EPILOGUE

Roy D. Shaffer, M.D.

AFTER LEAVING KENYA, Mother and Dad settled into a community of colleagues at Media near Clermont, Florida. Here, a band of pioneers, all retired AIMers, participate avidly through prayer, letters and family visits, in the growth of the church of Jesus Christ in modern Africa. Each sees it as a personal heritage.

In 1965, Dad died of a minute brain tumor with massive complications. Mother stayed at Media a few years with the old friends, Nixons, Teasdales, Lehrers, and many others. Even Papa Barnett was still there, with the sharpest memory of them all, in his 90s. But before long, Mother's Maasai instincts led her to seek new pastures and, more exactly, activity. This, she found at Prairie Bible Institute, in Alberta, Canada, where for five years she had the joy of introducing numbers of youth to stringed instruments — and Prairie never had a more avid ice hockey fan.

Much as she loves snow and icy weather, the chance was too great that a slip on the ice in Prairie's fierce winters might leave her a dependent invalid. So she moved to the Word of Life complex at Schroon Lake, New York. There, she became happily engrossed in the Overseas Office of the Word of Life International Headquarters for three years. Her recreation, in abundance, was in observing the Christian youth camp program and attending the music-saturated adult conference ministry. As at Prairie, she "vibrated" with everything that was going on.

Again, practicality, caution, age and probably the Maasai instinct led to another move, this time for another go at retirement at Media. However, for some time, visits back to Christ's Home in Warminster, Pa., in the course of her travels, always seemed more and more like going home. So now she is very happily retired in the Retirement Center at Christ's Home. There have been born to her family nineteen grandchildren and twenty-two great grandchildren to keep her pen busy, her interests growing and her conversations ever full of new material. But of course, she has not stayed put.

In 1977, after an absence of nineteen years, Mother was able to revisit Kenya. What a moving experience it was for us to share her reevocation of the people, places and events of this book. We were not surprised at her still perfect fluency with spoken Maasai, but we had not expected her retention of genealogies. During her visit, time after time, as an old friend was encountered, there would be a long questioning session, tracing out that person's extended family tree, with Mother supplying names and details from the old days. At Siyabei, Ngong, Kajiado, Kijabe, Nairobi and Loitokitok we "ate the news" with those brought close together in years past by a mutual love in Christ.

During this same visit, Mother had another round of safari life in Maasailand as she joined and helped me in a health research project for the University of Nairobi Medical School, in Amboseli, under the snows of Kilimanjaro. On another occasion we sorely missed Dad as we visited a still-useful waterwheel-powered grist mill, one of his many projects of practical evangelism.

Again in 1979 Mother came back to Africa, this time with Frieda Russ, manager of the Christ's Home Retirement Center. On this occasion, Mother received a visit from a grandson of the spirit, actually a grandson of Olduboi, one of the first nine converts Dad baptized when they first arrived at Siyabei in 1923: Tubula William Sankan, son of Stephen Sitoya and Tabitha Nolmusheni Sankan. William had graduated from Scott Theological College at Machakos, and was pastor of the AIC Church at Ngong. Subsequently,

William attended Grace Bible College in Omaha, Nebraska. On his return to Kenya, he married Christine Mulwa of Machakos, and God has blessed their home with two little ones. William serves as an assistant pastor at Ziwani Church in Nairobi. Following in the steps of his father, Sitoya, William has also taken up translation work. At the AIC headquarters office, he joined the committee working on a new translation of the Old Testament Scriptures into Maasai.

In 1983, they published the New Testament with a distinctive touch: a Maasai-red-ochre-colored cover! William wrote, "We rejoice with our fellow Maasais after getting our revised Maasai New Testament. The only part I played was to suggest the cover colour, which we felt should reflect the favorite colour of our people."

Mother and Dad's time among the Maasai spanned an important era in Kenya's history, from the peak of full colonialism to the eve of full independence.

During this era, the Maasai were relative bystanders, or at best, reluctant late-starters, as far as involvement in Kenya's developing nationhood. This was a reflection of the individualism and conservatism common to all pastoralists. Also, their population is scattered and their dry environment necessitates mobility. These two factors, conservatism and environment, posed an enormous challenge to development of both nationhood and church. Development, whether of church, school, water supply or clinic, calls for a static population.

The majority of Maasai have changed little since the 1930s. What Maasai will remain static if the only grass or water for his cattle is elsewhere, wherever the unpredictable rain happens to have fallen? Also, what are they to do if all the dry season grazing land, because it is arable, has been grabbed up for cultivation? Settling these pastoralists in this environment thus remains a problem with no immediate solution.

Back in the 1930s, Dad tried in vain to popularize ox plowing, the growing of beans, napier grass and fruit trees, and the use of stone grist mills — but he was forty years ahead of his time. Now there are Maasai farmers growing miles of wheat and acres of vegetables eaten by armies of tourists traversing both Amboseli and the Mara. When we were kids, Amboseli was "nothing," just a swampy, salt flat beyond Namanga. Now, three lodges accommodate hundreds of hungry tourists daily.

Some Maasai, particularly the Christians, are evolving a healthier, happier way of life by progressive adaptation to current circumstances. Regrettably, a few have gone backwards, and there are some Maasai communities housed in plastic trash "igloos," living off the detritus of tourism near the game park lodges. Both Jomo Kenyatta and my parents would wince in pain.

Still, past efforts were not altogether fruitless. Some modern mission or secular technocrats, speeding along on good roads in Landrovers and meeting only educated Maasai in major population centers, have said or implied that "little or nothing had been done" in Maasailand before them. This attitude comes from geographical ignorance or psychological unimaginativeness. It ignores, for example, a population density of only about 15 per square kilometer in Maasailand compared to about 600 in central Kenya. Only an unimaginative person can conceive of an African tribe resisting education earlier in this century. But that is the way it was.

Despite these and many other constraints, Mother and Dad did get through to the Maasai. I believe an important element in their acceptance by the Maasai was their straightforwardness. As one old Maasai said of Dad, "Unlike most *mzungus* (whites), your father was uncomplicated. His words had to do with God, you and me, and nothing more. We knew what he wanted of us."

Considering the practical hindrances to development in Maasailand, it is perhaps remarkable what progress the Maasai have made toward modernization, and what share they do have in East Africa's leadership. For example, a spiritual, and possibly genetic, descendant of the great

Oloiboni Sendeyo, Edward Sokoine, was the Prime Minister of Tanzania for a number of years. In Kenya, the Maasai have been represented by a Minister of Home Affairs, a Director of Medical Services, two Assistant Ministers, a Deputy Director of Wildlife, a Chief Accountant of Kenya Harbours, and numerous others in responsible national posts. This representation is far out of proportion to their one percent share of the total population. Incidentally, each of the above mentioned leaders has told me of the positive influence on their lives, directly or indirectly, of the Shaffers in Maasailand.

Kenya's esteemed President Moi has a personal motto: *Fuata nyayo* (follow the footprints). His intention is to create footprints so worthy that all patriotic citizens should follow them. Along the same line, many of us connected with Maasailand are proud to be following the *nyayo* of Roy and Ruth Shaffer, that uncomplicated couple who made some of the first footprints for Christ on the road to Kilimanjaro.

POSTSCRIPT

Some Maasai Trees and their Functions*

1. Olbili	Honey barrels are made from this tree.
2. Olerai	Bark boiled in water, induces vomiting.
3. Oldule	Leaves placed under iron ornaments of women, to prevent blisters.
4. Olngosua	Thorns used to pierce children's ear-lobes. Sap, chewed, mends broken gourds.
5. Osokonoi	Crushed bark is hot like pepper, mixed with blood or milk, for fever.
6. Olmatasia	Warriors carry leaves in hands at dances; they lie on the leaves; make tooth brush of its twigs.
7. Olmokotan	Bark mixed with milk, blood or soup as a purgative, or for worms.
8. Olderkesi	Liquid from bark, when drunk, makes warrior brave when he hunts lions.
9. Olkiloriti	Bark and roots mixed with beef soup and drunk from the stomach of a slaughtered ox, is given to a wounded warrior to quench thirst.

10. Oloisuki

Bits of bark are given to children to chew. It is said that fever is afraid of this tree so will depart from the children.

11. Olngeriandus

One kind gives a red dye, to color sheaths for swords. Another kind gives thorns used to tattoo foreheads and cheeks of girls, to produce coveted marks of beauty, also around the navel, which is status of beauty in their estimation. Warriors also produce these beauty marks on their bodies—a matter of voluntary choice. No one is forced.

*From THE MASAI by A. C. Hollis, Clarendon Press, Oxford, England, 1905.

AIM MAASAI WORKERS

Missionaries of the Africa Inland Mission who have continued the Lord's work first started just after the turn of the century by John and Florence Stauffacher with Molungit ole Sembele and his wife, Nyakeru.

Dallas and Charlotte Abendroth
Betty Alcock
Willard and Jane Anderson
Lanny and Janice Arenson
James and Charlotte Bisset
Vivien Des Forges
Lorna Eglin
Ann Ellis
Paul and Elizabeth Lehrer
Andrew and Dorothy Losier
Arnold and Marilyn Newman
Max and Fran Nicholaisen

Bea Noffsinger
Rosemary Russell
Marian Settles
Roy and Ruth Shaffer
Bertha Simpson
Olive Smith
Raymond and Sara Stauffacher
Claudon and Gladys Stauffacher
Wes and Frances Van Nattan
Bob and Sylvia Ward
Roger and Edith Weaver
Mary Wight

In 1985: Desmond and Ginny Hales

For additional copies of this book, please order through your nearest Africa Inland Mission office, or:

Africa Inland Mission International
P.O. Box 178
Pearl River, NY 10965
USA